بسم الله الرحمن الرحيم

DAJJAL THE QUR'AN AND AWWAL AL-ZAMĀN

The Antichrist, the Holy Qur'an, and the Beginning of History

IMRAN N. HOSEIN

IRONHEART PUBLISHING HOUSE
www.ironheartpublishing.com

ISBN-13: 978-1-989450-00-0

Published by Iron-Heart Publishing
www.ironheartpublishing.com

For my beloved son

Mujāhid

with the hope and prayer that he will be inspired
to reach for the stars—and then to travel on—
for beyond the stars there are many more worlds!

...فَذَكِّرْ بِالْقُرْآنِ مَن يَخَافُ وَعِيدِ...

(Qur'ān, Qāf, 50:45)

Remind, through this Qur'ān, those who fear Allah's warning. [This is an explanation, rather than a translation, of the Qur'ān, since the Arabic Qur'ān cannot be translated to another language.]

فَلَا تُطِعِ الْكَافِرِينَ وَجَاهِدْهُم بِهِ جِهَادًا كَبِيرًا

(Qur'ān, al-Furqān, 25:52)

Do not submit to and obey those who are hostile to Islam. Rather, wage a mighty Jihād against them by means of this Qur'ān.

بَلْ كَذَّبُوا بِمَا لَمْ يُحِيطُوا بِعِلْمِهِ وَلَمَّا يَأْتِهِمْ تَأْوِيلُهُ كَذَٰلِكَ
كَذَّبَ الَّذِينَ مِن قَبْلِهِمْ فَانظُرْ كَيْفَ كَانَ عَاقِبَةُ الظَّالِمِينَ

(Qur'ān, Yūnus, 10:39)

They rejected a scripture in which there is knowledge that they could not compass, and with verses whose Ta'wīl or interpretation had not as yet come unto them. There were others before them who also responded similarly; so they should remember the fate which befell such people.

"And there shall be signs in the sun,
and in the moon, and in the stars;
and upon the earth distress of nations, with perplexity;
the sea and the waves roaring;"
(Gospel, Luke: 21:25)

And I will show wonders in heaven above,
and signs in the earth beneath;
blood, and fire, and vapor of smoke:
(Gospel, Acts: 2:19)

"And ye shall hear of wars and rumors of wars:
see that ye be not troubled:
for all these things must come to pass,
but the end is not yet."
(Gospel, Matthew: 24:6)

Contents

PREFACE

I kept waiting for ten years before I could write this pioneering book on Dajjāl, the false Messiah or Anti-Christ, but this long wait was a blessing in disguise since my knowledge of the subject and, more importantly, my understanding of methodology for the study of the subject, has matured significantly over this time. Hence I suggest to those who now venture to write on the subject, to allow the river of thought and understanding to flow at its own speed.

I am grateful to a brother resident in New Zealand who was the first to assist in sponsoring the writing this new book, and to another Pakistani brother whose kind sponsorship allowed me to write a significant part of the book. Sponsors in UK then took over the sponsorship until, *Alhamdulillah,* this first book on Dajjāl was completed. I am also grateful to those who generously assisted in meeting the cost of printing this book. May Allah, Most High, bless them all for their kind assistance. Āmīn!

I will now resume work on my second book on Dajjāl entitled: *From Jesus the True Messiah to Dajjāl the False Messiah—A Journey in Islamic Eschatology*. I propose to write an additional three books on Dajjāl on the topics of *Dajjāl and 'Money', Dajjāl and the modern 'Feminist Revolution',* and finally, *Dajjāl, the Qur'ān and Ākhir al-Zamān*, or the end of history. May Allah Most Kind make it possible for me to accomplish this task *Insha' Allah.*

I know that these five books will not exhaust the subject of Dajjāl, but I hope and pray that they will provoke others Insha'Allah, to take up the challenge to write on those subjects which are yet to be explained.

I am grateful to those who read the manuscript of this book and assisted with valuable comments, as well as with proof-reading, and to my Assistant, Hasbullah, who was always there to assist me in searching for the texts of many Hadīth as well as references in the Sīrah, i.e., history of the life of Prophet Muhammad صلى الله عليه وسلم.

I have dedicated this book to my son, Mujāhid Fazlur Rahman, who was named after his grand-father, Maulānā Dr. Muhammad Fazlur Rahman Ansārī (*rahimahullah*). Mujāhid is also the great grand-son of Maulānā Muhammad Abdul Aleem Siddique (*rahimahullah*). I hope and pray that this dedication might inspire him to follow in their noble footsteps in serving the mission of Islam. *Āmīn!*

Imran N. Hosein
Published in Safar1439 / November 2017
San Fernando in the Caribbean island of Trinidad.
Revised in Dhul-Hijjah 1440 / August 2019

ANSĀRĪ MEMORIAL SERIES

The Ansārī Memorial Series of books is published in loving memory of *Maulānā* Dr. Muhammad Fazlur Rahmān Ansārī (1914–1974) who was a *Sufi Shaikh* of the *Qāderiyyah Sufi Order*, a philosopher, an outstanding Islamic scholar of the modern age, a roving missionary of Islam, and my teacher and spiritual mentor of blessed memory. My love for him, and my continuously increasing admiration for both his Islamic scholarship as well as his philosophical thought, more than 40 years after his death, is such that I cherish the very dust on which he walked.

I began writing the books of the Ansārī Memorial Series in 1994 while I was still resident in New York, and functioning as Director of Islamic Studies for the Joint Committee of Muslim Organizations of Greater New York. I started the Series of books in *Maulānā's* honor because I wanted to offer a gift to my teacher on the 25th anniversary of his death. The first six books of the Series were launched in the *Masjid* of the Muslim Centre of New York in Flushing Meadows, Queens, New York, in 1997, and in the years which have since passed, many more books were added to the Series. A complete list of books in the Series can be found at the end of this book.

The next book in the Series, entitled *From Jesus, the True Messiah, to Dajjāl, the False Messiah—A Journey in Islamic Eschatology,* promises to be the most difficult and challenging of all. The subject is both difficult and challenging because, among other things, it takes a scholar directly inside the Zionists' hornet's nest, and as a consequence there are few scholars who are prepared to risk writing or speaking on this subject. But let us recall that the blessed Prophet صلى الله عليه وسلم said:

فقَيِه وَاحِدٌ أَشَدُّ علَىَ الشَّيطْاَنِ مِنْ أَلفِ عاَبدٍِ

"One learned (scholar) is harder on Satan than a thousand worshippers".
(Sunan Ibn Mājah)

Hence scholarly books and lectures on Dajjāl, whose *Fitnah* (evil) is described by Prophet Muhammad صلى الله عليه وسلم as greater than that of Satan, will surely be a means through which our readers would be able to identify true scholars of Islam. I pray that my present humble pioneering book on Dajjāl entitled *Dajjāl the Qur'ān and Awwal al-Zamān,* i.e., the beginning of History, might pass the test of scholarship, and if it does do so, *Insha' Allah,* that it might encourage the learned scholars of Islam of the modern age to also address this important subject.

I recognize the subject of Dajjāl to be the ultimate test of Islamic scholarship, and that implies that it constitutes the ultimate test of methodology for study of the Qur'ān and for assessment of Hadīth. I am convinced that only an authentic *Sufi* scholar can write credibly on the subject of Dajjāl, because only he has the proper methodology for the study of the Qur'ān and the assessment of Hadīth, the *Sufi* epistemology of spiritual insight with which to interpret religious symbolism, as well as the tangible vibrating spiritual bond with Nabī Muhammad صلى الله عليه وسلم which are all indispensable for penetrating the subject; and this is why I have to devote attention to the religious thought of *Maulānā* Ansārī, the authentic *Sufi Shaikh.* I could never have written my book on Dajjāl without the benefit of his religious thought. The methodology of the scholars of 'Islamic Modernism', of the *Salafi, Shia, Deobandi, Brelvi* or of a *Tablīgh Jamaat,* for example, will not allow a scholar whose primary identification is with those sects, to successfully penetrate the subject of Dajjāl. I invite them, gently so, to prove me wrong.

I met *Maulānā* Ansārī for the first time in 1960 in my native Caribbean island of Trinidad when I was just 18 years of age. I had done some studies in science, and I was quite surprised to learn that a *Maulānā* (an Islamic religious scholar of a very high rank) would be visiting Trinidad from Pakistan, and that he would lecture at my Montrose Village Masjid on the subject of 'Islam and Science'. (The Masjid was subsequently named after him as *Masjid al-Ansārī*.) My response to the news was quite skeptical, since at that young age I new of no possible link between Islam and science. On the night of the lecture he astonished me with his scientific scholarship, as well as with knowledge of Islam of which I was hitherto quite ignorant. I was surprised to learn that the Qur'ān had, time and again, appealed to 'observation' and to 'inductive reasoning', and hence to what is today called 'scientific enquiry', as the method through which one should seek to penetrate and understand the reality of the material universe. I was also surprised to learn that knowledge which had come to the world these last few hundred years from some of the discoveries of modern science, such as in embryology, had already been present in the Qur'ān.

I was even more surprised when *Maulānā* lectured at Woodford Square in the capital city of Port of Spain, on 'Islam and Western Civilization' before an audience which filled the large Square to capacity, and with the Oxford University– trained Prime Minister of Trinidad and Tobago, Dr. Eric E. Williams, sitting on the platform beside him. Dr. Williams had himself already dealt a severe blow to Western Civilization in his PhD thesis at Oxford entitled 'Capitalism and Slavery'. The learned Prime Minister was clearly impressed by *Maulānā's* scholarship as he dissected the godless pagan foundations of a barbaric and oppressive civilization that had arrogantly and deceptively presented itself as the best that the world had ever experienced, and would ever experience.

Maulānā's dynamic Islamic scholarship, and the spiritual impact of his magnetic *Sufi* personality, changed my life. He inspired me to such an extent that I, also, wanted to become a scholar of Islam. By November 1963, and at the age of twenty-one, I became a student of Al Azhar University in Cairo, Egypt, which was the most famous institution of higher Islamic learning in the world. But I could not find in Al Azhar University the dazzling Islamic scholarship to which I was exposed three years earlier in *Maulānā* Ansārī. The scholars of Al Azhar appeared to me to have been stuck in time, and could not compare with *Maulānā* in their scholarly understanding of the reality of the strange and challenging modern age, nor in their capacity to offer an Islamic response for example, to challenges posed by the modern scientific and technological revolution, the feminist revolution, etc.

I left Egypt and travelled to Pakistan in August 1964 to become *Maulānā's* student at the Aleemiyah Institute of Islamic Studies in Karachi, and that was the best decision that I have ever taken in life. [The Institute still exists to this day at the Islamic Center in Block B of the Karachi suburb of North Nazimabad.]

I remained his student until I graduated from the Institute seven years later in 1971 at the age of twenty-nine with the degree of Al-Ijāzah Al-'Āliyah, and returned to Trinidad. I never met him again in life, since he died three years later in 1974 in Pakistan at the age of 60.

There are many things about *Maulānā* that I would love to write and to record for history, but by far the most important of all aspects of his rich and multi-faceted life was his religious thought, and that is what I have attempted to explain in my brief essay on the subject. It was crucially important for me to do so, not only because his exceptional scholarship offers some assistance for modern Islamic scholarship to extricate itself from its present sorry and miserable plight (one cannot find a single prominent Islamic scholar today who dares to declare the present paper-money monetary system to be bogus, fraudulent and Harām), but also because his scholarship has played such an important role in guiding and assisting me in writing my present pioneering book on Dajjāl, the false Messiah, which is the latest book in the Ansārī Memorial Series.

That essay can be found in the Appendix to my book on *'Methodology for Study of the Qur'ān'.*

INTRODUCTION

DR. BURHĀN AHMAD FĀRŪQĪ – THE PHILOSOPHER OF HISTORY

No one can possibly write a book concerning Dajjāl, the Anti- Christ, and the beginning of history, without a knowledge of the philosophy of history. The seed of this book may have been planted in the 1930s, at the Aligarh Muslim University in India, when two students, who were dear friends, Muhammad Fazlur Rahmān Ansārī and Burhān Ahmad Fārūqī, pursued studies for their PhDs in Philosophy under the guidance of Prof. Dr. Syed Zafar-ul-Hassan.

Dr. Fārūqī eventually wrote a masterpiece of *'Ilm al- Kalām*, or Islamic Philosophy, entitled *'A Mujaddid's Conception of Tauheed'*, and *Maulānā* Dr. Ansārī wrote a masterpiece of *'Ilm al-Akhlāq'* or Islamic Moral Philosophy, entitled *The Quranic Foundations and Structure of Muslim Society* (in 2 vols.).

This writer was blessed, thirty years later in the 1960s, when both of the scholars had reached the zenith of their scholarly lives, to have them both as his teachers at the Aleemiyah Institute of Islamic Studies in Pakistan. Dr. Fārūqī taught the philosophy of history, and Dr. Ansārī taught the Qur'ān and, vastly more importantly, the methodology for study of the

Qur'ān. That methodology was explained in his 'Quranic Foundations' book, but was simplified and expanded in this writer's recent book entitled *'Methodology for Study of the Qur'ān'.*

More than fifty years have passed since that dazzling moment in scholarly time at the Aleemiyah Institute of Islamic Studies in Pakistan, when two truly gifted scholars of Islam taught and inspired just a handful of students, and built the foundation on which this pioneering book on Dajjāl, as well as the others which will now follow *Insha' Allah,* now rests.

How do we explain an Aleemiyah Institute of Islamic Studies with a curriculum of studies and a methodology for study of the Qur'ān that differed so significantly from the traditional *Dār al-'Ulūm,* or the *Jāmi'ah,* i.e., Islamic seminary or university? The answer lies in the intellectual response of part of the Indian Muslim community to the challenge of modern western civilization. One part of the Indian Muslim community recognized that the traditional Islamic education imparted in the *Dār al-'Ulūm* was woefully inadequate for a student to even understand the modern world that had come into being in consequence of the dramatic emergence of modern western civilization on the stage of the world. Dr. Muhammad Iqbal, for example, mourned over the fact that, according to him: "During the last five hundred years religious thought in Islam has been practically stationary" (*Reconstruction of Religious Thought in Islam;* Essay entitled *'Knowledge and Religious Experience'*). Iqbal was referring, of course, to the religious scholarship that was emerging from the *Dār al-'Ulūm.*

That part of the Indian Muslim community which recognized the inadequacy of the *Dār al-'Ulūm* education, proceeded to establish an academically independent institution of higher Islamic learning which would not only teach the religion of Islam, but would also introduce the student to the modern world of knowledge that had emerged from western civilization. And so the seed of this book was planted when the Aligarh Muslim University was established in the rural town of Aligarh in India. It was truly an academic institution, since it was free of government control.

We will demonstrate *Insha' Allah,* that it was Dajjāl who brought the new modern western world into being, and it is he who is constantly changing it—and with it, the rest of the world —to bring stranger new worlds into being. Since Dajjāl is Allah's supreme test for mankind, surpassing everything that preceded him, Dajjāl is also the supreme test for the *Dār al- 'Ulūm*. Not only has the *Dār al-'Ulūm* continuously failed that test for the last few hundred years, but these books on Dajjāl will conclusively demonstrate that it continues to fail that test even to this day. Indeed, the book on Dajjāl and Money would suffice, *Insha' Allah,* to remove any lingering doubts concerning that subject.

Not only has the *Dār al-'Ulūm* failed the test, but even the graduates of western universities and government-sponsored Islamic universities as well as government-paid Muftis and other such scholars of Islam, have also failed, sometimes miserably so, in responding adequately and appropriately to the intellectual challenges posed by the modern west.

Aligarh-trained Dr. Fārūqī was an intellectual rebel who defied conventional thought as he waved and thrust his scholarly sword with nary a concern for conventional sensibilities in the world of knowledge, and in the pursuit of truth. He built the foundation of his philosophy of history on 'perennial truth', with which history commenced, and insisted that history must end with the triumph of that same truth. But in-between the beginning of history with 'truth', and the end of history with the 're-realization of that truth', he declared that history moves up and down in what he described as 'the zig-zag movement of history'.

The conclusion that emerged from that philosophy of history was that the arrogant Zionist Western world, and Dajjāl's Impostor State of Israel, could weave their full spectrum dominance on the world on whichever cloth they chose, it would make no difference to the end of history. Truth would still triumph over falsehood, lies, injustice, oppression and false-flag acts of terrorism in which the alleged Muslim terrorist is always killed, or commits suicide, hence conveniently avoiding, again and again, the possibility of a court case.

Without *Maulānā* Dr. Ansārī's amazing methodology for study of the Qur'ān however, it would not have been possible for the Aleemiyah Institute of Islamic Studies to offer a higher Islamic education which allowed the student to integrate all knowledge into a coherent whole while critically assessing with the Qur'ān, all knowledge that came from the west. Without that critical intellectual effort at integration of knowledge, the student would have emerged with a split personality as he straddled dual intellectual worlds without a bridge with which to cross between them. He would have studied Islam with one mind, and studied the modern world with a second mind that was disconnected from the first. Such a scholar would have been, and would still be, a misfit in both worlds.

It was not possible for Dr. Fārūqī's philosophy of history to be grounded in the Qur'ān without the application of Dr. Ansari's methodology for the study of the Qur'ān. And so it was with the combined thought of these two amazing scholars that this book on 'Dajjāl the Qur'ān and the Beginning of History' could be written.

A serious book written at this time—the late afternoon of history—on the subject of Dajjāl the false Messiah or Anti- Christ, and firmly grounded in the Qur'ān, is sure to attract the attention of many Christians and Jews, in addition, of course, to the scholars of Islam and the literate world of Islam. This initial book on Dajjāl however, as well as the books on the subject which will now follow this book, might very well be judged to be a pioneering attempt to present the scholarly viewpoint of Islam on this subject. As such it may attract even more attention. For this reason we invite serious comments, and even critical responses which can be published in a second edition *Insha' Allah.* Responses can be sent by email to *inhosein@hotmail.com,* or to our website *www.imranhosein.org* where this text will be placed for free download and for comments.

Islamic Scholarship and Eschatology

Islamic scholarship should not be blamed for ignoring eschatology; rather, it would be more appropriate to recognize that Islamic eschatology could not properly be developed as a branch of knowledge until events had unfolded sufficiently in the historical process to allow the discerning scholar to penetrate and recognize the meaning and implication of several verses of the Qur'ān as well several prophecies of Prophet Muhammad صل الله عليه و سلم pertaining to *Ākhir al-Zamān* or the End-time.

The Qur'ān has given notice that the world is yet to know the *Ta'wīl* or 'interpretation' of certain of its verses perhaps because 'interpretation' would be possible only with the passage of time and the unfolding of events in history:

...وَلَمَّا يَأْتِهِمْ تَأْوِيلُهُ...

(Qur'ān, Yūnus, 10:39)

Allah Most High, discloses above that there are verses of the Book whose interpretation have not as yet come unto them . . .

It would be helpful to the gentle reader if we were to provide an example of such an event which had to occur before an important prophecy located in Islamic eschatology, i.e., pertaining to the End-time, could be interpreted and explained.

Prophet Muhammad صل الله عليه و سلم prophesied more than 1400 years ago, in a Hadīth recorded in Sahīh Bukhārī: *that the River Euphrates would uncover a mountain of gold, and that people would fight for that gold.* He declared that *99 out of every 100 who fight for that gold would be killed, but that each would believe that he would be the one who would survive.* He ended by warning the believers that they must not touch that gold.

Here is the Arabic text of the Hadīth:

عَنْ أَبِي هُرَيْرَةَ، أَنَّ رَسُولَ اللَّهِ صلى الله عليه وسلم قَالَ:
لاَ تَقُومُ السَّاعَةُ حَتَّى يَحْسِرَ الْفُرَاتُ عَنْ جَبَلٍ مِنْ ذَهَبٍ
يَقْتَتِلُ النَّاسُ عَلَيْهِ فَيُقْتَلُ مِنْ كُلِّ مِائَةٍ تِسْعَةٌ وَتِسْعُونَ
وَيَقُولُ كُلُّ رَجُلٍ مِنْهُمْ لَعَلِّي أَكُونُ أَنَا الَّذِي أَنْجُو.

There are those who, in consequence of using a defective methodology of study, await a mountain of the metal that would one day emerge from underneath the River. They have already waited in vain for the fulfillment of this prophecy for more than 1400 years, and our view is that they will still wait in vain for another 1400 years. We, however, have recognized the Hadīth to be *Mutashābihah*, i.e., allegorical, and that it must hence be interpreted in order for its meaning to be penetrated.

Our interpretation of the Hadīth is that when US Secretary of State, Henry Kissinger, succeeded in making a satanic deal with Saudi Arabia's King Faisal in 1974, for oil to be sold for only USD, the US dollar became a petrodollar, and an ocean of oil underneath the 'river' began to function as a mountain of gold supporting the US dollar. This event was the fulfillment of the Prophet's ominous prophecy; and Allah Knows best!

If our interpretation of the Hadīth is correct, then the current rival BRICS monetary system represents an attack on the mountain of gold petrodollar monetary system that will lead, inevitably so, to that Great War in which 99% of combatants will be killed. Only a nuclear war, or a war in which weapons of mass destruction are used, can result in such a great percentage of fatalities.

Most of the Hadīth pertaining to Dajjāl are similar to the above Hadīth since they have to be interpreted in order to be understood; and it was not possible for anyone to interpret that Hadīth until certain events had unfolded in the world of money. First there was the birth of modern Western civilization with an agenda of perpetrating universal *Fasād* on earth (*Fasād* is that which corrupts to the extent that it can destroy). The Qur'ān identified Gog and Magog as the perpetrators of that universal *Fasād*. It did so by first identifying Gog and Magog with *Fasād* on earth:

قَالُوا يَا ذَا الْقَرْنَيْنِ إِنَّ يَأْجُوجَ وَمَأْجُوجَ مُفْسِدُونَ فِي الْأَرْضِ
فَهَلْ نَجْعَلُ لَكَ خَرْجًا عَلَى أَنْ تَجْعَلَ بَيْنَنَا وَبَيْنَهُمْ سَدًّا

(Qur'ān, Al-Kahf, 18:94)

After they solved the language problem of communication, those people informed Dhūl Qarnain that Gog and Magog were inflicting Fasād, i.e., that which corrupts to the extent that it can cause destruction, in their territory. They then asked whether they could pay him to build a barrier that would protect them from Gog and Magog.

The Qur'ān then said that Gog and Magog would one day be released into the world, and that the world would then be subjected to their *Fasād* as a universal phenomenon:

وَحَرَامٌ علَى قَر يْةٍ أَهْلَكْنَاهَا أَنَّهُمْ لَا يرْجِعوُن حَتَّىٓ إِذَا فتُحِتْ
يأْجُوجُ وَمَأْجُوجُ وَهمُ مِّن
كلِّ حدَبٍ ينَسِلوُن

(Qur'ān, al-Anbiyāh, 21:95–6)

Allah Most High, disclosed that there was a Divine ban on the people of a Town (which we identify as Jerusalem) which was destroyed and from which those people were expelled by Divine decree, that they could never return to reclaim that town as their own until Gog and Magog were released, and they then spread out in all directions and hence take control of the world in the world-order of Gog and Magog.

Since it is the West which made possible the return of the Jews to Jerusalem to reclaim it as their own, it is as clear as daylight that Gog and Magog are located within modern Western civilization. Russia, incidentally, is not a part of the decadent West. A man cannot marry another man in Russia and get a marriage certificate. Rather the decadent West is now preparing to wage nuclear war on an Orthodox Christian Russia which they have hated from the day that the modern West was mysteriously born.

No one could have understood the prophecy of the 'mountain of gold' until the decadent West had corrupted the world of money by printing paper and using it as money. They then waged wars of naked aggression in order to colonize the rest of the world and to impose, through the Bretton Woods Accord, and the International Monetary Fund (IMF), a monetary system in which one paper-money, i.e., the US dollar, became the ruling money in the world. However France had a great ruler in General Charles De Gaulle, and he could see through the deception and injustice of that monetary system. The French challenge to the system eventually forced the US to abandon it in 1971, and to replace it in 1974 with the petrodollar monetary system that was made possible through the 'mountain of gold'.

The Hadīth concerning the ocean of oil functioning as a mountain of gold is also connected to Dajjāl since this book argues that Dajjāl will have to demonstrate his capacity to succeed the Prophet-Kings David and Solomon, i.e., Nabī Dāud and Nabī Sulaimān عليه السلام , for whom Allah caused the earth to bring forth its treasures:

... وَأَسَلْنَا لَهُ عَيْنَ الْقِطْرِ...

(Qur'ān, Saba', 34:12)

Allah Most High caused a lake of molten copper to flow at David's behest.

Prophet Muhammad صل الله عليه و سلم prophesied (as only a true Prophet can prophesy) that the earth would one day bring forth its treasures for Dajjāl:

He would then walk through the waste land and say to it: Bring forth your treasures, and the treasures would come out and collect (themselves) before him like the swarm of bees.

(Sahīh Muslim)

Hence, there is a direct connection between Dajjāl and the bogus Bretton Woods monetary system which was eventually replaced by the petrodollar monetary system in which the earth sent forth its treasures to help Dajjāl to continue, and even expand, his control over the world of money.

For more information and analysis on this subject readers may wish to view the following of my entitled lectures available on the internet:

- Islam, the Petrodollar and Beyond
- Beyond the Petrodollar—An Islamic Response to the Bogus Monetary System
- Islam, the Petrodollar and Russia's Tryst with Destiny
- Islam, the Petrodollar and the Great War

Outline of book

We commence, in Chapter One, our explanation of the subject of Dajjāl, or the Anti-Christ, appropriately so, with a description of his profile. This includes data concerning him which has to be literally understood, as well as other data which must be interpreted. It is in that latter exercise that we are led to the startling discovery in the Qur'ān that Dajjāl is a *Jasad*, i.e., a human body without a spirit. This leads us to important conclusions which will intrigue the reader as well as the Zionist Judeo-Christian world.

We then go on to recognize, through a process of logical deduction, that the Jews must await a Messiah who would match the Prophet-Kings David and Solomon, i.e., Nabī Dāud and Nabī Sulaimān عليه السلام , in respect of power, as well as in respect of divinely-bestowed miraculous capacities. Solomon was blessed, for example, with a measure of control over the weather, and Dajjāl will therefore have to demonstrate that he has a similar capacity.

Chapter Two is devoted to our methodology for study of the subject in which we demonstrate that there is a link between the beginning and the end of history.

In Chapter Three we take up our subject with the response of the Rabbis in Yathrib to the query of the *Quraish* asking how they could determine whether or not Muhammad, the Arab from Makkah, was indeed a true Prophet of the Lord-God. In their response, the Rabbis had posed three questions which, according to them, only a Prophet could answer. One of the questions was about the *Rūh* or Spirit. This chapter is devoted to the subject of the *Rūh* and in doing so it exposes the Jewish claim to be the chosen people of the Lord-God, to be false.

Chapter Four is devoted to an analysis of the most important event that occurred at the beginning of history, i.e., the Divine Command to the Angels, as well as to a Jinn named *Iblīs*, to bow down in prostration before Ādam عليه السلام . The analysis of this event further confirms our conclusion that the Jewish claim to be the chosen people of the Lord-God is false.

The substance of this book is located in Chapter Five in which we describe and analyze other events occurring at the beginning of history which have a direct link with Dajjāl's mission at the end of history to seek to replicate Solomon's Holy State of Israel.

Our readers should note that neither the Qur'ān nor the Hadīth have referred by name to the Holy State which was created by David, i.e., Nabi' Daūd عليه السلام, and over which his son also ruled. When we use the name, 'Holy State of Israel', we refer to that Holy State for which Solomon, i.e., Nabi' Sulaimān عليه السلام , prayed to Allah Most High, that "it can belong to none after him". Hence this book reminds Dajjāl and his Zionist followers, that it can never be restored.

The Arabic Text of the Qur'ān

This book, on Dajjāl and the Beginning of History, is based on the Qur'ān, and hence the very substance of the book is located in the verses of the Qur'ān which we have quoted extensively. We hasten to remind readers that the Qur'ān was not revealed in English, French or Swahili. It was revealed in Arabic, and we have come to the conclusion, after a life-time of study, that the Qur'ān cannot be translated to another language. Rather, the most that we can do is to try to explain the Qur'ān with the caveat that no one explanation can possibly exhaust its meaning. Readers must also be made aware that whenever an effort is made to translate the Arabic text to another language, the scholarship of the translator as well as his limited understanding of the Arabic text, always influences his translation.

For the above reasons it is necessary for us to always quote the Arabic text of every verse of the Qur'ān quoted in this book. That text has been Divinely-preserved since the Book was revealed more than 1400 years ago, and it remains today beyond the reach of those who may still wish to pursue a futile effort to challenge its claim to absolute authenticity and integrity. Whenever a verse of the Qur'ān is quoted in this book we make an effort to explain its meaning in the English language.

It should not surprise the reader, nor those who will translate this book to other languages, that an explanation sometimes conveys a meaning of a verse that is different from a translation.

It would benefit the reader if we now provide an example of a translated verse in which our explanation differs in meaning from translations of the verse. It pains us that wrong understanding of the Qur'ān derived from some translations, has caused, and continues to cause, great damage to those who are thereby misguided. We provide an example of such in verse 51 of *Sūrah al-Māidah* in which Allah Most Wise has ordered (in Arabic) as follows:

يَا أَيُّهَا الَّذِينَ آمَنُوا لَا تَتَّخِذُوا الْيَهُودَ وَالنَّصَارَىٰ أَوْلِيَاءَ بَعْضُهُمْ أَوْلِيَاءُ بَعْضٍ وَمَنْ يَتَوَلَّهُمْ مِنْكُمْ فَإِنَّهُ مِنْهُمْ إِنَّ اللَّهَ لَا يَهْدِي الْقَوْمَ الظَّالِمِينَ

(Qur'ān, Al-Māidah, 5:51)

Almost all translations of this verse to the English language could lead the reader, Christian, Jewish, Muslim or otherwise, to believe that the Qur'ān has prohibited Muslim friendship and alliance with Christians and Jews. But such an understanding of the Qur'ān would be false. The Qur'ān has most certainly not prohibited Muslims from being friends and allies of all Christians and all Jews; rather, it has prohibited friendship and alliance with specific Christians and specific Jews.

The gentle reader may wish to judge for himself the conclusion that can be arrived at from reading fifteen different translations of the above verse 51 of *Sūrah al-Māidah:*

Muhammad Asad: *O you who have attained to faith! Do not take the Jews and the Christians for your allies: they are but allies of one another and whoever of you allies himself with them becomes, verily, one of them; behold, God does not guide such evildoers.*

Sahīh International: *O you who have believed, do not take the Jews and the Christians as allies. They are [in fact] allies of one another. And whoever is an ally to them among you—then indeed, he is [one] of them. Indeed, Allah guides not the wrongdoing people.*

Pickthall: *O ye who believe! Take not the Jews and the Christians for friends. They are friends one to another. He among you who taketh them for friends is (one) of them. Lo! Allah guideth not wrongdoing folk.*

Yusuf Ali: *O ye who believe! Take not the Jews and the Christians for your friends and protectors: They are but friends and protectors to each other. And he amongst you that turns to them (for friendship) is of them. Verily Allah guideth not a people unjust.*

Shakir: *O you who believe! Do not take the Jews and the Christians for friends; they are friends of each other; and whoever amongst you takes them for a friend, then surely he is one of them; surely Allah does not guide the unjust people.*

Muhammad Sarwar: *Believers, do not consider the Jews and Christians as your intimate friends for they are only friends with each other. Whoever does so, will be considered as one of them. God does not guide the unjust people.*

Hilāli and Muhsin Khan: *O you who believe! Take not the Jews and the Christians as Auliya' (friends, protectors, helpers, etc.), they are but Auliya' to one another. And if any amongst you takes them as Auliya', then surely he is one of them. Verily, Allah guides not those people who are the Zālimūn (polytheists and wrongdoers and unjust).*

Allama Nooruddin: *O you who believe! Do not take these Jews and the Christians for allies. They are allies of one to another (when against you), and whoso from amongst you takes them for allies, is indeed one of them. Verily, Allah does not guide the unjust people to attain their goal.*

Arberry: *O believers, take not Jews and Christians as friends; they are friends of each other. Whoso of you makes them his friends is one of them. God guides not the people of the evildoers.*

Muhammad Ali: *O you who believe, take not the Jews and the Christians for friends. They are friends of each other. And whoever amongst you takes them for friends he is indeed one of them. Surely Allah guides not the unjust people.*

Talāl Itāni: *O you who believe! Do not take the Jews and the Christians as allies; some of them are allies of one another. Whoever of you allies himself with them is one of them. God does not guide the wrongdoing people.*

Rashad Khalīfah: *O you who believe, do not take certain Jews and Christians as allies; these are allies of one another. Those among you who ally themselves with these belong with them. God does not guide the transgressors. (This writer has inserted the italics above)*

Abdul Mājid Daryabādī: *You who believe! Do not take the Jews and the Nazarenes for friend; friends they are to each other, and if any of you befriends them, verily he is one of them. Surely Allah does not guide a transgressing people.*

Abdal Haq and Aisha Bewley: *You who have Imān! do not take the Jews and Christians as your friends; they are the friends of one another. Any of you who takes them as friends is one of them. Allah does not guide wrongdoing people.*

Sher Ali: *O ye who believe! take not the Jews and the Christians for friends. They are friends one to another. And whoso among you takes them for friends is indeed one of them. Verily, Allah guides not the unjust people.*

It should be readily apparent that, other than the translation of Rashad Khalīfa, all these well-known translations of the Qur'ān to the English language translate the verse the same way: i.e., prohibiting Muslims from taking Christians and Jews as their friends and allies. None of the translators, other than Rashad Khalīfa, seem to have realized that such translation of the verse has placed it in conflict with another verse of the Qur'ān which recognizes certain Christians as a people who will be closest in love and affection for Muslims (*Al-Māidah, 5:82*), and with another verse which permits marriage with Christian and Jewish women, and which also permits Muslims to eat food which has been made *Halāl* or permissible for Christians and Jews (*Al-Māidah, 5:5*). But the Qur'ān itself declares that is free from all inconsistencies or contradictions:

أَفَلَا يَتَدَبَّرُونَ الْقُرْآنَ وَلَوْ كَانَ مِنْ عِنْدِ غَيْرِ اللَّهِ لَوَجَدُوا فِيهِ اخْتِلَافًا كَثِيرًا

(Qur'ān, An-Nisa', 4:82)

Allah Most High, invites an examination of the credentials of the Qur'ān as Divine revelation. He boldly declares that if the Qur'ān had come from any but Allah, they would surely have found in it many contradictions! Hence no verse of the Qur'ān contradicts any other verse.

There would be a manifest contradiction if the same Qur'ān were to declare that certain Christians would be closest in love and affection for Muslims, and also declare that Muslims are prohibited to be friends and allies of all Christians and all Jews.

There is yet another problem with the several translations of this verse of the Qur'ān since the translators make the Qur'ān declare something which is factually false! According to Asad, the Qur'ān declares of Christians and Jews that *they are but allies of one another;* Sahīh International: *they are [in fact] allies of one another;* Pickthall: *they are friends one to another;* Abdullah Yusuf Ali: *they are but friends and protectors to each other;* Shākir: *they are friends of each other;* Sarwar: *for they are only friends with each other;* Mohsin Khan: *they are but Auliya' to one another;* Noorddin: *they are allies of one to another (when against you);* Arberry: *they are friends of each other;* Muhammad Ali: *they are friends of each other;* etc.

The Qur'ān was revealed more than six hundred years after the Jews boasted that they had crucified Jesus, and so the Qur'ān appeared in a world in which, for almost six hundred years, Christians and Jews had hated each other. That Christian hatred for Jews continued for more than a thousand years after the revelation of the Qur'ān. It is therefore manifestly false for anyone to declare, at the time when the Qur'ān was revealed and for more than a thousand years after, that Christians and Jews are friend and allies of each other. In fact, Christian-Jewish friendship and alliance emerged as a clearly visible phenomenon of contemporary history only after the birth of the Zionist Movement in 1897.

The proper understanding of the verse of the Qur'ān is that it anticipates such a Jewish-Christian reconciliation and friendship as would pave the way for a certain part of the Christian world, and a certain part of the Jewish world, to reconcile and to then establish friendship and an alliance. Whenever that alliance were to come into being or is established, Muslims are prohibited to be friends and allies with such Christians and such Jews. That alliance has now appeared in the world in the form of the Judeo-Christian Zionist alliance which has brought the State of Israel into existence, and which continues to work to ensure that Israel will one day rule the whole world with a Pax Judaica. (See my two books entitled Jerusalem in the Qur'ān, and Explaining Israel's Mysterious Imperial Agenda.)

Those who attempted to translate the verse (Al-Māidah, 5:51) made the mistake of breaking it into parts or sentences, and to then translate each part or sentence separately. In this way they arrived at a first sentence which was translated to prohibit friendship and alliance with Jews and Christians. They then proceeded to a second part or sentence which was understood in isolation, or stand alone, from what preceded it. They thus declared the Qur'ān to say, falsely so, that Jews and Christians are friends and allies of each other. If they had studied the verse as a whole, they would have understood that their second part or sentence in the verse, was not a second part or sentence at all. Rather it was a phrase which qualified what preceded it. Hence what the Qur'ān actually did, and which escaped the understanding of those who translated the verse, was to prohibit Muslim friendship and alliance with Jews and Christians who were friends and allies of each other, and hence with a Judeo-Christian alliance.

Here is my explanation of the verse which removes all possible contradiction with other verses of the Qur'ān and which does not attribute a manifest falsehood to the Qur'ān:

يَا أَيُّهَا الَّذِينَ آمَنُوا لَا تَتَّخِذُوا الْيَهُودَ وَالنَّصَارَىٰ أَوْلِيَاءَ
بَعْضُهُمْ أَوْلِيَاءُ بَعْضٍ وَمَنْ يَتَوَلَّهُمْ مِنْكُمْ فَإِنَّهُ مِنْهُمْ إِنَّ اللَّهَ لَا
يَهْدِي الْقَوْمَ الظَّالِمِينَ

(Qur'ān, Al-Māidah, 5:51)

> *Allah Most High addresses those who believe in this Qur'ān as the Word of Allah and commands them not to take 'such' Jews and 'such' Christians as their friends and allies who are, themselves, friends and allies of each other. The verse then goes on to declare that whoever from among the Muslims were to take 'such' Christians and Jews as their friends and allies, would be recognized to belong to them, or would eventually belong to them, rather than to the community of Muslims. It ends by declaring that Allah surely or certainly does not guide wicked people.*

I urge readers to study the scholarly analysis of this very important verse of the Qur'ān by the young and brilliant Singaporean scholar, Hasbullah Shafi'iy, which we have included in this book as Appendix 1.

We have shared the above with our readers in order to alert them concerning the dangers posed by translations of the Qur'ān to other languages, and hence the absolute need to quote and to study the actual Arabic text of the Qur'ān whenever we turn to that Book for information or guidance.

For the Christian and Jewish Reader

While we expect that this book will be read by many Muslims, it is also written for the benefit of those to whom the Torah of Moses, i.e. Mūsa عليه السلام, and the Gospel of Jesus, i.e. 'Īsa عليه السلام, was sent, and who, today, refer to themselves as Christians and Jews. They will find in this book a view from the Qur'ān of the beginning of history, which differs sometimes from the Christian and Jewish view of that subject. How should a Christian or a Jew respond when faced with conflicting views emerging from revealed scriptures? The Qur'ān itself answers that question when it declares that Truth that was sent down in the Qur'ān was supported by rational proofs (*Bayyināt min al-Huda*). Hence it is with the rational faculty—which receives its data both externally and internally—that judgment must be made.

The Qur'ān presents excellent credentials with which its claim to be a divinely-revealed scripture can be judged. It presents a text that is absolutely authentic and uncorrupted.

We have presented in our book entitled Methodology for Study of the Qur'ān, the credentials of the Qur'ān to be recognized as absolutely authentic. We urge our Christian and Jewish readers to examine those credentials.

This book will surely test the patience of the English speaking reader who is unfamiliar with the Arabic language, since we have insisted in using Arabic terms that are essential for a presentation of the view of the Qur'ān. However, we always hasten to provide an English equivalent to each Arabic term. As the reader becomes familiar with the Arabic words, the book will hopefully become easier to be read and understood.

وَنَزَّلْنَا عَلَيْكَ الْكِتَابَ تِبْيَانًا لِكُلِّ شَيْءٍ وَهُدًى وَرَحْمَةً
وَبُشْرَى لِلْمُسْلِمِينَ

(Qur'an, al-Nahl, 16:89)

The Qur'ān was sent down as Divine revelation which would explain all things, would provide guidance, and as grace, and glad tidings unto all who submit to Allah Most High.

وَأَنْ أَتْلُوَ الْقُرْآنَ فَمَنِ اهْتَدَى فَإِنَّمَا يَهْتَدِي لِنَفْسِهِ وَمَنْ ضَلَّ
فَقُلْ إِنَّمَا أَنَا مِنَ الْمُنْذِرِينَ

(Qur'ān, al-Naml, 27:92)

Allah Most High has ordered that the Qur'ān be conveyed to mankind. Whoever then chooses to follow the right path, would follow it for his own good. A warning must be given to those who choose to go astray that: I am only a warner.

CHAPTER ONE

INTRODUCING DAJJĀL, THE JASAD

A Gentle Warning

The subject of Dajjāl is perhaps the most difficult that a student or scholar can ever encounter, hence readers are gently cautioned to be patient whenever the understanding of any part of the subject becomes difficult, and not rush to premature judgment on the basis of doubt. As knowledge of the subject expands, it would become easier to connect the many parts of the subject and eventually grasp the subject as a harmonious whole. At that time, and not before, many doubts will be cleared up *Insha' Allah,* i.e., if Allah so Wills.

The Basic Description

Christians know him as the 'Anti-Christ', but Prophet Muhammad صل اللہ علیه و سلم referred to him as *Al-Masīh al-Dajjāl,* i.e., the Dajjāl the Messiah. It is important for our readers to understand that the Prophet has not given to the Anti-Christ, the name—'Dajjāl', for it is not a name! Rather it is a descriptive term which describes him as a 'liar', or as one who 'deceives'. Hence whenever he is referred to in this book as Dajjāl, readers are advised to remember that he should properly be referred to as the Dajjāl.

Since the Qur'ān has identified Nabī 'Īsā, or Jesus, the son of the Virgin Mary عليه السلام, as the Messiah, the implication of the description *'Al-Masīh Al-Dajjāl'* used by the Prophet, is that Dajjāl is someone who would seek to impersonate the Messiah by claiming, falsely so, to be the Messiah. It is for this reason that he is referred to in this book as Dajjāl the false Messiah.

Prophet Muhammad صل الله عليه و سلم prophesied that Nabī 'Īsā or Jesus عليه السلام the true Messiah, would one day return to this world, and that his miraculous return would be a major sign of the End-Time. This writer intends to demonstrate in his second book on Dajjāl entitled 'From Jesus the True Messiah to Dajjāl the False Messiah—A Journey in Islamic Eschatology', that the Qur'ān supports this prophecy of a miraculous return of the true Messiah. But the Prophet went on to prophesy that Dajjāl, the false Messiah, would appear in person in the world just before the return of the true Messiah, and would seek to convince the Jews in particular, that he is indeed the true Messiah. Since Dajjāl, or the Anti-Christ, is a being who belongs to the evil which was created by Allah Most High (see Qur'ān, *Sūrah al-Falaq, 113:2*), and he was thus programmed by Allah Most High to fulfill that evil mission of impersonation, one can expect that he will do so with astonishing accuracy.

It is with this fact constantly in mind that we can now proceed to attempt to deliver to the reader a profile of that extraordinary being, i.e., Dajjāl, the false Messiah, who, according to our interpretation, is described in the Qur'ān as a *Jasad*, i.e., a human body without a soul. He was placed by Allah Most High to sit on Solomon's throne so that, as Solomon feared, he would seek to rule over Holy Israel. This subject is explained later in this chapter.

The Qur'ān confirms that the Messiah, Jesus the son of Mariam, was a human being, and that both he and his mother ate food (the Lord-God, however, does not eat food and indeed, is free from any such need):

مَا الْمَسِيحُ ابْنُ مَرْيَمَ إِلَّا رَسُولٌ قَدْ خَلَتْ مِنْ قَبْلِهِ الرُّسُلُ
وَأُمُّهُ صِدِّيقَةٌ كَانَا يَأْكُلَانِ الطَّعَامَ انْظُرْ كَيْفَ نُبَيِّنُ لَهُمُ

الْآيَاتِ ثُمَّ انْظُرْ أَنَّىٰ يُؤْفَكُونَ

(Qur'ān, al-Māidah, 5:75)

The Christ, son of Mary, was but a messenger of Allah Most High, and hence he was not God—nor was he the son of God! All those who preceded him as messengers of Allah Most High, have died. His mother was someone who never deviated from the truth; and they both ate food like other mortals; Behold how Allah makes clear these clarifying statements for them: and then behold how perverted are their responses!

It is clear therefore, that the Jews expected a Messiah who would be a human being.

Prophet Muhammad صلى الله عليه و سلم gave a description of the Anti-Christ or Dajjāl, as follows: "He would be a Jew, a young man, powerfully built, and with curls in his hair . . ." (Sahīh Muslim). Orthodox Jews, and, it appears, no others besides them, wear these curls in the form of sideburns (Payot) because of a Biblical injunction against shaving the "corners" of one's head:

Do not cut off the hair on the sides of your head.
— Leviticus: 19:27

Although he is a *Jasad*, i.e., a human body without a soul, it should be obvious to our readers that the Anti-Christ or Dajjāl would have to appear as a human being, and as a Jew, since his mission is to convince the Jews that he is indeed the Messiah whom they await. Unless he is a Jew, they would not accept him as the Messiah. Hence when Prophet Muhammad صلى الله عليه و سلم described Dajjāl in the way that he did, i.e., as a being who would appear as a 'person', and a 'Jew', the Islamic view is that the above description of Dajjāl has to be understood literally. This view from Islam differs dramatically from other well-known and sometimes frivolous views which identified the Anti-Christ, for example, with the Roman Catholic Christian Pope in Rome, or former US President Barak Obama, or with a system rather than a person, etc.

Christians face some difficulties in identifying the Anti- Christ or Dajjāl as a person, and as a Jew, because of several scriptural references to him which depart from the single most important fact which emerges from Islamic eschatology, to wit, that he is someone who will seek to impersonate the true Messiah. Consider the following:

Many deceivers have gone out into the world, those who do not confess that Jesus Christ has come in the flesh; any such person is the deceiver and the Antichrist!

— 2 John 1:7

Who is the liar but the one who denies that Jesus is the Christ? This is the Antichrist, the one who denies the Father and the Son.

— 1 John 2:22

By this you know the Spirit of God: every spirit that confesses that Jesus Christ has come in the flesh is from God, and every spirit that does not confess Jesus is not from God. This is the spirit of the Antichrist, which you have heard is coming and now is in the world already.

— 1 John 4:2–3

Despite the above, this writer urges the gentle reader to seriously consider the arguments and evidence now presented in this book for understanding and recognizing the Anti-Christ as someone who was created by the Lord-God and was sent into the world with an evil mission to impersonate Jesus, the True Messiah; as someone who would be a Jew and who would claim to be the true Messiah, and as someone who should therefore be known, properly so, as the false Messiah!

The Complexity of the Subject—Dajjāl is One-Eyed

While it is true that Prophet Muhammad صل الله عليه و سلم did declare that there would be many Dajjāl's who would appear in the world as liars (he said they would number close to thirty) before the appearance of al-Masīh al-Dajjāl himself (Ref. Sunan Tirmīdhī, Sahīh Muslim, etc.), it remains true that he did deliver a basic Prophetic description of al-Masīh al-Dajjāl as a Jew, a young man who would be powerfully built and who would have the curls required by the law of the Torah, etc. This book has already argued that the above description has to be understood literally. The complexity of this subject becomes apparent when we now proceed to argue that a further part of the description of the Anti-Christ or Dajjāl, given by the Prophet, cannot be understood literally but, rather, must be interpreted in order to be understood. Indeed, the Christian or Jewish reader would readily show understanding when told that a significant amount of information in the religion of Islam concerning the Anti-Christ or false Messiah, is presented in language that is allegorical and symbolic. Indeed this is true for the most important Hadīth of all, concerning Dajjāl.

Prophet Muhammad صلى الله عليه و سلم said:

عَنْ عَبْدَ اللَّهِ بْنَ عُمَرَ . رضى الله عنهما . قَالَ قَامَ رَسُولُ اللَّهِ
صلى الله عليه وسلم فِي النَّاسِ فَأَثْنَى عَلَى اللَّهِ بِمَا هُوَ أَهْلُهُ
ثُمَّ ذَكَرَ الدَّجَّالَ فَقَالَ: إِنِّي لأُنْذِرُكُمُوهُ، وَمَا مِنْ نَبِيٍّ إِلاَّ وَقَدْ
أَنْذَرَهُ قَوْمَهُ، وَلَكِنِّي سَأَقُولُ لَكُمْ فِيهِ قَوْلاً لَمْ يَقُلْهُ نَبِيٌّ لِقَوْمِهِ،
إِنَّهُ أَعْوَرُ وَإِنَّ اللَّهَ لَيْسَ بِأَعْوَرَ

Abdullah ibn 'Umar said... The Messenger of Allah then stood up in front of the people, praised Allah with words worthy of Him and then he mentioned Dajjāl and said: I warn you about him, and there is no Prophet who has not warned his people about him. Noah warned his people about him. But I will say to you something about him that no Prophet has ever said to his people. You should know that he is one-eyed, and Allah is not one-eyed.

(Sahīh Bukhārī)

يَا عِبَادَ اللَّهِ أَيُّهَا النَّاسُ فَاثْبُتُوا فَإِنِّي سَأَصِفُهُ لَكُمْ صِفَةً لَمْ
يَصِفْهَا إِيَّاهُ نَبِيٌّ قَبْلِي إِنَّهُ يَبْدَأُ فَيَقُولُ أَنَا نَبِيٌّ وَلاَ نَبِيَّ بَعْدِي
ثُمَّ يُثَنِّي فَيَقُولُ أَنَا رَبُّكُمْ . وَلاَ تَرَوْنَ رَبَّكُمْ حَتَّى تَمُوتُوا وَإِنَّهُ

أَعْوَرُ وَإِنَّ رَبَّكُمْ لَيْسَ بِأَعْوَرَ وَإِنَّهُ مَكْتُوبٌ بَيْنَ عَيْنَيْهِ كَافِرٌ
يَقْرَؤُهُ كُلُّ مُؤْمِنٍ كَاتِبٍ أَوْ غَيْرِ كَاتِبٍ

(The Prophet warned) Oh people, be firm! I describe him, i.e., Dajjāl, to you as no Prophet before me ever did. He will commence by declaring: "I am a Prophet", but there will be no Prophet after me (hence he will lie). Then he will praise himself and declare "I am your Lord-God", but you will not see your Lord-God until you die. And (in addition) he is one-eyed, and your Lord-God is not one-eyed. And between his eyes is written (the word) KAFIR, i.e., disbeliever, which every believer (who has faith in his heart) will be able to read—whether he be literate or illiterate.

(Sunan Ibn Mājah)

In another Hadīth recorded in Sahīh Bukhārī, the Prophet declared that Dajjāl sees with one eye—the left eye, and that he is so blind in the right eye:

وَإِنَّهُ أَعْوَرُ عَيْنُهُ الْيُمْنَى

that it looks like a bulging grape:

كَأَنَّ عَيْنَهُ عِنَبَةٌ طَافِيَةٌ

In yet another Hadīth, also recorded in Sahīh Bukhārī, the Prophet again made mention of Dajjāl's blind right eye:

While sleeping near the Ka'aba last night, I saw in my dream a man of brown color, the best one can see amongst brown color and his hair was long that it fell between his shoulders. His hair was lank and water was dribbling from his head and he was placing his hands on the shoulders of two men while circumambulating the Ka`aba. I asked, Who is this? They replied: This is Jesus, son of Mary. Behind him I saw a man who had very curly hair and was blind in the right eye,* *resembling Ibn Qatān, i.e. an infidel, in appearance. He was placing his hands on the shoulders of a person while performing Tawāf around the Ka`aba. I asked: Who is this? They replied, Al-Masīh Al-Dajjāl.

How can it be possible for someone who has 'faith', but is 'illiterate', to be able to read what is written between the eyes— on the forehead of the Anti-Christ? Our response is that such would be impossible if we were to understand the act of reading literally. As soon as we dismiss a literal understanding, and we turn consequently to search for an interpretation, it becomes readily apparent that the illiterate believer would have the capacity to read because he would be reading with 'eyes' other than those located on the face. The epistemology of the Qur'ān, like that of all other divinely-revealed scriptures, recognizes that the heart can see. In other words, human beings have a capacity for internal sight, i.e., in addition to external sight. It is with internal sight therefore, that the illiterate believer would be able to read what is written on the forehead of the Anti-Christ.

The Qur'ān and Internal Sight

In the following verses in which the Qur'ān directs attention to a fate which can await those who are blind, it is quite obvious that the reference to blindness is not to be understood literally. Rather, the verses of the Qur'ān obviously refer to internal blindness:

قُلْ هَلْ يَسْتَوِي الْأَعْمَى وَالْبَصِيرُ أَفَلَا تَتَفَكَّرُونَ

(Qur'ān, al-An'ām, 6:50)

Allah Most High asks whether someone who is blind, can be deemed equal with someone who can see. Obviously they cannot be equal— hence, will people not think?

قَدْ جَاءَكُمْ بَصَائِرُ مِنْ رَبِّكُمْ فَمَنْ أَبْصَرَ فَلِنَفْسِهِ وَمَنْ عَمِيَ
فَعَلَيْهَا وَمَا أَنَا عَلَيْكُمْ بِحَفِيظٍ

(Qur'ān, al-An'ām, 6:104)

ur'ān declares above, that means of insight have now come unto nd from their Lord-God through this revealed Book.

Whoever, therefore, chooses to 'see' and recognize the Truth, does so for his own good; and whoever chooses to remain 'blind' to the Truth, does so to his own detriment. And (say unto the blind): I am not your keeper.

أَوَّلَ مَرَّةٍ وَنَذَرُهُمْ فِي طُغْيَانِهِمْ يَعْمَهُونَ

(Qur'ān, al-An'ām, 6:110)

Those who reject this Qur'ān will pay a price for that rejection. Allah Most High will keep their hearts and their eyes turned away from the truth, even as they did not believe in it in the first instance; and so they will be left in their overweening arrogance blindly stumbling to and fro.

فَكَذَّبُوهُ فَأَنْجَيْنَاهُ وَالَّذِينَ مَعَهُ فِي الْفُلْكِ وَأَغْرَقْنَا الَّذِينَ كَذَّبُوا
بِآيَاتِنَا إِنَّهُمْ كَانُوا قَوْمًا عَمِينَ

(Qur'ān, Al-'Arāf, 7:64)

When his people rejected Noah and Allah Most High responded to punish them, Allah saved him and those who stood by him, in the Ark, the He caused those who had rejected the Truth sent with Noah to drown. The Qur'ān then declared that they were a people who were 'blind'!

الْعُمْيَ وَلَوْ كَانُوا لَا يُبْصِرُونَ

(Qur'ān, Yūnus, 10:43)

Among the people there are those who pretend to look towards the Prophet: but can he show the right way to the 'blind'—when they are a people who cannot 'see'?

مَثَلُ الْفَرِيقَيْنِ كَالْأَعْمَى وَالْأَصَمِّ وَالْبَصِيرِ وَالسَّمِيعِ هَلْ
يَسْتَوِيَانِ مَثَلًا أَفَلَا تَذَكَّرُونَ

(Qur'ān, Hūd, 11:24)

The Qur'ān directs attention to two kinds of men who may be likened to the 'blind' and 'deaf', on the one hand, and the 'seeing' and 'hearing', on the other. Can these two be deemed alike in their nature? Will people not, then, keep this in mind?

أَفَمَنْ يَعْلَمُ أَنَّمَا أُنْزِلَ إِلَيْكَ مِنْ رَبِّكَ الْحَقُّ

(Qur'ān, al-R'ad, 13:19)

The Qur'ān asks whether one who knows and accepts that whatever has been bestowed from on high upon the Prophet by the Lord-God is the Truth, be deemed equal to one who is 'blind'? Only they who are endowed with insight keep this in mind.

وَمَنْ كَانَ فِي هَذِهِ أَعْمَى فَهُوَ فِي الْآخِرَةِ أَعْمَى وَأَضَلُّ سَبِيلًا

(Qur'ān, al-Isra', 17:72)

The Qur'ān declares that whoever is 'blind' in this world will be 'blind' in the life to come as well, and still farther astray from the path of truth.

We can now conclude that Dajjāl's capacity to see with his left eye, and his blindness in his right eye, ought to be recognized as information that is *Mutashābihah*, i.e., allegorical, and hence subject to *Ta'wīl*, or interpretation.

Our interpretation of the description given by Prophet Muhammad صل الله عليه و سلم is that Dajjāl has external sight, but he is internally blind!

There is an ominous implication which follows from the above interpretation. All those from amongst mankind who follow Dajjāl will all eventually be similar to him, i.e., internally blind; and since he has the word *Kāfir* or 'disbeliever' written on his forehead, the further implication is that all those who follow him would become *Kuffār* (plural of *Kāfir*) or 'disbelievers', and thus be debarred from entering into *Jannah* or paradise.

It is, perhaps, because of this implication that the Qur'ān has delivered a truly ominous warning to those who remain internally blind, that the hellfire can await them, since Dajjāl can get them to dance to every tune he plays:

وَلَقَدْ ذَرَأْنَا لِجَهَنَّمَ كَثِيرًا مِنَ الْجِنِّ وَالْإِنْسِ لَهُمْ قُلُوبٌ لَا يَفْقَهُونَ بِهَا وَلَهُمْ أَعْيُنٌ لَا يُبْصِرُونَ بِهَا وَلَهُمْ آذَانٌ لَا يَسْمَعُونَ بِهَا أُولَئِكَ كَالْأَنْعَامِ بَلْ هُمْ أَضَلُّ أُولَئِكَ هُمُ الْغَافِلُونَ

(Qur'ān, Al-'Arāf, 7:179)

Allah Most High has warned that huge numbers of Jinn and men who have hearts with which they fail to grasp the truth, 'eyes' with which they fail to 'see', and 'ears' with which they fail to 'hear', are destined to enter the Hell-fire. He considers them to have a status like unto cattle—nay, they are even less conscious of the right way: it is they, they who are the truly heedless!

Protestant Islam, which seems, mysteriously so, to be a carbon-copy of Protestant Christianity, may remain unconvinced by our argument in favor of an interpretation that Dajjāl's blind eye should be interpreted to mean internal blindness, and may consequently remain steadfastly adamant in their literal understanding of his 'blind' right eye. Such a people would obviously refuse to recognize Dajjāl when he eventually appears in Jerusalem with the claim to be the Messiah, unless he is literally blind in the right eye. Protestant Islam should reflect over the mysterious incapacity of all disbelievers, regardless of how perfect their eyesight may be, to be able to read what all believers would be able to read, namely the word *Kāfir* which would be written between Dajjāl's eyes—on his forehead! Such die-hards, who cling to a literal understanding of Dajjāl's blind right eye, and to the word *Kāfir* written on his forehead, must explain to us why the Prophet singled out the *Mu'min*, i.e., believer, and hence excluded the *Kāfir*, i.e., disbeliever, when he declared that the believer would be able to read what was written on Dajjāl's forehead? Why can the believer read what the disbeliever cannot read? Protestant Islam must either deliver an answer which is convincing, or abandon its defective methodology. Indeed, unless they change their defective methodology they will never be able to explain why *Tamīm al-Dāri,* who saw Dajjāl (who is so blind in his right eye that it looks like a bulging grape), failed to mention anything about his blind right eye when he reported the event to the Prophet:

> *It was narrated that Fatimah bint Qays (may Allah be pleased with her) said...(what follows are the words spoken by Tamīm al-Dāri)... Then we set off, rushing, until we came to that monastery, where we found the hugest man we had ever seen, bound strongly in chains with his hands tied to his neck and his legs bound from the knees to the ankles with iron shackles...*
>
> (Sahīh al-Bukhārī)

Protestant Islam has an even greater obstacle to overcome when they attempt to offer a credible explanation how Prophet Muhammad صل الله عليه و سلم could suspect Ibn Sayyād, a Jewish youth in Medina, to be Dajjāl, when he was not blind in the right eye?

While the above exhausts our physical description of Dajjāl, the false Messiah, derived from a literal understanding of scriptural texts in Islam, there is more information concerning Dajjāl's unique profile which can be discovered through a process of deduction from those texts; and it is to that process of deduction that we now direct attention.

Deducing Dajjāl's Greater Profile

The historical record reveals that a large number of Jewish tribes were resident in Yathrib (a city located north of Makkah in Arabia) prior to the birth of Prophet Muhammad صل الله عليه و سلم. We know that they were present in Yathrib when the Prophet arrived in that city—having migrated from his native Makkah, since the *Mīthāq* or constitutional agreement successfully negotiated by the Prophet upon his arrival in Yathrib, with which he brought into being (a plural model of) a state, makes mention of several Jewish tribes who were party to the agreement. Muhammad Hamidullah mentions in his book entitled 'First Written Constitution in the World' (Ashraf, Lahore 1994) that " . . . the Arab section of the population was divided into twelve tribes of *Aws* and *Khazraj*, the Jews were divided into the ten tribes of *Banū Nadir* and *Banū Qurayzah*". It should thus be clear that Jews, who were a non-Arab people who considered themselves superior to Arabs, constituted a substantial proportion of the population of an Arab city located close to the very heart of Arabia, i.e., close to Makkah.

It is quite appropriate that we enquire what brought so many Jewish tribes to the city of Yathrib. It is not enough to claim, as some do, that they were expelled by the Christians from Jerusalem and hence they fled to Yathrib. Refugees, who considered themselves, arrogantly so, to be superior to a native population, would be courting grave danger if they allowed themselves to grow in numbers to such an extent that they approached half the size of the whole population. There had to be a compelling reason which would justify such growth in numbers of an arrogant alien population in an Arab city.

We recall that they had rejected the claim of Jesus, the son of the Virgin Mary, who claimed that he was their Promised Messiah. They had rejected that claim on the grounds that his mother had conceived him without being married (which was, of course, true) and they had concluded, falsely so, that he was born in sin. They therefore remained adamantly in wait of the Messiah promised to them by the One God.

They were privy to information conveyed to them through the many Prophets who were raised from their midst, that a divinely-appointed person would appear in Yathrib. It was clear that they perceived it possible that he could be their Messiah since they even boasted to the Arabs in Arabia that he would so empower them that they would then have the upperhand against the Arabs. This fact is mentioned in several books of *Sīrah*, i.e., biographies of the Prophet.

When Prophet Muhammad صل الله عليه و سلم arrived in Yathrib with the startling claim that he was a divinely-appointed Prophet and Messenger, they were shocked and rattled since he did not conform to their profile of the expected Messiah, or even of a Prophet.

Is it possible for us to deduce what kind of person the Jews were expecting, and are still expecting, who would be their Messiah? If we can discover that profile, we would then know more of the profile of Dajjāl who is divinely-programmed to impersonate the Messiah. What was, and is, that profile?

Firstly, the Jews believed, and still believe, that they are the chosen people of the One God to the exclusion of the rest of mankind. The Qur'ān rejected this (false) belief of theirs. It did so in verses which challenged them to seek death if they really believed they were Allah's chosen people. Here is one such verse:

قُلْ يَا أَيُّهَا الَّذِينَ هَادُوا إِنْ زَعَمْتُمْ أَنَّكُمْ أَوْلِيَاءُ لِلَّهِ مِنْ دُونِ النَّاسِ فَتَمَنَّوُا الْمَوْتَ إِنْ كُنْتُمْ صَادِقِينَ

(Qur'ān, al-Jumu'ah, 62:6)

The Qur'ān addresses the Jews and invites them, bluntly so: If you believe that you are the chosen people of Allah, to the exclusion of all other people, then why do you not long for death—if what you say is true?

In consequence of their (false) belief that they are the chosen people of the Lord-God, it was clear to them that the Messiah had to belong to the chosen people, hence he had to be a Jew. Muhammad صل الله عليه و سلم was not a Jew!

Secondly, they believed that the advent of the Messiah would result in a return of the golden age of power that they had enjoyed when the Lord-God chose David, i.e., Nabī Dāud عيه السلام, as a King and ruler, and bestowed on him a mighty kingdom. That kingdom subsequently became a ruling State in the time of his son, Solomon, i.e., Nabī Sulaimān عليه السلام. It is possible for us to deduce that the Jews awaited a Messiah who would restore Holy Israel as a ruling State, and whose lineage could be traced to David, the divinely-appointed King of Israel. The Jews would also expect him to display the unique powers that both David and Solomon possessed. The Messiah could not be just another King; rather he would have to possess a unique stature and status comparable to that of David and Solomon, and he would also have to possess divinely-bestowed miraculous powers comparable to that which they possessed.

If the above deduction is correct, then it would be essential for us to carefully study the profile of those two Prophet-Kings who were the founding fathers of Holy Israel, since it would be that profile which Dajjāl would have to emulate or match.

Profile of the Two Great Prophet-Kings

The Qur'ān confirmed that David, i.e., Nabī Dāud عليه السلام , was chosen by Allah Most High as the ruler on earth who was given a kingdom (or State) over which he was required to rule or govern on the basis of Truth:

فَهَزَمُوهُمْ بِإِذْنِ اللَّهِ وَقَتَلَ دَاوُودُ جَالُوتَ وَآتَاهُ اللَّهُ الْمُلْكَ وَالْحِكْمَةَ وَعَلَّمَهُ مِمَّا يَشَاءُ

(Qur'ān, al-Baqarah, 2:251)

And thereupon, by Allah's leave, the Israelites routed them, and David slew Goliath; and Allah then granted him a Kingdom or State, and wisdom, and imparted to him the knowledge of whatever He willed. . .

It is universally recognized that when the Qur'ān referred in the above verse to a *Mulk* which was granted to David, i.e., Nabī Dāud عليه السلام , it meant a kingdom or State which eventually became known as Holy Israel.

We deduce from the above that the Anti-Christ, or Dajjāl, the false Messiah, must also be a man (and not a woman) who would rule over a *Mulk*, i.e., kingdom or State, which will lay claim to be Holy Israel, and that he must also possess knowledge and wisdom.

يَا دَاوُودُ إِنَّا جَعَلْنَاكَ خَلِيفَةً فِي الْأَرْضِ فَاحْكُمْ بَيْنَ النَّاسِ بِالْحَقِّ وَلَا تَتَّبِعِ الْهَوَى فَيُضِلَّكَ عَنْ سَبِيلِ اللَّهِ إِنَّ الَّذِينَ يَضِلُّونَ عَنْ سَبِيلِ اللَّهِ لَهُمْ عَذَابٌ شَدِيدٌ بِمَا نَسُوا يَوْمَ الْحِسَابِ

(Qur'ān, Sād, 38:26)

Allah Most High addressed the Prophet David and informed him that he was appointed as a ruler who would rule or govern on Allah's behalf on earth. David was then ordered to judge between men on the basis of Truth. Hence he had to judge on the basis of the Law which came from Allah Most High, and he should not follow vain desire by adopting a substitute secular law of his own. If he did so, it would lead him astray from the path of Allah: verily, for those who go astray from the path of Allah, there is suffering severe in store for having forgotten the Day of Reckoning!

In consequence of this divine appointment, David, i.e., Nabī Dāud عليه السلام, established in the Holy Land the Holy State of Israel as a *Khilāfah* State, i.e., a State in which rule and governance was based on divinely-revealed truth, and in which Allah's Law was enforced as the supreme law.

We can deduce from the above that Dajjāl would also have to establish what he would claim to be a *Khilāfah* State, in the Holy Land, and that such a State would have to (appear to) enforce the Divine Law as the supreme law. Dajjāl's Israel cannot, therefore, be a member-State of a United Nations Organization and be subject to the supreme authority of the UN Security Council. It cannot, also, be a member-State of the International Monetary Fund which prohibits the use of gold as money. The Jews would expect the Messiah to rule or govern on the basis of Truth. For this reason Dajjāl, the false Messiah, cannot expect the Jews to accept him as the true Messiah if his Israel is using fake money in the form of paper, plastic or electronic money. Israel will thus have to return to the monetary system of gold and silver coins. Every Jew in the world knows that the present monetary system is bogus, fraudulent and *Harām*, i.e., prohibited. Perhaps, the only ones now left on earth who cannot recognize what every Jew recognizes, are the learned scholars and leaders of the world of Islam—both in and out of the (hitherto) American Republic of Pakistan!

Both David and Solomon, i.e., Nabī Dāud and Nabī Sulaimān عليه السلام, became kings who were raised by Allah Most High to a very high status in His creation, and who ruled over a mighty kingdom:

وَلَقَدْ آتَيْنَا دَاوُودَ وَسُلَيْمَانَ عِلْمًا وَقَالَا الْحَمْدُ لِلَّهِ الَّذِي
فَضَّلَنَا عَلَىٰ كَثِيرٍ مِنْ عِبَادِهِ الْمُؤْمِنِينَ

(Qur'ān, al-Naml, 27:15)

Allah Most High granted true knowledge unto both David and Solomon, and they both responded with praise for Allah Who favored them above many of His believing servants!

وَشَدَدْنَا مُلْكَهُ وَآتَيْنَاهُ الْحِكْمَةَ وَفَصْلَ الْخِطَابِ

(Qur'ān, Sād, 38:20)

Allah Most High caused David's Kingdom, i.e., the Holy State of Israel, to become a very powerful State or Kingdom. Allah also gave him wisdom and sound judgment in speech and decision.

In consequence of the above, Jews would expect the Messiah to rule over a Holy State of Israel that would compare positively with the mighty Kingdom of Israel under the rule of David and Solomon, i.e., Nabī Dāud and Nabī Sulaimān عليه السلام .

We can now deduce from the above that Dajjāl would have to seek to establish today's Israel as precisely such a mighty kingdom and ruling State—hence *Pax Judaica!*

An Impostor on Solomon's Throne

The Qur'ān proceeded to reveal a truly astonishing event in religious history, the likes of which one can hardly, if ever, find a parallel. The description of the event has led us to the view that Solomon had a vision from Allah Most High in which he saw that a soulless impostor would one day sit on his throne, and hence seek to establish a bogus State with a claim that he has restored Holy Israel; and it was precisely because of his knowledge of that ominous future event that he immediately made an extra-ordinary prayer to Allah Most High. Here are the two relevant verses of the Qur'ān:

وَلَقَدْ فَتَنَّا سُلَيْمَانَ وَأَلْقَيْنَا عَلَى كُرْسِيِّهِ جَسَدًا ثُمَّ أَنَابَ

(Qur'ān, Sād, 38:34)

Allah Most High caused distress to Solomon when He placed upon his throne a Jasad, i.e., a human body without a soul; and when Solomon saw what was shown to him, he thereupon turned penitently towards Allah and made a prayer.

In the very next verse of the *Sūrah* Allah Most High described Nabī Sulaimān's response to the *Jasad* which he saw sitting on his throne:

قَالَ رَبِّ اغْفِرْ لِي وَهَبْ لِي مُلْكًا لَا يَنْبَغِي لِأَحَدٍ مِنْ بَعْدِي إِنَّكَ أَنْتَ الْوَهَّابُ

(Qur'ān, Sād, 38:35)

Solomon responded with the prayer that Allah Most High might forgive him his sins, and ordain that his Holy State of Israel could never belong to any after him: verily, Thou alone can grant such a thing.

Proper methodology for studying this subject, in order to understand and identify the *Jasad*, requires that these two verses be studied as a whole. It is indeed regrettable that Islamic scholars failed to apply proper methodology in their efforts to explain the *Jasad* and, as a consequence they have delivered very strange explanations of the subject.

When the two verses are studied as a whole, the entirely plausible deduction can be derived that the human body that was devoid of a soul, and hence described as a *Jasad*, which was placed on Solomon's throne, terrified him into making the prayer that he made because he could see that it would attempt to usurp his throne—which is his rule over Holy Israel, and to create an unholy State in the Holy Land—in Holy Israel's name—that would seek to compare with Holy Israel.

Our view, therefore, is that Nabī Sulaimān saw the Anti- Christ or Dajjāl, the false Messiah, sitting on his throne in Jerusalem, with a mission of eventually ruling over a State of Israel that would claim to be Holy Israel, and hence he made the prayer to Allah Most High in order to ensure that such an effort should never succeed. The *Jasad* who was sitting on the throne was Dajjāl!

We can now recognize that Dajjāl is not an angel, nor a Jinn, but, rather, a *Jasad*, i.e., a human body that is without a soul.

We do not know of anyone who has previously identified the *Jasad* of the Qur'ān with Dajjāl, and hence it is possible that such an identification has been made in this book for the first time. Since this is the most important of all our views presented in this book, our readers would naturally be interested in knowing what were the explanations and interpretations of the verse that were given in particular, by the classical commentators of the Qur'ān. For this reason we have included a summary of those views in Appendix Two.

Since this writer is of the view that Dajjāl, or the Anti- Christ, is the *Jasad* that Allah placed on Solomon's throne, it would follow that he is a special one-of-a-kind created being who would appear as a human being because he has a human body, but who would not be a complete human being since he would be without a soul (*Nafs*). Since he does not possess a soul, he would not have a free will, or a self-directed-will, and hence he would not be responsible for his conduct. It would follow therefrom that he would not be judged on Judgment Day as would all other human beings. It may be difficult, if not impossible, for some readers to even understand, much less to eventually accept, this view of Dajjāl expressed above. Hence we advise that such readers should move on with the subject and not allow this view of Dajjāl to become a bone that sticks in the throat.

We need to make one more comment concerning the *Jasad* however, before we can move on with our subject.

If Dajjāl is, indeed, a *Jasad*, i.e., a human body without a soul or spirit, then it would follow that Dajjāl does not possess intrinsic intelligence. He does not, and cannot think for himself. Rather his intelligence and his process of thinking is externally programmed. He is similar to a robot, and we can thus better understand Dajjāl, and sometimes even recognize his footprints, in whatever functions through artificial intelligence. Nowhere are the Dajjāl's footprints more visible today than in the world of money where real money in the form of gold and silver have been replaced by a monetary *Jasad* of artificial money. This will be the subject of a subsequent book, *Insha' Allah.*

The Qur'ān went on to describe the success of that *Jasad* in getting the Jinn to continue to work for him and to serve him for long years while believing that they were working for Solomon. The explanation for Dajjāl's success in that act of deception is that, upon the death of Solomon, the Jinn saw only the *Jasad* sitting on the throne and holding on to Solomon's staff, and assumed that it was Solomon. The Jinn were bonded to Sulaimān by divine decree, and hence did not have the freedom to observe what was occurring in the world (see *Qur'ān, Saba, 34:12–14*).They were unaware that Sulaimān was dead and buried. They had no knowledge of *Ākhir al-Zamān* and, as a consequence, there was no way that they could realize that they were working as slaves for an impostor. Thus the unholy State of Israel would receive the continuous support of the Jinn during the long struggle for its eventual creation, upon the birth of Israel, and all through its life, so long as Dajjāl continued to sit on Solomon's throne while holding on to his holy staff.

Dā'bbatul Ard (i.e., a beast or creature of the earth)

Allah Most Wise created those who would incrementally chip away at the authority of Dajjāl's Israel—symbolized by Solomon's *Minsa'ah*—until the *Minsa'ah* loses its *Fitrah*, i.e., divinely-bestowed constitution, and then collapses. It would only be when it collapses that the *Jasad* would lose his ability to convince the Jinn that it was Solomon who was sitting on the throne. At that moment when this fact dawns upon the Jinn, Dajjāl's unholy State of Israel will lose the support of the Jinn with consequences that must terrify every Zionist Jew and Zionist Christian supporter of that Israel. Here is the verse of the Qur'ān which has delivered this extra-ordinary information:

فَلَمَّا قَضَيْنَا عَلَيْهِ الْمَوْتَ مَا دَلَّهُمْ عَلَى مَوْتِهِ إِلَّا دَابَّةُ الْأَرْضِ
تَأْكُلُ مِنْسَأَتَهُ فَلَمَّا خَرَّ تَبَيَّنَتِ الْجِنُّ أَنْ لَوْ كَانُوا يَعْلَمُونَ
الْغَيْبَ مَا لَبِثُوا فِي الْعَذَابِ الْمُهِينِ

(Qur'ān, Saba, 34:14)

When Allah Most High decreed that Solomon should die, the Jinn never realized that he was dead, and that there was an impostor sitting on his throne in his place in possession of his Minsa'ah, until Dā'bbatul Ard consumed the Minsa'ah. And when it consequently collapsed in the sense that it lost its miraculous powers, the Jinn, who were subservient to Solomon by Allah's command, then realized that he was dead and that they had been working all this time since his death for an impostor sitting on his throne and in possession of his Minsa'ah. Allah Most Wise then commented that if they had the knowledge of al-Ghaib, i.e., knowledge of events located beyond their capacity to perceive or observe while they remained bonded to Sulaimān, they would not have continued to toil in the shameful punishing servitude doing all the evil things the impostor decreed that they must do on Israel's behalf.

It is clear that it was because of his possession of Solomon's *Minsa'ah* that the *Jasad*, who was sitting on Solomon's throne, could succeed in having the Jinn continue working for him. Solomon's *Minsa'ah* had to possess certain divinely-bestowed miraculous powers or properties to have that effect on the Jinn. We can recall to advantage that it was with his staff (which also possessed similar divinely-bestowed power and properties) that Nabī Mūsa, i.e., Moses عليه السلام , struck the Red Sea, which then parted miraculously to make a track of dry land through which the Israelites could pass to safety (See *Qur'ān, al-Shurā, 26:63*). It was also with his staff that Moses struck the rock and twelve streams of water then flowed miraculously from the rock—one stream for each of Israel's twelve tribes (See *Qur'ān, Al-Baqarah, 2:60*). It was with that same staff that Moses defeated Pharaoh's magicians when his staff became a serpent which miraculously swallowed all that they produced as magic (See *Qur'ān, Al-'Arāf, 7:107–117*). But it was with Yusuf's shirt which was thrown on his father, Yakūb's face, that his sight was miraculously restored.

The commentators of the Qur'ān are universally agreed that the word *Minsa'ah* above means 'staff' or 'walking stick'. If we accept this explanation of the meaning of the word *Minsa'ah*, then the implication would be that the Jasad was holding on the Solomon's staff and benefiting from its miraculous powers which prevented the Jinn from knowing that Solomon was dead, and that there was someone else sitting on his throne.

Dā'bbatul Ard would then have to be something which incrementally dismantles and eventually succeeds in nullifying or destroying the miraculous properties of Solomon's staff. The above verse of the Qur'ān suggests the analogy of termites eating away at the base of a standing staff which then, eventually loses its balance and collapses. Our view is that one of the possible ways of identifying *Dā'bbatul Ard* would then be the invisible electronic waves emitted from cellular phones and wireless internet which pollute the atmosphere. Perhaps it is these electronic waves which eventually cause Solomon's staff to lose its miraculous properties, and that loss is described in the Qur'ān as a collapse—and Allah Knows best! Already, bees have difficulty in navigating their way to and from the pollen in flowers, and as a consequence the production of honey in the mysterious modern world is in constant and alarming decline.

But proper methodology requires that the Qur'ān itself be used to explain the meaning of the word *Minsa'ah*. We must begin the application of proper methodology by recognizing that the Qur'ān has always used another word for 'staff', i.e., *Asāh*. Why then should Allah Most High depart from a word *Asāh* which He has consistently used to mean 'staff', and in this solitary instance, use another word, *Minsa'ah*, to mean the same thing? This would be a strange and mysterious departure from the principle of literary consistency.

When we proceed to apply proper methodology in searching the Qur'ān for any other instance in which the *Minsa'ah* occurs, we find one solitary instance in *Sūrah al-Taubah* as follows:

إِنَّمَا النَّسِيءُ زِيَادَةٌ فِي الْكُفْرِ يُضَلُّ بِهِ الَّذِينَ كَفَرُوا يُحِلُّونَهُ
عَامًا وَيُحَرِّمُونَهُ عَامًا لِيُوَاطِئُوا عِدَّةَ مَا حَرَّمَ اللَّهُ فَيُحِلُّوا
مَا حَرَّمَ اللَّهُ زُيِّنَ لَهُمْ سُوءُ أَعْمَالِهِمْ وَاللَّهُ لَا يَهْدِي الْقَوْمَ
الْكَافِرِينَ

(Qur'ān, al-Taubah, 9:37)

Allah Most High has denounced in the above verse the Arab practice of interfering with 'time' and has declared such to be one more instance of their refusal to acknowledge the truth—a means by which those who are bent on denying the truth are led astray. They declare this practice of adding an extra month every third year in order that the lunar year may synchronize with the solar year to be permissible in one year and forbidden in another year, in order to conform outwardly to the number of months which Allah has hallowed: and thus they make permissible what Allah has prohibited. Goodly seems unto them the evil of their own doings, since Allah does not grace with His guidance people who refuse to acknowledge the truth.

The above verse of the blessed Qur'ān has very clearly used the word to mean 'time'. In this case it is the change in the system of measurement of the passage of time in which Allah Most High, has ordained that a year should comprise of twelve lunar months.

When the Prophet صل الله عليه و سلم used the same word, he also used it to mean 'time' in the sense of 'life-time':

عَنْ أَنَسٍ، قَالَ قَالَ رَسُولُ اللَّهِ صلى الله عليه وسلم: مَنْ سَرَّهُ أَنْ يُبْسَطَ لَهُ فِي رِزْقِهِ وَيُنْسَأَ لَهُ فِي أَثَرِهِ فَلْيَصِلْ رَحِمَهُ

Whoever wishes that he be granted more wealth and that his lease of life be pro longed, he should keep good relations with his kith and kin.
(Bukhārī, Muslim)

Hence neither does the Qur'ān, nor does the Prophet صل الله عليه و سلم support the meaning of 'staff' which has been given by the Commentators of the Qur'ān to the word *Minsa'ah*.

We are now left with only one alternative, i.e., that *Minsa'ah* refers to some miraculous capacity in Solomon's relationship with 'time'.

It is possible that *Dā'bbatul Ard* destroys the miraculous capacity of the 'staff' to permit simultaneous travel back and forth through different dimensions of time. It was through this back and forth travel that the young men who were asleep in the cave could remain in two dimensions of time simultaneously (See *Qur'ān, al-Kahf, 18:16–20*). If the *Jasad* could manipulate different dimensions of time, he could thereby present to the Jinn a Solomon who is still alive, while concealing from them, Solomon's death.

If Dajjāl, the *Jasad*, can manipulate different dimensions of time through his possession of Solomon's staff, and hence advance his agenda of eventually ruling the world from Holy Jerusalem, we will have to accept that the major function of *Dā'bbatul Ard* is to eventually check-mate Dajjāl, the *Jasad* by depriving him of that miraculous staff. They do so by consuming the staff and thereby depriving the staff of its miraculous properties and functions. And Allah Knows best!

In another verse, the Qur'ān further describes *Dā'bbatul Ard* as something which will 'speak' (or injure):

وَإِذَا وَقَعَ الْقَوْلُ عَلَيْهِمْ أَخْرَجْنَا لَهُمْ دَابَّةً مِنَ الْأَرْضِ تُكَلِّمُهُمْ
أَنَّ النَّاسَ كَانُوا بِآيَاتِنَا لَا يُوقِنُونَ

(Qur'ān, al-Naml, 27:82)

Now, as for the deaf and blind of heart, when the word of truth stands revealed against them, We shall bring forth unto them out of the earth a creature, which will speak to, or injure them, because mankind had no real faith in Our messages. The emergence of the beast or creature of the earth i.e., Dā'bbatul Ard, is therefore directly linked to the negligence of a world of people who allow themselves to become brain-washed.

The same Arabic word تكلمهم can have two different meanings based on different punctuation. If it is written as تُكَلِّمُهُمْ (*tukallimuhum*) then it would mean 'speak to them'. But if it is written as تَكْلِمُهُمْ (*taklimuhum*) it would mean 'wound them'. Both meanings would appear to apply if we interpret *Da'butul Ard* in the manner which we have just done. The learned companion of the blessed Prophet صل الله عليه و سلم , Ibn Abbas, held this view. (See *Tafsīr al-Qurtubi*)

Already electronic communication through so-called 'Smart Phones' and other such cellular phones is rapidly transforming much of the thus 'connected world' into a virtual talk city in which the 'cattle' of the world spend endless, hours, days, weeks—and eventually a lifetime, communicating with each other in what may best be described as a 'Talk City'. Eventually the 'cattle' become so addicted to what is sometimes known as 'Bla Bla', that they cannot bear to live without those devices. They remain unaware that this explosion in 'talk' is not happening by accident. Rather a divine plan is unfolding in which the electronic waves emitted into the atmosphere, and into the human ear-drum and brain, will not only cause the miraculous properties of Solomon's staff to be consumed electronically, but will also damage peoples' brains to such an extent that brain cancer, dementia and a form of dementia known as Alzheimer would become common-place. Indeed there may be an epidemic in the making. Alzheimer's is a brain disease that causes a slow decline in memory, thinking and reasoning skills. One of the most common signs of Alzheimer's is memory loss, especially forgetting recently learned information. It should be a cause for major concern that children as young as six and eight years of age are now falling victims to childhood dementia—i.e., Alzheimer's.

Our view is that *Dā'bbatul Ard* can be identified with this electronic storm which has emerged out of the earth and is sweeping all of mankind into its deadly embrace in which the human mind itself, is being dismantled. Instead of living in the real concrete world, negligent mankind is being swept into the deadly embrace of what is called the virtual world. They eventually lose contact with spiritual reality, and they lose the consciousness of their own status as beings in whom reside the Divinely-breathed *Rūh*, or Spirit.

The Qur'ān has delivered an ominous warning on precisely such a state of affairs:

وَلَا تَكُونُوا كَالَّذِينَ نَسُوا اللَّهَ فَأَنْسَاهُمْ أَنْفُسَهُمْ أُولَئِكَ هُمُ الْفَاسِقُونَ

(Qur'ān, al-Hashr, 59:19)

Allah warns mankind not to be like those who are oblivious of Allah, and whom He therefore causes to become oblivious of their own status as human beings: for it is they, they who are truly depraved!

Those who are not comfortable with the above identification of *Dā'bbatul Ard,* may choose instead to await a Beast described elsewhere as follows:

Its head is like the head of a bull, its eyes are like the eyes of a pig, its ears are like the ears of an elephant, its horns are like the horns of a stag, its neck is like the neck of an ostrich, its chest is like the chest of a lion, its color is like the color of a tiger, its haunches are like the haunches of a cat, its tail is like the tail of a ram, and its legs are like the legs of a camel.

This function of *Dā'bbatul Ard* must be very convenient for Dajjāl, who has precisely the same goal of incrementally dismantling every rival to Israel that now exists in the world— hence the explanation for the fate which is now embracing such great States of the modern West as USA, UK, France, Germany, etc. These ruling States and their greatest allies which gave to the world the likes of *Pax Britannica* and *Pax Americana,* are being incrementally dismantled by hidden forces akin to termites which are constantly nibbling away at the staff that maintains the balance of a soulless body sitting on the throne reserved for the ruling State. The rivals to Israel's status as ruling State in the world will one day collapse. It is just a matter of time.

This writer pauses to advise all those who have faith in the One God (Muslim, Christian, Jew or otherwise) and who are living within the embrace of Dajjāl's electronically-connected world, to seek protection and healing through continuous recitation (of the Arabic text) of the blessed Qur'ān. This is particularly important for those who continuously use (foolishly so) their so-called Smart Phones and other cellular phones. This writer pauses to remind such people of the divine declaration that the Qur'ān can 'heal':

وَنُنَزِّلُ مِنَ الْقُرْآنِ مَا هُوَ شِفَاءٌ وَرَحْمَةٌ لِلْمُؤْمِنِينَ وَلَا يَزِيدُ
الظَّالِمِينَ إِلَّا خَسَارًا

(Qur'ān, al-Isra', 17:82)

Thus, step by step, has Allah Most High bestowed through this Qur'ān that which heals, and is a grace unto those who believe in the One God, the while it only adds to the ruin of evildoers.

David and Solomon—the Miraculous Profile

David, i.e., Nabī Dāud عليه السلام, was more than just a King who ruled over a kingdom. Both he, and his son Solomon, i.e. Nabī Sulaimān عليه السلام, were unique in Allah's creation since the Qur'ān disclosed that Allah Most High caused the mountains and the birds to sing with David in His divine praise, and that Solomon was taught the language of the birds:

وَسَخَّرْنَا مَعَ دَاوُودَ الْجِبَالَ يُسَبِّحْنَ وَالطَّيْرَ وَكُنَّا فَاعِلِينَ

(Qur'ān, al-Anbiyāh, 21:79)

...And Allah Most High, caused the mountains to join David in extolling His limitless glory, and likewise the birds: for Allah is able to do all things.

وَوَرِثَ سُلَيْمَانُ دَاوُودَ وَقَالَ يَا أَيُّهَا النَّاسُ عُلِّمْنَا مَنْطِقَ الطَّيْرِ
وَأُوتِينَا مِنْ كُلِّ شَيْءٍ إِنَّ هَذَا لَهُوَ الْفَضْلُ الْمُبِينُ

(Qur'ān, al-Naml, 27:16)

And in respect of this miraculous profile, Solomon was truly David's heir; and he would say: Oh people! We have been taught the speech of birds, and have been given in abundance of all good things: this, behold, is indeed a manifest favor from Allah!

Not only were these two Prophet-Kings blessed as described above but, in addition, Solomon could control the weather:

وَلِسُلَيْمَانَ الرِّيحَ عَاصِفَةً تَجْرِي بِأَمْرِهِ إِلَى الْأَرْضِ الَّتِي بَارَكْنَا
فِيهَا وَكُنَّا بِكُلِّ شَيْءٍ عَالِمِينَ

(Qur'ān, al-Anbiyāh, 21:81)

And Allah made the stormy wind subservient unto Solomon, so that it sped at his behest towards the land which Allah had blessed, i.e., the Holy Land: for it is Allah Who has knowledge of all things.

When the ants spoke, Solomon, i.e., Nabī Sulaimān عليه السلام could understand what they said:

حَتَّىٰ إِذَا أَتَوْا عَلَىٰ وَادِ النَّمْلِ قَالَتْ نَمْلَةٌ يَا أَيُّهَا النَّمْلُ ادْخُلُوا مَسَاكِنَكُمْ لَا يَحْطِمَنَّكُمْ سُلَيْمَانُ وَجُنُودُهُ وَهُمْ لَا يَشْعُرُونَ

(Qur'ān, al-Naml, 27:18)

Solomon and his forces travelled until they came upon a valley full of ants. An ant then exclaimed: Oh ants! Go quickly into your dwellings, lest Solomon and his hosts crush you without even being aware of you!

The Qur'ān disclosed that even the Jinn were divinely bonded, at the pain of great punishment for deviation from Allah's command, to work for Solomon, i.e., Nabī Sulaimān عليه السلام in the manufacture of numerous items of copper that were of use to Holy Israel in the Temple, i.e., Masjid, which he had built. They obtained that metal from a fountain of copper which Allah Most High bestowed on him. As a consequence the Jews will expect their Messiah to do the same:

وَأَسَلْنَا لَهُ عَيْنَ الْقِطْرِ وَمِنَ الْجِنِّ مَنْ يَعْمَلُ بَيْنَ يَدَيْهِ بِإِذْنِ رَبِّهِ وَمَنْ يَزِغْ مِنْهُمْ عَنْ أَمْرِنَا نُذِقْهُ مِنْ عَذَابِ السَّعِيرِ

(Qur'ān, Sabā, 34:12)

Allah caused a fountain of molten copper to flow at Solomon's behest; and among the Jinn there were some that had been constrained to labour for him by his Lord-God's leave and whichever of them deviated from Allah's command, him would Allah let taste suffering through a blazing flame.

يَعْمَلُونَ لَهُ مَا يَشَاءُ مِنْ مَحَارِيبَ وَتَمَاثِيلَ وَجِفَانٍ كَالْجَوَابِ وَقُدُورٍ رَاسِيَاتٍ اعْمَلُوا آلَ دَاوُودَ شُكْرًا وَقَلِيلٌ مِنْ عِبَادِيَ الشَّكُور

(Qur'ān, Sabā, 34:13)

The Jinn made for Solomon whatever he wished of sanctuaries, and statues, and basins as large as great watering-troughs, and cauldrons firmly anchored. Allah said: Labour, Oh David's people, in gratitude towards Me, and remember that few are the truly grateful—even among My servants!

اصْبِرْ عَلَى مَا يَقُولُونَ وَاذْكُرْ عَبْدَنَا دَاوُودَ ذَا الْأَيْدِ إِنَّهُ أَوَّابٌ

(Qur'ān, Sād, 38:17)

Allah Most High advised Prophet Muhammad to bear patiently with whatever those opposed to him may say, and to remember His servant David who was endowed with so much inner strength! He, verily, would always turn unto Allah.

Perhaps one of the events in the life of Nabī Sulaimān عليه السلام that was revealed in the Qur'ān allows us to anticipate the kind of assistance that the Jinn can provide to Dajjāl in *Ākhir al-Zamān*. The event concerns the wondrous throne of the Queen of *Saba'*, i.e., Sheba. Nabī Sulaimān عليه السلام wanted the throne to be brought to his court prior to the Queen's arrival at his court. A Jinn offered to bring it in the twinkling of an eye.

Here is what the Qur'ān has to say concerning the assistance provided by the Jinn in this matter:

قَالَ يَا أَيُّهَا الْمَلَأُ أَيُّكُمْ يَأْتِينِي بِعَرْشِهَا قَبْلَ أَنْ يَأْتُونِي مُسْلِمِينَ ۝

قَالَ عِفْرِيتٌ مِنَ الْجِنِّ أَنَا آتِيكَ بِهِ قَبْلَ أَنْ تَقُومَ مِنْ مَقَامِكَ

وَإِنِّي عَلَيْهِ لَقَوِيٌّ أَمِينٌ ۝
قَالَ الَّذِي عِنْدَهُ عِلْمٌ مِنَ الْكِتَابِ أَنَا آتِيكَ بِهِ قَبْلَ أَنْ يَرْتَدَّ
إِلَيْكَ طَرْفُكَ فَلَمَّا رَآهُ مُسْتَقِرًّا عِنْدَهُ قَالَ هَذَا مِنْ فَضْلِ رَبِّي
لِيَبْلُوَنِي أَأَشْكُرُ أَمْ أَكْفُرُ وَمَنْ شَكَرَ فَإِنَّمَا يَشْكُرُ لِنَفْسِهِ وَمَنْ
كَفَرَ فَإِنَّ رَبِّي غَنِيٌّ كَرِيمٌ ۝
قَالَ نَكِّرُوا لَهَا عَرْشَهَا نَنْظُرْ أَتَهْتَدِي أَمْ تَكُونُ مِنَ الَّذِينَ لَا
يَهْتَدُونَ ۝

(Qur'ān, al-Naml, 27:38–41)

When Solomon learned that the Queen of Sheba was coming to visit him, he said to his council: Oh you nobles! Which of you can bring me her throne ere she and her followers come unto me in willing surrender to Allah? An 'Ifreet of the Jinn said: I shall bring it to you before you rise from your council-seat—for, behold, I am powerful enough to do it, and worthy of trust! Thereupon one of the Jinn who had knowledge of the Book said: I will bring it to thee within the twinkling of an eye! Then when Solomon saw it placed firmly before him, he said: This is by the Grace of my Lord, to test me whether I am grateful or ungrateful! And if any is grateful, truly his gratitude is a gain for his own soul; but if any is ungrateful, truly my Lord is Free of all Needs, Supreme in Honor! Solomon then requested that the throne be so altered or disguised that she may not know it as hers: let us see whether she allows herself to be guided [to the truth] or remains one of those who will not be guided.

The assistance provided to Solomon by the Jinn who, according to the Qur'ān, had 'knowledge of the book', anticipates modern television, and the holographic casting of three-dimensional objects in mid-air without using any kind of screen, and other such seemingly miraculous things beside.

While the Qur'ān does not identify the 'book' which provided the knowledge which, in turn, made it possible for a Jinn to relocate an object instantaneously to a new location thousands of miles away, it does confirm the existence of such a book. But we must consider the possibility that the word 'book' may have been used to represent a branch of knowledge. If so, then the possibility exists that Dajjāl may have access to that branch of knowledge and hence, that the modern scientific and technological revolution is assisted by the Jinn, and that there are scientific and technological miracles waiting to occur in history which will attempt to replicate this event described above.

We conclude by observing that the profile of the Messiah whom the Jews await, must compare favorably with what has been described above of the profiles of both David and of Solomon, i.e., Nabī Dāud and Nabī Sulaimān عليه السلام There is an abundance of evidence which convincingly demonstrate that Dajjāl has already made substantial progress in establishing for himself precisely such a profile.

هُوَ الْأَوَّلُ وَالْآخِرُ وَالظَّاهِرُ وَالْبَاطِنُ وَهُوَ بِكُلِّ شَيْءٍ عَلِيمٌ

(Qur'ān, al-Hadīd, 57:3)

He—Allah Most High—is the First and He is the Last. He is the outwardly manifest as well as the inwardly hidden, and He has full knowledge of all things; from first to last, as well as from outward to inward.

CHAPTER TWO

Methodology of Connecting the Beginning of History with the End

History Begins and Ends with Allah Most High

The Qur'ān has, time and again, affirmed that with Allah resides both the beginning and the end of all affairs, and that His Will prevails both at the beginning as well as at the end.

Here are some relevant verses:

...أَلَا إِلَى اللَّهِ تَصِيرُ الْأُمُورُ

(Qur'ān, al-Shūra, 42:53)

. . . verily, with Allah is the beginning and the end of all affairs and events!

...وَإِلَى اللَّهِ تُرْجَعُ الْأُمُورُ

(Qur'ān, al-Hajj, 22:76)

. . . for all affairs return to Allah as their source.

وَأَنَّ إِلَىٰ رَبِّكَ الْمُنْتَهَىٰ

(Qur'ān, al-Najm, 53:42)

And that with thy Lord-God is the beginning and the end of all that exists, and this includes history.

إِلَىٰ رَبِّكَ مُنْتَهَاهَا

(Qur'ān, al-Nāziāt, 79:44)

With thy Lord-God alone rests the beginning and the end of all knowledge pertaining to the End-time.

... كَمَا بَدَأَكُمْ تَعُودُونَ

(Qur'ān, al-'Arāf, 7:29)

. . . As it was, when He who brought you into being at the beginning, so also it shall be when you return to it.

When we view all the verses of the Qur'ān that connect the 'beginning' with the 'end', and when we locate the system of meaning which binds them into a harmonious whole, we arrive at a marvelous philosophy of history in which we recognize— not only that Truth is One—but that the same One Truth Methodology of Connecting the Beginning of History with the End pervades the totality of the historical process as it weaves or meanders its way through history from sunrise to sunset. In other words, history commenced with that One Truth and will end with the same Truth. Hence there is no linear ascent or descent of history (i.e., in the movement of history) from 'falsehood' to 'truth' or vice versa; nor is the movement of history cyclic. Rather, it is movement from Truth to Truth despite all the meanderings of history. This should be known as the Islamic philosophy of history.

Nowhere, perhaps, has the Qur'ān delivered a more eloquent declaration of that unity and harmony in the historical process which both locks and binds 'beginning' with 'end' in a harmonious whole, than in the following verse:

مَا خَلْقُكُمْ وَلَا بَعْثُكُمْ إِلَّا كَنَفْسٍ وَاحِدَةٍ إِنَّ اللَّهَ سَمِيعٌ بَصِيرٌ

(Qur'ān, Luqmān, 31:28)

The creation of mankind, as well as the resurrection of mankind, is in no wise but as that of an individual soul: for Allah is He Who hears and sees all things.

Another verse of the Qur'ān has declared that the stamp of Allah's authority is established both in the beginning, as well as in the end; i.e., in events which occurred previously, and this necessarily includes the beginning of history, and that which will occur subsequently, and this, also, necessarily includes the end of history. The *Āyah*, i.e., verse, which has made this declaration concludes, significantly so, with 'good news' at that end for those who have faith in the One God:

...لِلَّهِ الْأَمْرُ مِنْ قَبْلُ وَمِنْ بَعْدُ وَيَوْمَئِذٍ يَفْرَحُ الْمُؤْمِنُونَ

(Qur'ān, al-Rūm, 30:4)

. . . with Allah resides all authority in respect, for example, of events that will occur in history previously, which includes the beginning, as well as later, which includes the end of history, and on that day at the end, when Allah's authority will prevail, those who have faith in the One God will celebrate.

While the immediate context of the revelation of the above *Āyah*, i.e., verse, with its dramatic declaration of victory with Allah's help, was the (Orthodox) Christian Byzantine victory over pagan Persia (pagan in the same sense in which Arabia was also pagan at that time), the *Āyāt* or verses of the Qur'ān have a universal import and cannot be restricted to a specific historical context; hence this verse of the Qur'ān has actually delivered a declaration that the beginning and the end of history are connected and impressed with Divine authority in such wise Methodology of Connecting the Beginning of History with the End that history will end with the triumph of truth over all rivals, and of faith and justice over injustice and oppression. Orthodox Christian Russia, which today leads the Orthodox Christian world, must find great comfort in this assurance in the Qur'ān of victory again at the end of history. Muslims also, will surely be pleased to celebrate that victory once again, as they did the first time, the only difference being an alliance with *Rūm*, i.e., the Orthodox Christian world, the second time around. The Prophet himself prophesied that alliance:

> *"You will make peace with the Romans, i.e. Christians/'Rum', in a secure truce/alliance, and you and they will fight an enemy who is behind you, and you will be victorious"*
> (We omit the rest of this Hadīth since the rest is in conflict with the part which we have quoted, in addition to being in conflict with the Qur'ān.)
>
> (Sunan Abū Dāud)

Victory for Truth at the end of history was affirmed in the following thrice-repeated *Āyah* (verse) of the Qur'ān:

هُوَ الَّذِي أَرْسَلَ رَسُولَهُ بِالْهُدَى وَدِينِ الْحَقِّ لِيُظْهِرَهُ عَلَى الدِّينِ كُلِّهِ وَكَفَى بِاللَّهِ شَهِيدًا

(Qur'ān, al-Fath, 48:28); (al-Saff, 61:9); (al-Taubah, 9:33)

He it is who has sent forth His Messenger, i.e., Prophet Muhammad, with the task of spreading guidance and the religion of truth, to the end that He make it prevail over every false religion; and none can bear witness to the truth as Allah does.

Muslims and Orthodox Christians, who both share many eschatological similarities, are assured of victory at the end of history. We are, in fact, on firm foundations when we anticipate a Muslim-Orthodox alliance in the military struggle for the conquest of Constantinople which, according to the prophecy of Prophet Muhammad صل الله عليه و سلم , will follow immediately after the *Malhama* or Great War (Christians refer to it as Armageddon) in which 99 out of every 100 combatants will be killed. (Sahīh Bukhārī, Sahīh Muslim)

It is important for us to note at this juncture that Islam has never claimed that Truth came to the world for the first time with Nabī Muhammad صل الله عليه و سلم, nor has the Qur'ān ever claimed a monopoly on Truth! Rather the Qur'ān has consistently affirmed that the Truth which came to the world with Nabī Muhammad, also came with previous Prophets of the One God such as Nabī Ibrahīm, i.e., Abraham, Nabī Mūsa, i.e., Moses, Nabī Dāud, i.e., David, Nabī Īsa, i.e., Jesus, etc. عليه السلام, and in the scriptures such as the *Taurāt*, i.e., Torah, and the *Injīl*, i.e., Gospel, which were divinely-revealed to them. Indeed the Qur'ān declared that it came to not only confirm and validate that previously–revealed truth, but to also guard and protect it (See Qur'ān, *Al-Māidah, 5:48*). And so, it is 'perennial truth' which was revealed for the last time in the last scripture, i.e., the Qur'ān, and it is that truth which will triumph in the end of history. Only two communities of people (in addition of course to individual Jews, as well as other individuals) will be holding on to that truth at the end of history—i.e., the community of true Muslims and the community of true Christians.

Truth does not require an army, navy and air force, in order to prevail over all rivals. Truth does not ever wage endless wars to establish full-spectrum political, economic and military dominion or rule over the whole world in order to prevail over all rivals; hence the arrogant blood-stained Zionist claim to Truth is manifestly bogus and false. Rather Truth requires believers to resist oppression, and to respond to the oppressor by all means lawful and necessary, in order to liberate the oppressed and to ensure that justice triumphs in the world. The Judeo-Christian Zionist alliance and its allies around the world, pursue their claim to Truth with an oppression that is unprecedented in history, and with a mountain of lies. The modern Judeo-Christian West also sought to brain-wash the non-Western world which they attacked and colonized, into believing that they were a civilization of people who had been raised with a divine mission of civilizing the peoples of the non-Western world. They pursued this so-called divine mission with an arrogant belief that they were created superior to all other people. This book recognizes Dajjāl as the mastermind who brought into being the arrogant Zionist Judeo-Christian Western civilization.

Islam is not imperialism, and it was not an imperial Islam which spread so rapidly in its early history. Rather, the oppressed of the world welcomed Islam. Whenever Muslims fought and conquered territory for reasons other than liberating the oppressed and resisting aggression, as they did in Hindu India as well as in the Orthodox Christian world in the Balkans, and perhaps elsewhere as well, such wars were bogus *Jihād*, and they naturally left in their trail eternal hatred for Islam!

It was a bogus Islam which made a deal with Henry Kissinger to sell oil for only US dollars and to thus force upon the world a bogus and fraudulent petrodollar monetary system. It is bogus Islam which now forces upon the world of Islam a *Harām* so-called Islamic Banking system, and which legalizes *Harām* Bit-coin as money. And it is bogus Islam which dances with every tune that comes out of Dajjāl's feminist revolution, to prohibit the marriage of a girl who is seventeen years of age, and to thrust women forward to occupy every possible public office until the ominous prophecy of Prophet Muhammad concerning 'Dajjāl and women' is fulfilled, as 'night' becomes 'day'.

The Qur'ān has linked the beginning of history with the end, in another *Āyah* (or verse) as follows:

هُوَ الْأَوَّلُ وَالْآخِرُ وَالظَّاهِرُ وَالْبَاطِنُ وَهُوَ بِكُلِّ شَيْءٍ عَلِيمٌ

(Qur'ān, al-Hadīd, 57:3)

He, Allah, is the First and He is the Last. He is the outwardly manifest as well as the inwardly hidden: and He has full knowledge of all things.

The above verse again suggests a connection between the beginning and the end of history—to wit, that the end of history cannot be fully understood without a study of events that occurred at the beginning of history.

If the Qur'ān declares that Allah Most High, is the first, last, manifest and hidden, and if the verse concludes with the statement that "He has (full) knowledge of all things", the implication is that references to first, last, manifest and hidden were all made in the context of knowledge; hence, when the Qur'ān declared that Allah Most High, is the first, and that He has knowledge of all things, it indicates that with Him is the knowledge of the beginning of history; and when it declared that He is the last, the implication is the same; hence, with Him, also, is the knowledge of the end of history. When first and last are juxtaposed together, as in the above *Āyah*, i.e., verse, it logically indicates a Divine connection between knowledge of the end of history and knowledge of the beginning. Since the Qur'ān addresses the subject of the beginning of history, the implication is that Islamic scholarship has a capacity to make an eschatological contribution to the understanding and explanation of history, the historical process and the movement of history.

My teacher of the philosophy of history, Dr. Burhān Ahmad Fārūqī (*rahimahullah*) taught an Islamic philosophy of history which recognized the purpose and end of history in "the re-realization of perennial truth". In other words, Truth was established at the beginning of history, and will again be established at the end. By 'establishment' of Truth, he meant the triumph of Truth over all rivals. The world got a taste of that conclusion of the historical process when history witnessed the advent of the last of the Prophets or Messengers of Allah Most High, i.e., Nabī Muhammad صل الله عليه و سلم. Truth triumphed over all rivals in Arabia 1400 years ago, and Truth will again triumph over all rivals at the end of history.

The Book of 'Revelation' of the Gospel of Jesus, i.e., Nabī 'Īsa عليه السلام, has a statement concerning the Lord-God which is almost identical to the verse of the Qur'ān, quoted above, which connected the 'beginning' with the 'end' of history:

I am Alpha and Omega, the beginning and the end, the first and the last. ('Alpha' and 'Omega' are the first and last letters of the Greek alphabet).
— Revelation, 22:13

The Torah that was sent to Nabī Mūsa i.e., Moses, عليه السلام also says the same thing:

"This is what the Lord says—Israel's King and Redeemer, the Lord Almighty: I am the first and I am the last; apart from me there is no God."
— Isaiah, 44:6

Our readers may wish to examine Jewish and Christian eschatology to locate what connections have been made by Christian and Jewish scholarship between the 'beginning' and the 'end' of history, and with what results.

The Beginning, the End, and Dajjāl

The main events that occur in our subject of the advent of *Al-Masīh Al-Dajjāl,* or Dajjāl, the false Messiah (some refer to him as the Anti-Christ), and the return of Nabī Īsa, i.e., Jesus the true Messiah عليه السلام, are both located at the end of history. Muslims and Christians are the only two people among mankind who believe in these two events as a matter of religious faith. As a consequence both Muslims and Christians must seek to determine whether these End-time events are in any way connected with events which may have occurred at the beginning of history.

Muslims can embark on that effort with confidence of positive results since Prophet Muhammad صل الله عليه و سلم declared that "every Prophet before him (and he is the last of them all) warned his people about Dajjāl, or the Anti-Christ". He even went on to make it quite clear that he included the Prophets who were located at the beginning of history. He did so when he made specific mention of Nabī Nūh, i.e., Noah عليه السلام, in that connection:

عَنْ عَبْدَ اللَّهِ بْنَ عُمَرَ - رضى الله عنهما - قَالَ قَامَ رَسُولُ اللَّهِ صلى الله عليه وسلم فِي النَّاسِ فَأَثْنَى عَلَى اللَّهِ بِمَا هُوَ أَهْلُهُ ثُمَّ ذَكَرَ الدَّجَّالَ فَقَالَ: إِنِّي لأُنْذِرُكُمُوهُ، وَمَا مِنْ نَبِيٍّ إِلاَّ وَقَدْ أَنْذَرَهُ قَوْمَهُ، وَلَكِنِّي سَأَقُولُ لَكُمْ فِيهِ قَوْلاً لَمْ يَقُلْهُ نَبِيٌّ لِقَوْمِهِ، إِنَّهُ أَعْوَرُ وَإِنَّ اللَّهَ لَيْسَ بِأَعْوَرَ

Abdullah ibn 'Umar said: . . . . The Messenger of Allah then stood up in front of the people, praised Allah with words worthy of Him and then he mentioned Dajjāl and said: I warn you about him, and there is no prophet who has not warned his people about him. Noah warned his people about him . . .

(Sahīh Bukhārī)

If every Prophet warned his people about Dajjāl, it follows that there must be information about him, or connected to him, at the beginning of history. Let us therefore turn to the first pages of history in an effort to understand a most momentous event located close to the end of history and without which there would be no Dajjāl.

If there had been no Jewish rejection of Jesus, the son of the Virgin Mary, as the promised Messiah, no demand for his crucifixion, and no boasting when they saw him crucified before their very eyes, there would have been no need for an advent of a false Messiah or Anti-Christ prior to a return of the true Messiah, or of a world-order of Gog and Magog to work for the Anti-Christ to assist him in realizing his mission, and no return of the true Messiah, at the end of history.

Since the return of the true Messiah, and the advent of a false Messiah prior to that miraculous return, are located at the very heart of the end of history, the implication for Christians and for Muslims, i.e., the two people who believe that Jesus will one day return, is that the dramatic conclusion of the historical process itself cannot be explained unless we can locate the explanation for the Jewish rejection of Jesus عليه السلام. Our view is that the main reasons for that rejection are located in the beginning of history—hence the need for us to address this subject.

Jesus عليه السلام was born into an Israelite community, and hence belonged to a people who claimed, and still claim to this day, that they are a special people with the Lord-God who chose them from amongst all of mankind and conferred upon them a special status with Himself. They were expecting a Messiah who was promised to them by the Lord-God, and who when he came, would restore the golden age when Jews ruled the world. When Jesus claimed to be that Messiah, and it was well-known that he was born to a mother who was not married, they rejected his claim to be the Messiah on the basis of their charge that he was a 'bastard' child. They were also very angry when they saw him performing miracles as a boy despite his alleged 'bastard' status; for example he took mud, shaped it in the form of birds, blew into them, and, by Allah's leave, they became living birds (Qur'ān, *Ale 'Imrān, 3:49*). But they were also very angry with him for other reasons. The Qur'ān has consistently accused them of having corrupted Divine revelation by changing and rewriting the word of the One God. It has identified, for example, a change which made *Halāl*, i.e., permissible, what Allah had made *Harām*, i.e., prohibited. They took *Ribā* or usury, even though they had been prohibited from doing so (Qur'ān, *An-Nisa', 4:161*).

It was also a scriptural crime for them to claim, arrogantly so, that they are the chosen people of the Lord-God to the exclusion of the rest of mankind, and hence no gentile could ever be the equal of even the lowest of the Jews. They do not believe that they will be judged individually on Judgment Day, but rather believe in their unique collective judgment as a people (all others being judged individually), and that heaven is reserved for them.

Here is what the Torah has to say concerning their status as a chosen people:

"For you are a holy people to Yahweh your God, and God has chosen you to be His treasured people from all the nations that are on the face of the earth."
— Deuteronomy, 14:2

"Now therefore, if you will obey My voice indeed, and keep My covenant, then you shall be a peculiar treasure unto Me from all the peoples, for all the earth is mine."
— Exodus, 19:5

"And I will establish My covenant between Me and you and your descendants after you in their generations, for an everlasting covenant, to be God to you and your descendants after you."
— Genesis, 17:7

"And you shall be unto Me a kingdom of priests, and a Holy nation."
— Exodus, 19:6

"The Lord did not set his love upon you, nor choose you, because you were more in number than any people; for you were the fewest of all people; but because the Lord loved you, and because he would keep the oath which he had sworn unto your ancestors."
— Deuteronomy, 7:7–8

"You only have I singled out of all the families of the earth: therefore will I visit upon you all your iniquities."

— Amos, 3:2

It is quite strange and, indeed, mysterious, that modern western civilization emerged in history with unprecedented power, and then went on a rampage of oppression around the world, subjugating untold millions to western colonial and imperial rule while raising the same claim to superiority over the non-European peoples of the world. They also used this same claim to justify western slavery over Africans. The outstanding West Indian scholar and politician, Dr. Eric E. Williams, has documented and exposed the western slavemaster's claim to racial superiority in his masterly-written book entitled 'British Historians and the West Indies' (Andre Deutsch, London. 1966).

It was because Jesus challenged this Jewish belief that they firmly and vehemently rejected him as the promised Messiah, and demanded his execution by crucifixion. When they saw him crucified before their very eyes, it conclusively validated their rejection of his claim to be the true Messiah since the Torah itself had declared that "anyone who is hung on a pole is under God's curse (Deuteronomy, 21:22–23). Since he was the "cursed of the Lord-God" it followed logically that he could not have been the Messiah.

If history is to end with a validation of the Jewish claim to Truth, and if that Truth recognizes the Jews as God's chosen people, chosen eternally and unconditionally to the exclusion of all of mankind, then this astonishing and ethically questionable supposedly Divine preference must find support in the beginning of history. If it has no support in the beginning of history, then this claim to truth must be questioned! If the Jewish claim to truth is to be validated, then history must end with the advent of a Messiah other than Jesus عليه السلام since they rejected him as the Messiah.

Jesus, the Jews and the Chosen People The Jews had a major problem with Nabī 'Īsa, i.e., Jesus, عليه السلام because he condemned them with very powerful language while dismissing their claim to have a special status with Allah Most High as His chosen people.

Jesus declared of the Jews that the Devil was their father. In other words, instead of recognizing them as the chosen people of the Lord-God, he declared that they were, in effect, the chosen people of Satan since their conduct was satanic. He considered them to be one-eyed, i.e., internally blind, and declared them to be "a nation of vipers":

"Ye are of your father the devil, and the lusts of your father ye will do. He was a murderer from the beginning, and abode not in the truth, because there is no truth in him. When he speaketh a lie, he speaketh of his own: for he is a liar, and the father of it."

— John 8:44

"You brood of vipers, how can you who are evil say anything good? For the mouth speaks what the heart is full of."

— Matthew 12:34

"For this people's heart has become calloused; they hardly hear with their ears, and they have closed their eyes. Otherwise they might see with their eyes, hear with their ears, understand with their hearts and turn, and I would heal them."

— Matthew 13:15

The Qur'ān supported the response of Nabī 'Īsā, i.e., Jesus عليه السلام . In fact it not only rejected the Jewish claim to that special status with the Lord-God as false, but went on to challenge them to seek or desire death if they were convinced of the truth of their claim:

قُلْ يَا أَيُّهَا الَّذِينَ هَادُوا إِنْ زَعَمْتُمْ أَنَّكُمْ أَوْلِيَاءُ لِلَّهِ مِنْ دُونِ النَّاسِ فَتَمَنَّوُا الْمَوْتَ إِنْ كُنْتُمْ صَادِقِينَ ۝

وَلَا يَتَمَنَّوْنَهُ أَبَدًا بِمَا قَدَّمَتْ أَيْدِيهِمْ وَاللَّهُ عَلِيمٌ بِالظَّالِمِينَ ۝

قُلْ إِنَّ الْمَوْتَ الَّذِي تَفِرُّونَ مِنْهُ فَإِنَّهُ مُلَاقِيكُمْ ثُمَّ تُرَدُّونَ إِلَىٰ عَالِمِ الْغَيْبِ وَالشَّهَادَةِ فَيُنَبِّئُكُمْ بِمَا كُنْتُمْ تَعْمَلُونَ ۝

(Qur'ān, al-Jumu'ah, 62:6–8)

Say: O you who follow the Jewish faith! If you claim that you alone are close to Allah, i.e., chosen by Allah Most High, to the exclusion of all other people, then you should be longing for death—if what you say is true! But never will they long for it, because they are aware of what their hands have wrought in this world, i.e. their sinful evil conduct; and Allah has full knowledge of evildoers. Say: Behold, the death from which you are fleeing is bound to overtake you—and then you will be brought back unto Him Who knows all that is beyond the reach of a created being's perception as well as all that can be witnessed by a creature's senses or mind, whereupon He will make you truly understand all that you were doing in life.

The Qur'ān again challenged them concerning their belief that heaven is reserved for them:

قُلْ إِنْ كَانَتْ لَكُمُ الدَّارُ الْآخِرَةُ عِنْدَ اللَّهِ خَالِصَةً مِنْ دُونِ النَّاسِ فَتَمَنَّوُا الْمَوْتَ إِنْ كُنْتُمْ صَادِقِينَ ۝
وَلَنْ يَتَمَنَّوْهُ أَبَدًا بِمَا قَدَّمَتْ أَيْدِيهِمْ وَاللَّهُ عَلِيمٌ بِالظَّالِمِينَ

(Qur'ān, al-Baqarah, 2:94–5)

Say: If an afterlife with Allah, i.e., the abode of heaven, is to be for you alone, to the exclusion of all other people, then you should long for death—if what you say is true! But never will they long for it, because (they are aware) of what their hands have sent ahead in this world: and Allah has full knowledge of evildoers.

The Qur'ān asked with great logical compulsion, if the Lord-God chose you to be His 'special', 'chosen' and 'beloved' people, why then, does He punish you for your sins?

وَقَالَتِ الْيَهُودُ وَالنَّصَارَى نَحْنُ أَبْنَاءُ اللَّهِ وَأَحِبَّاؤُهُ قُلْ فَلِمَ يُعَذِّبُكُمْ بِذُنُوبِكُمْ بَلْ أَنْتُمْ بَشَرٌ مِمَّنْ خَلَقَ يَغْفِرُ لِمَنْ يَشَاءُ وَيُعَذِّبُ مَنْ يَشَاءُ وَلِلَّهِ مُلْكُ السَّمَاوَاتِ وَالْأَرْضِ وَمَا

بَيْنَهُمَا وَإِلَيْهِ الْمَصِيرُ

(Qur'ān, al-Māidah, 5:18)

And both the Jews and the Christians say: We are Allah's children, and His beloved ones. Say: Why, then, does He cause you to be punished for your sins? Nay, you are but human beings of His creating. He forgives whom He wills, and He causes to be punished whom He wills: for Allah's is the dominion over the heavens and the earth and all that is between them, and with Him all journeys end.

The Qur'ān laid this alleged Divine preference for the Jews to rest when it declared that the Divine classification of human beings is based on piety rather than on lineage:

يَا أَيُّهَا النَّاسُ إِنَّا خَلَقْنَاكُمْ مِنْ ذَكَرٍ وَأُنْثَى وَجَعَلْنَاكُمْ شُعُوبًا وَقَبَائِلَ لِتَعَارَفُوا إِنَّ أَكْرَمَكُمْ عِنْدَ اللَّهِ أَتْقَاكُمْ إِنَّ اللَّهَ عَلِيمٌ خَبِيرٌ

(Qur'ān, al-Hujurāt, 49:13)

O men! Behold, We have created you all out of a male and a female, and have made you into nations and tribes, so that you might come to know one another, i.e., in respect of classification of humankind. Verily, the noblest of you in the sight of Allah is the one who is most pious. Behold, Allah is all-knowing, all-aware.

Prophet Muhammad صل الله عليه و سلم also dismissed that Jewish claim to a special (birthright) status with Allah when he declared: النّاسُ سواء كأسنانِ المشْطِ *i.e., that all of mankind are as equal in His sight as are the teeth of a comb".* (Sahīh Bukhārī)

We must now ask,—wherefrom came this arrogant Jewish claim to a birthright of superiority over all of mankind?

The Qur'ān confirms that the Israelite people descended from Nabī Ibrāhīm, i.e., Abraham عليه السلام , and also confirms that Allah Most High conferred on Abraham the status of *Imām*, i.e., spiritual or religious leader, of mankind. Abraham responded, however, with a request that his seed should also share in that status conferred upon him. As a consequence the Jews came to the conclusion that since they were from the seed of Abraham, they had a special status divinely conferred upon them. But the Qur'ān explained that Allah's response to Abraham's request was to grant it conditionally:

وَإِذِ ابْتَلَى إِبْرَاهِيمَ رَبُّهُ بِكَلِمَاتٍ فَأَتَمَّهُنَّ قَالَ إِنِّي جَاعِلُكَ
لِلنَّاسِ إِمَامًا قَالَ وَمِن ذُرِّيَّتِي قَالَ لَا يَنَالُ عَهْدِي الظَّالِمِينَ

(Qur'ān, al-Baqarah, 2:124)

And remember that event when his Lord-God tried Abraham by His commandments and the latter fulfilled them. He said: Behold, I shall make thee an Imām, i.e., leader, of men. Abraham asked: And will You make leaders of my offspring as well? Allah answered: My covenant does not embrace the wicked.

The condition was that this status would not be conferred on those of his seed who were unjust, wicked in conduct, or oppressors. Allah Most High went on to fulfill that favor unto Abraham by choosing Imams from his seed, hence the phenomenon of a continuous line of Prophets chosen from the seed of Abraham who were all sent to the Israelite people. The most that the Jews could claim, therefore, is that Allah Most High accepted the request of Abraham and blessed his righteous seed by choosing a continuous line of Imams or Prophets from that righteous seed. Believing Israelites, who are righteous, can therefore claim that Allah Most High chose Prophets from 'our' ranks.

Hence it was that Prophets of Allah were always chosen and appointed from the righteous seed of Abraham (since the Covenant excluded those who were wicked). This continued uninterruptedly until the birth of the Messiah, Jesus the son of the Virgin Mary عليه السلام. Mary's mother is referred to in the Qur'ān as a woman of the House of 'Imrān, and Mary herself is called "sister of Harūn" who, himself, is the son of 'Imrān. It is very strange indeed that there is no evidence of 'Imrān having the status of a Nabī, i.e., Prophet of Allah Most High. Yet he is a father of two Prophets—Mūsa, i.e., Moses, and Harūn, i.e., Aaron عليه السلام. The Qur'ān mentioned the names of Ādam عليه السلام and Noah عليه السلام as Prophets who were raised to a special status over all of mankind. It then mentioned that the same status was conferred on the progeny of Abraham عليه السلام, but it then went on to provide the additional information that this status was also conferred, strangely so, on the progeny of an unknown Israelite named 'Imrān, who resided in Egypt. The Qur'ān is otherwise silent on this strange subject.

Epistemology and Methodology

When the *Āyah*, or verse, of the Qur'ān declared that Allah Most High, in addition to being the first and last, is also the outwardly manifest as well as the inwardly hidden, and that He has full knowledge of all things, it implies that knowledge of the beginning, and of the end, and of that which connects them together, can be accessed only through an epistemology which harmoniously integrates *Zāhir*, i.e., the externally observable historical process, with *Bātin*, i.e., the internal reality of that externally observable historical process. Hence it integrates visible historical events with their hidden or concealed eschatological reality.

The verse of the Qur'ān (*Al-Hadīd, 57:3*) has thus provided a quartet of 'beginning', 'end', 'observable' and 'hidden' which have to be fully integrated by the research student into a harmonious whole for the proper study of both history and eschatology. Only those who are firmly grounded in knowledge can therefore penetrate and grasp the movement of history and the events which unfold at the end of history. This explains why we cannot attempt to understand Dajjāl, the False Messiah, who is a major actor at the end of history, without studying the beginning of history to attempt to locate at the beginning, that which connects to our subject in the end of history. This, perhaps, explains why so few are even conscious of the implications of such monetary events as the IMF ban of the use of gold as money. There are many Christians who cannot see the mark of the beast in the present bogus monetary system of paper, plastic and electronic or digital money!

The Qur'ān has directed attention to the epistemology with which this subject must be studied. It has done so in a passage in *Sūrah Al-Kahf* of the Qur'ān which describes the encounter between Nabī Mūsa (Moses) and an elusive mystical sage known as *Khidr* (عليه السلام). The word *Khidr* in Arabic means Green. An Orthodox Christian friend once commented to this writer that *Khidr* bears an uncanny resemblance to Jesus. We have analyzed that passage of the Qur'ān in our book entitled *Sūrah al-Kahf and the Modern Age.*

There is another reference in *Sūrah al-Kahf* to the importance of epistemology in respect of methodology for study of history. Two major evil actors in the historical process are to be released into the world in the end-time. They are Gog and Magog. (See my book entitled An Islamic View of Gog and Magog in the Modern World). The Qur'ān informs us that when the time comes for their release, Allah Most High will destroy a barrier built by *Dhūl Qarnain,* which effectively contained them and protected mankind from their evil. When that happens, then disbelieving people who suffer from an incapacity to see and to hear, would find themselves living in a hellish world spread out before them:

وَعَرَضْنَا جَهَنَّمَ يَوْمَئِذٍ لِّلْكَافِرِينَ عَرْضًا ۚ
الَّذِينَ كَانَتْ أَعْيُنُهُمْ فِي غِطَاءٍ عَن ذِكْرِي وَكَانُوا لَا
يَسْتَطِيعُونَ سَمْعًا

(Qur'ān, al-Kahf, 18:100–101)

On that day Allah Most High will present hell to the disbelievers, plain to view; those whose eyes were hoodwinked from His reminder, and who could not bear to hear the truth which He sent down.

It should be obvious that the Qur'ān has referred in the above to internal sight as well as to an internal capacity to hear.

We now return to *Sūrah al-Hadīd* to note that the first two verses of the *Sūrah,* which precede the third verse concerning the first and last, expand a conception of the philosophy of history to include a vertical dimension, i.e., above with below, which complements the horizontal dimension of first with last:

سَبَّحَ لِلَّهِ مَا فِي السَّمَاوَاتِ وَالْأَرْضِ وَهُوَ الْعَزِيزُ الْحَكِيمُ ۝ لَهُ مُلْكُ السَّمَاوَاتِ وَالْأَرْضِ يُحْيِي وَيُمِيتُ وَهُوَ عَلَى كُلِّ شَيْءٍ قَدِيرٌ

(Qur'ān, al-Hadīd, 57:1–2)

All that is in the heavens or parallel universes, and on earth or the material universe, glorify Allah; for He alone is Mighty and Wise! To Him belongs sovereignty over the heavens, or the parallel universes, and the earth, or the material universe; He gives life and He takes life, i.e., He causes death; and this should provide evidence enough that He has power over all things.

The implication of the above two verses of the Qur'ān, when studied in the context of the third verse, is that cosmology continuously impacts upon the historical process in such wise that events here-under cannot be fully understood without reference to cosmological reality located in the world above, i.e., *Al-Ghaib* or the unseen world. The most dramatic evidence of the relationship between these two worlds can be found in true dreams and visions,—and hence the abiding importance of *Sūrat Yūsuf* of the Qur'ān.

But even more important for our subject is the need for us to recognize that it is not possible to connect the dots of history—from the beginning to the end—without such interaction with the world above that would deliver both spiritual 'strength' and 'spiritual light'. Unless we can see with the 'internal eye' we would not recognize an even more important eschatological implication with which, we hope, Orthodox Christian eschatology will agree,—to wit, that there is more to the end of history than the mere unfolding of events already prophesied. Rather, the Lord-God can intervene in the historical process with events that will occur at the end of history concerning which neither Islamic nor Christian eschatology have any information or knowledge at this time.

If anyone is to have any knowledge of coming events, it can only come through true dreams or visions. This reconfirms the strategic importance of dreams and visions which is the topic of one of my books. At the request of one of my students, I now disclose precisely such a dream which I saw when I was 26 years of age and still studying at the Aleemiyah Institute of Islamic Studies in Pakistan. I saw a mighty river which was in very high flood and with dangerous currents, and I saw all my fellow students (as well as many others) struggling in the dangerous currents of the river, and in great danger of drowning; and I saw myself swimming to them one by one, and taking hold of them, and swimming with them to safety. I went to *Maulānā* Ansārī next morning and narrated to him my dream. He responded immediately to declare that I was destined to do precisely that in real life.

In consequence of this dream, and my teacher's interpretation of the dream, I have consistently persisted in my mission in the cause of truth all through life, even though I have so often been a lone voice crying in the wilderness!

We now turn to the description in the Qur'ān of enigmatic events that occurred at the beginning of history which, we believe, have significant eschatological implications,— significant for Judaism, Christianity and Islam, as well as all the rest of mankind. All these events occurred in a transcendental realm of existence before the commencement of man's biological or material life on earth, i.e., in the material universe.

فَإِذَا سَوَّيْتُهُ وَنَفَخْتُ فِيهِ مِنْ رُوحِي

(Qur'ān, al-Hijr, 15:28–29)

… So when Allah Most High has formed him fully, and breathed into him of His Divine Rūh, i.e., Divine Spirit …

CHAPTER THREE

The Human Rūh, The Divine Rūh, The Rūh al-Qudus and The Messiah Who Is Himself Rūh

Relevance of this subject

This chapter deals exclusively with the *Rūh* or Spirit. It is relevant to our subject of Dajjāl and *Awwal al-Zamān*, i.e., the beginning of history, since, without an explanation of this subject, we cannot proceed to our next chapter in which we analyze what must be recognized as the most important event to have occurred in *Awwal al-Zamān*, to wit: Allah's command to the Angels to prostrate themselves before Nabī Ādam عليه السلام, and the implications of the arrogant refusal to prostrate by an Iblīs who believed that he possessed a birth-right of superiority over Ādam.

The subject is also of importance because of the three questions which the Rabbis of Yathrib chose for the Prophet to be asked to answer in order for his claim to be a Prophet to be validated or invalidated (see my book entitled *'Surah al-Kahf and the Modern Age'* p. 91). The third of the three questions was: Ask him about the *Rūh*, or Spirit?

The question was difficult since the *Rūh*, or Spirit, could refer to the Divine *Rūh*, or to the *Rūh* that was breathed into Nabī Ādam عليه السلام, or it could refer to the *Rūh Al-Qudus* or Holy Spirit. But, surprisingly so, the *Rūh* could also refer to the Messiah himself.

Our initial view was that the Rabbis had posed the questions concerning the *Rūh* as a distraction, since we could see no eschatological connection to the question—as was readily discernible in the other two questions (which we understood to be connected to Gog and Magog, and to the interaction between the different dimensions of 'space' and of 'time' that is the key to understanding an important part of the subject of Dajjāl). It was only subsequently that we realized that there were more implications to the subject of the *Rūh* than we had initially understood.

There is an abundance of evidence that some of the most learned Jews of all times believed that the Divine *Rūh*, i.e., soul or spirit, was breathed into only the so-called 'chosen people', and that, while other human beings may be said to possess a soul, it was akin to an animal soul rather than a divine soul.

(See the scholarly essay written by the Jewish scholar, Hanan Balk, entitled: The Soul of a Jew and the Soul of a Non-Jew—An Inconvenient Truth and the Search for an Alternative. Published in ' akirah', the The Human Rūh, The Divine Rūh, The Rūh Al-Qudus ... 113 Flatbush Journal of Jewish Law and Thought. http://www.hakirah.org/. There are several other quotations from the views of prominent Jewish scholars which confirm their belief in a birth-right of Jewish supremacy over mankind, and which can be found in the following essay: https://stopcg.wordpress.com/jewish-supremacism.)

Hence the question concerning the *Rūh* may have been posed by the Rabbis in order to tease a view out of the Prophet, while forcing him to respond to this popular Jewish view. Perhaps, also, the Jews had secret knowledge that the *Rūh Al-Qudus* or Holy Spirit had a special End-time role to play in the advent of the Messiah, and they wanted to test Muhammad صل الله عليه و سلم to see whether he had any knowledge of that subject. It is quite possible that prior to revelations that were subsequently sent down in the Qur'ān on the subject of the *Rūh*, no one knew, for example, that Nabī Īsā, i.e., Jesus, the true Messiah عليه السلام, was strengthened with the *Rūh Al-Qudus* or Holy Spirit, or that he was himself, a *Rūh* or spirit that Allah Most High had breathed into Maryam, in consequence of which he became known as *Rūhullah* or Allah's Spirit (*Qur'ān, al-Anbiyāh', 21:91*).

Perhaps, also, other than the Jews, no one knew that Allah Most High had ordered the Angels at the dawn of creation to prostrate themselves before Ādam عليه السلام, in an act of respect for him, and that the order to prostrate was made only after the Divine *Rūh* was breathed into him. It has therefore become necessary for us to devote attention to explaining what the Qur'ān has to say on this subject of the *Rūh*, or spirit.

What is the Rūh?

When the Qur'ān described the event of the creation of the human being, it located that event in the spiritual realm, before human beings were excluded from *Al-Jannah*, i.e., heaven, and sent down to the material universe. Even so, it declared of that event that man was created from 'humble clay':

هُوَ الَّذِي خَلَقَكُمْ مِنْ طِينٍ ثُمَّ قَضَىٰ أَجَلًا وَأَجَلٌ مُسَمًّى عِنْدَهُ ثُمَّ أَنْتُمْ تَمْتَرُونَ

(Qur'ān, al-An'ām, 6:2)

He it is who has created man out of clay, and then has decreed a term for him—a term known only to Him Most High. And yet people doubt.

وَإِذْ قَالَ رَبُّكَ لِلْمَلَائِكَةِ إِنِّي خَالِقٌ بَشَرًا مِنْ صَلْصَالٍ مِنْ حَمَإٍ مَسْنُونٍ

(Qur'ān, al-Hijr, 15:28)

Allah Most High declared to the angels that He was about to create mortal man out of potter's clay, out of dark mud molded into shape.

The only way that mankind could have been created of 'clay' in a spiritual realm, prior to being transformed to material form in this world of space and time, is if that 'clay' was, itself, spiritual in nature and form, i.e., 'clay' which existed as spiritual substance, and which had not as yet been transformed to material form. Can there be such a thing as 'spiritual' clay?

When the Qur'ān declared of Allah Most High that He is the *Nūr* (light) of the *Samawāt* (or the parallel universes, i. e., the seven worlds of space and time that exist beyond our material universe) and the earth (or the material universe), (*Al-Nūr, 24:35*) the implication is that all of creation is ultimately resolvable or reducible to *Nūr*, i.e., light, and that all of creation must have emerged from *Nūr*. Hence, at the level of spiritual substance all things must exist as *Nūr* or 'light'. It is that 'light' which is, perhaps, heated up to become 'smokeless fire', from which the Jinn were created, and then cooled down to be transformed to 'material clay', in which form human beings emerged in this material universe. (For a better explanation of this complex subject see Dr. Muhammad Fazlur Rahman Ansari's two books entitled 'Foundations of Faith' and '*Quranic Foundations and Structure of Muslim Society*'. World Federation of Islamic Missions, Karachi.)

We may conclude from the above that all human beings existed in the form of spiritual clay before emerging in the form of material clay in the material universe. Hence all human beings existed in the spiritual realm with a spiritual body prior to emerging in this material universe with a material body. We may recall, in support of the above, that the Qur'ān has declared that all human beings—including those who have not as yet been born in the material universe—were created at the dawn of creation (i.e., in the spiritual realm) and endowed with the means with which to 'see', to 'hear' and to 'understand':

وَإِذْ أَخَذَ رَبُّكَ مِنْ بَنِي آدَمَ مِنْ ظُهُورِهِمْ ذُرِّيَّتَهُمْ وَأَشْهَدَهُمْ
عَلَى أَنْفُسِهِمْ أَلَسْتُ بِرَبِّكُمْ قَالُوا بَلَى شَهِدْنَا أَنْ تَقُولُوا يَوْمَ
الْقِيَامَةِ إِنَّا كُنَّا عَنْ هَذَا غَافِلِينَ

(Qur'ān, al A'raf 7:172)

And mankind must know that when their Lord-God brought forth from the progeny of Ādam, at the dawn of creation, their offspring, generation after generation until the last, and caused them to bear witness to their divinely-ordained status, He asked them: Am I not your Lord-God? They replied: Yea, indeed, we do bear witness thereto! Allah has reminded us about this event lest some people complain on the Day of Resurrection that they were unaware of this.

We may now also recall to advantage an incident which occurred in the Battle of Uhud when the companions saw the Prophet صل الله عليه و سلم looking up in the sky while uttering the words *"Subhān Allah"* (سبحان الله i.e., Glory be to Allah!) A companion of his, Sayyiduna Hanzalah bin Abī `Āmir Rāhib رضي الله عنه , was killed in the fighting while he was still in a state of *Janāba* (the state of ritual impurity that exists after sexual intercourse, and which requires a *Ghusl,* or bath, to be taken in order for a state of ritual purity to be restored), and the Prophet observed the Angels in the sky giving *Ghusl,* i.e., a bath, to the body of that companion.

While the material dead body with its distinctive shape and form, was lying on the battlefield, a spiritual body of identical shape and form as the material body, was observed in the sky, and that is why it could be recognized as the Companion who had just been killed. Both bodies were created from the same original clay; but the body in the sky appeared in clay in its spiritual form, while the body lying on the battlefield was comprised of clay in its material form.

The supra-rational bond which connected the spiritual body with the material body was such that when some Companions who had heard the comment of the Prophet, went to examine Hanzala's material body on the battle-field, they found drops of water on the body. (See *Kitāb al-Maghāzi* by Al-Wāqidi; edited by Rizwi Faizar, translated to English by Rizwi Faizer, Amal Ismail, and Abdul Kader Tayob, and published in Routledge Studies in Classical Islam, Routledge. Oxford. 2011. p. 134).

There is a similar incident which revealed to us that the spiritual body of Uwais Al-Qarni lingered on in Yathrib (renamed Madina despite the fact that the Qur'ān refers to it as Yathrib), even after his material body had left Yathrib on a sorrowful return to his native Yemen. He had traveled all the way from Yemen to Yathrib just to see the Prophet صل الله عليه و سلم but when he arrived in Yathrib he learnt, to his sorrow, that the Prophet had traveled out of the city. Since he could not stay in Yathrib long enough to await his return, he had to leave without seeing the Prophet. Shortly after Uwais's departure the Prophet returned to Yathrib and experienced a heavenly fragrance. When he subsequently learnt about the visitor from Yemen, the Prophet identified that fragrance to belong to Uwais. The fragrance came from Uwais's spiritual body, even though his material body had already departed.

Visions also provide data which assist us to understand how the spiritual can be connected to the material. I once delivered a lecture many years ago on the subject of 'Dreams and Visions in Islam' at the Pertapis Hall in Singapore (prior to the Government of Singapore banning my entry into that country), and when the program was over, a young man approached me to confide in me the following vision which he had experienced. He said that he was asleep in Yathrib, the city of the blessed Prophet صل الله عليه و سلم when he saw the Prophet entering his room. There was a heavenly fragrance which enveloped the room while the Prophet remained in the room in which he was sleeping. The young man then confided in me that when he woke up from his sleep, that wonderful fragrance still lingered in the room for some time.

We have provided sufficient evidence above to confirm both the creation of a spiritual human body prior to its emergence in material form in this world of space and time, and of the existence of a supra-rational connection between the spiritual human body and the material body.

Having created man from spiritual clay, the Qur'ān provided further information concerning the process through which he developed into a sentient and rational being. The Qur'ān declared that Allah Most High then proceeded to fashion him and, astonishingly so, to breathe into him of His own *Rūh* or Divine spirit:

وَإِذْ قَالَ رَبُّكَ لِلْمَلَائِكَةِ إِنِّي خَالِقٌ بَشَرًا مِنْ صَلْصَالٍ مِنْ حَمَإٍ مَسْنُونٍ ۝

فَإِذَا سَوَّيْتُهُ وَنَفَخْتُ فِيهِ مِنْ رُوحِي فَقَعُوا لَهُ سَاجِدِينَ ۝

(Qur'ān, al-Hijr, 15:28–29)

Allah Most High declared to the angels that He was about to create mortal man out of potter's clay, out of dark mud molded into shape; Then, when Allah Most High formed him fully, He breathed into him of His Rūh, i.e., Divine Spirit . . .

The *Rūh*, or Divine Spirit, is not a created thing. It is not a 'thing' that exists apart from Allah Most High, even though it belongs to Him and it proceeds from Him. While the *Rūh* can be breathed into a 'thing', but it is not a 'thing'. Rather it is with *Rūh* that 'life' is activated, and when *Rūh* is withdrawn, death occurs. It is necessary for us to offer this explanation in order to prevent any pantheistic interpretation to be attributed to the breathing of the Divine *Rūh* into the human being. Allah says in the Qur'ān that to Him belongs *Al-Khalq*, i.e. the created world, and *Al-Amr*, i.e., the world of command through which events occur:

أَلَا لَهُ الْخَلْقُ وَالْأَمْرُ تَبَارَكَ اللَّهُ رَبُّ الْعَالَمِينَ

(Qur'ān, al-'Arāf, 7:54)

Verily, to Allah belongs all creation, i.e., the world of creation, and all command, i.e., a world of command which does not belong to the created world. Hallowed is Allah, the Lord-God of all the worlds!

And He then went on to explain that the *Rūh* belongs to the world of *Amr* (and hence, does not belong to the world of *Khalq*):

... قُلِ الرُّوحُ مِنْ أَمْرِ رَبِّي ...

(Qur'ān, al-Isra', 17:85)

When the Jews question you Oh Muhammad, about the Rūh. Say to them that the Rūh is from Allah's Command;

Unlike the *Nafs*, i.e., the human 'self', and the physical human body, which both belong to the world of *Khalq* or creation, the *Rūh* does not belong to that world of 'creation', rather it belongs to the world of *Amr* or command.

The world of created things emerges through a divine command—'Be!':

إِنَّمَا أَمْرُهُ إِذَا أَرَادَ شَيْئًا أَنْ يَقُولَ لَهُ كُنْ فَيَكُونُ

(Qur'ān, Yasīn, 36:82)

Allah's Command is such that when He wills a thing to be, He but says unto it, Be!—and it is.

فَإِنَّمَا يَقُولُ لَهُ كُنْ فَيَكُونُ

(Qur'ān, al-Baqarah, 2:117)

He is the Originator of the heavens and the earth: and when He Wills a thing to be, He but says unto it, Be!— and it is.

Similarly the *Rūh* manifests itself in a human being through the Divine command: The *Rūh* is from Allah's Command (see 17:85 above).

The human *Rūh* proceeds therefore from the Divine *Amr* through which creation takes place. Hence the human *Rūh* partakes in the Divine capacity to create, and this explains why the Qur'ān recognizes Allah Most High as the best of those who create:

...فَتَبَارَكَ اللَّهُ أَحْسَنُ الْخَالِقِينَ

(Qur'ān, al-Mu'minūn, 23:14)

Hallowed, therefore, is Allah, the best of those who create!
Since the Divine Rūh was breathed into man, the implication is that he now possessed creative capacity in a creative faculty of rational thought potentially enriched (because of the Rūh) by intuitive internal spiritual insight:

ثُمَّ سَوَّاهُ وَنَفَخَ فِيهِ مِنْ رُوحِهِ وَجَعَلَ لَكُمُ السَّمْعَ وَالْأَبْصَارَ
وَالْأَفْئِدَةَ قَلِيلًا مَا تَشْكُرُونَ

(Qur'ān, al-Sajda, 32:9)

And then Allah formed him in accordance with what he is meant to be, and breathed into him of His Divine spirit: and thus, O men, did He endow you with hearing, and sight, and hearts as well as minds through which you can acquire knowledge, yet how seldom are you grateful!

How can the Divine Rūh be bestowed on all and sundry when we are the Chosen People of the Lord-God?

We tried the patience of the readers in offering the above explanation of the subject of the *Rūh*, in order that they might understand the question that must now be asked: How could it be possible that Allah Most Wise could choose a people as His chosen people with a status far superior to all the rest of mankind, and then bestow this supreme Divine gift of the *Rūh* to all of mankind while making no distinction between the so-called chosen people and the rest of mankind?

The Rabbis were convinced that such was not possible, and they wanted to know whether Nabī Muhammad صل الله عليه و سلم would confirm it; and that is why they asked the third of three questions: Ask him about the *Rūh*? (See my book entitled *Sūrah al- Kahf and the Modern* Age p. 91).

A study of the subject in the Qur'ān indicates that at no time did Allah Most High ever declare that the Divine *Rūh* was breathed into only the Israelite people, to the exclusion of all other human beings. Rather, all human beings possess the Divine *Rūh* within them. However, when the Divinely-revealed answer to that third question was sent down in the Qur'ān, it was humiliatingly curt, and it must have left the world of Jewish scholarship in a state of agony and frustration:

وَيَسْأَلُونَكَ عَنِ الرُّوحِ قُلِ الرُّوحُ مِنْ أَمْرِ رَبِّي وَمَا أُوتِيتُم مِّنَ الْعِلْمِ إِلَّا قَلِيلًا

(Qur'ān, al-Isra', 17:85)

And they, the Jews, question you Oh Muhammad, about the Rūh. Say to them in reply that the Rūh is by Allah's command, and you, the Jews, have been granted but little knowledge of this subject.

This revelation was sent down while the Prophet was still in Makkah, i.e., prior to the *Hijrah,* or migration to Yathrib. It represented the initial response in the Qur'ān to the questions posed by the Rabbis. Subsequent revelations which came down after the *Hijrah* to Yathrib, delivered more information of the subject. The Qur'ān went on to inform us, for example, that Allah Most High not only created every human being at the dawn of creation, and breathed into each of them of His Divine *Rūh*, but also endowed them with the capacity to recognize Him as their Lord-God:

وَإِذْ أَخَذَ رَبُّكَ مِنْ بَنِي آدَمَ مِنْ ظُهُورِهِمْ ذُرِّيَّتَهُمْ وَأَشْهَدَهُمْ عَلَى أَنْفُسِهِمْ أَلَسْتُ بِرَبِّكُمْ قَالُوا بَلَى شَهِدْنَا أَنْ تَقُولُوا يَوْمَ الْقِيَامَةِ إِنَّا كُنَّا عَنْ هَذَا غَافِلِينَ

(Qur'ān, al-An'ām, 7:172)

And you must know that when your Lord-God brought forth from the progeny of Ādam their offspring, generation after generation until the last, and caused them to bear witness to their divinelyordained status, He asked them: Am I not your Lord- God? to which they replied: Yea, indeed, we do bear witness thereto! We remind you of this lest you say on the Day of Resurrection, Verily, we were unaware of this.

After having disclosed all of the above (perhaps for the first time in a divinely-revealed Book that could be read by all, rather than by a select few) the Qur'ān then proceeded to deliver the coup-de-grace in demolishing the claim of a so-called chosen people to have a special status with the Lord-God to the exclusion of the rest of mankind. It did so when it declared that Allah Most High honored all the progeny of Ādam عليه السلام , hence all of mankind (without exception—and this includes the Africans who were enslaved by the West, and the native Indians who were to be robbed of their land, in order for bright and shining America to be established in that land) were honored, and that they had all thereby been raised to a status above most of Allah's creation. Here is the declaration honoring all human-beings:

وَلَقَدْ كَرَّمْنَا بَنِي آدَمَ وَحَمَلْنَاهُمْ فِي الْبَرِّ وَالْبَحْرِ وَرَزَقْنَاهُمْ مِنَ الطَّيِّبَاتِ وَفَضَّلْنَاهُمْ عَلَى كَثِيرٍ مِمَّنْ خَلَقْنَا تَفْضِيلًا

(Qur'ān, al-Isra', 17:70)

Now, indeed, Allah Most High has conferred honor and dignity on the progeny of Ādam, hence all of mankind without exception, and borne them over land and sea, and provided for them sustenance out of the good things of life, and favored them far above most of His creation.

The honor that was bestowed on all of mankind had to be the *Rūh* which was breathed into every human being. This had to be so since it was after Ādam عليه السلام had received that divine gift that the Angels were ordered to prostrate (in honor and in respect) before him. This subject is explained in greater detail in the chapter which follows.

Before we proceed further with this discussion however, it is interesting to observe the remarkable similarity which has existed between this Jewish claim to be the chosen people of the Lord-God, and hence their preoccupation with the subject of whether non-Jews possessed a Divine *Rūh*, and a modern western civilization which emerged in history with the jingoistic agenda of civilizing non-European humanity. When the West declared its manifest destiny in waging wars of continuous territorial expansion (and military dominance) which continue to this day, and in dragging all mankind into an age which they described as one of unprecedented progress, democracy and freedom, their undeclared belief which explained that manifest destiny was that they were the chosen people of the Lord-God.

While Popes in Rome issued (infallible) 'Bulls' concerning the possession of a soul by American Indians (and Africans) and then revoked them, the enslavement of Africans in the western slave trade flourished because of the general western Christian belief that slavery was religiously permitted since the slaves were not truly human beings. They did not possess the divinely-bestowed *Rūh* or spirit which made them truly human. Not only was it permissible to enslave the Africans and sell them to plantation-owners in the Americas, but it was similarly permissible to enslave the American Indians since they, also, did not possess a *Rūh*. In addition, since the divine *Rūh* was conferred on Ādam, who was male, there were many who believed that women did not have a *Rūh* or soul.

The Holy Spirit (Al-Rūh Al-Qudus)

There are four verses of the Qur'ān which make mention by name of someone called the *Rūh Al-Qudus* or Holy Spirit. In the other verses, the same *Rūh Al-Qudus* is referred to simply as the *Rūh*.

In the first verse we are informed that Allah Most High strengthened Nabī Īsa, i.e., Jesus عليه السلام, with the Holy Spirit. This verse is repeated twice in the Qur'ān:

...وَآتَيْنَا عِيسَى ابْنَ مَرْيَمَ الْبَيِّنَاتِ وَأَيَّدْنَاهُ بِرُوحِ الْقُدُسِ...

(Qur'ān, al-Baqarah, 2:87, 2:253)

Allah Most High gave to Jesus, the son of Mary revelation which functions as evidence of the truth, and strengthened him with the Holy Spirit.

Who or what is the Holy Spirit? Is the Holy Spirit of the Qur'ān the same as the Holy Ghost in the Christian belief in a third person in a Divine Trinity?

In the third reference in the Qur'ān to the Holy Spirit we are informed that, as a consequence of being strengthened with the Holy Spirit, Jesus was able to perform miracles:

إِذْ قَالَ اللَّهُ يَا عِيسَى ابْنَ مَرْيَمَ اذْكُرْ نِعْمَتِي عَلَيْكَ وَعَلَى
وَالِدَتِكَ إِذْ أَيَّدْتُكَ بِرُوحِ الْقُدُسِ تُكَلِّمُ النَّاسَ فِي الْمَهْدِ
وَكَهْلًا وَإِذْ عَلَّمْتُكَ الْكِتَابَ وَالْحِكْمَةَ وَالتَّوْرَاةَ وَالْإِنْجِيلَ وَإِذْ
تَخْلُقُ مِنَ الطِّينِ كَهَيْئَةِ الطَّيْرِ بِإِذْنِي فَتَنْفُخُ فِيهَا فَتَكُونُ طَيْرًا
بِإِذْنِي وَتُبْرِئُ الْأَكْمَهَ وَالْأَبْرَصَ بِإِذْنِي وَإِذْ تُخْرِجُ الْمَوْتَى بِإِذْنِي

(Qur'ān, al-Māidah, 5:110)

Lo! Allah Most High would say: O Jesus, son of Mary! Remember the blessings which I bestowed upon you and your mother—how I strengthened you with Holy Spirit in consequence of which you could speak unto men miraculously while you were a baby in the cradle, and again speak miraculously as a grown man having returned to the material universe after departing more than 2000 years earlier; and how I imparted unto you revelation and wisdom, including the Torah and the Gospel; and how by My leave you created a bird out of clay, and then breathed into it, and by My leave, it miraculously became a living bird; and how you healed the blind by miraculously restoring their sight, and the leper by miraculously curing the leper of his leprosy, and how you raised the dead by My leave . . .

When the Qur'ān referred for a fourth and last time to the 'Holy Spirit', it finally gave us the means with which to identify him as the Archangel who brought down divine revelation upon Prophet Muhammad صل الله عليه و سلم

قُلْ نَزَّلَهُ رُوحُ الْقُدُسِ مِنْ رَبِّكَ بِالْحَقِّ لِيُثَبِّتَ الَّذِينَ آمَنُوا وَهُدًى وَبُشْرَى لِلْمُسْلِمِينَ

(Qur'ān, al-Nahl, 16:102)

Say: A Holy Spirit has brought the Qur'ān down from thy Lord-God by stages, setting forth the truth, so that it might give firmness of resolve, conduct, speech, etc., to those who have faith, and provide guidance and a glad tiding unto all who have surrendered themselves to Allah Most High.

The Qur'ān went on to declare that it was the Angel Gabriel عليه السلام who brought down the divine revelation (i.e., the Qur'ān) from Allah Most High:

قُلْ مَنْ كَانَ عَدُوًّا لِجِبْرِيلَ فَإِنَّهُ نَزَّلَهُ عَلَى قَلْبِكَ بِإِذْنِ اللَّهِ مُصَدِّقًا لِمَا بَيْنَ يَدَيْهِ وَهُدًى وَبُشْرَى لِلْمُؤْمِنِينَ

(Qur'ān, al-Baqarah, 2:97)

Say Oh Prophet: Whosoever is an enemy of Gabriel— who, verily, by

Allah's leave, has brought down upon thy heart this divine writ which confirms the truth of whatever there still remains of earlier revelations, and is a guidance and a glad tiding for the believers.

It is quite clear that when the Qur'ān referred to a *Rūh Al-Qudus,* or Holy Spirit, it was referring to the Archangel Gabriel. This was again made clear when the Qur'ān referred to the *Rūh* coming down on *Lailatul Qadr*, i.e., the night of power, to perform all errands (assigned to it by Allah Most High):

لَيْلَةُ الْقَدْرِ خَيْرٌ مِنْ أَلْفِ شَهْرٍ ۝
تَنَزَّلُ الْمَلَائِكَةُ وَالرُّوحُ فِيهَا بِإِذْنِ رَبِّهِمْ مِنْ كُلِّ أَمْرٍ

(Qur'ān, al-Qadr, 97:3–4)

The Night of Destiny is better than a thousand months because, among other things, the Angels descend in hosts by Allah's leave during that night, and so too the Rūh, with all decrees.

But the verse also disclosed that there were those who considered that Archangel to be their enemy. It was of course, the Jews (i.e., the Israelites who rejected Jesus as the Messiah), who considered Gabriel to be their enemy, and it should be obvious that their hatred for Gabriel arose from the fact that he played a crucial role in the test to which they were subjected when the Messiah appeared in the world as the son of a virgin mother,—and it was a test which they failed (this will be explained in greater detail in my next book on Dajjāl entitled *From Jesus the True Messiah to Dajjāl the False Messiah—A Journey in Islamic Eschatology*).

He also brought down the Qur'ān which confirmed and validated that which had previously been revealed to the Israelite people in the Torah and Gospel, and in so doing, exposed whatever had been concealed or corrupted over time.

Perhaps the most glaring example of such corruption of divinely-revealed scripture was the verse of the Torah which permitted money being lent on interest to those who were not Jews, while upholding the prohibition of such transactions with fellow Jews (*Deuteronomy, 23:19–20*). The Qur'ān denounced them for their money-lending (to non-Jews of course) in the strongest language. (See *An-Nisa'*, 4:161).

And finally, the Angel Gabriel brought the Qur'ān down to an Arab (i.e., Prophet Muhammad) when they, the Jews, believed that only an Israelite could qualify to receive divine revelation since the Israelites believed (falsely so) that they were the chosen people of the Lord Most High to the exclusion of all of the rest of mankind. As a consequence they hated Angel Gabriel (see Qur'ān, *Al-Baqarah*, 2:97–98).

While it is outside of the scope of this book to examine the hypothesis, it nevertheless remains worthy of study to determine to what extent did Jewish hatred for Gabriel provoke an attack on Christianity which culminated in the Holy Ghost or Holy Spirit (i.e., Gabriel) being worshiped as the third person in a divine trinity (i.e., God the Father, God the Son and God the Holy Ghost).

More importantly, we must determine whether the Holy Spirit can descend on human beings who are not Jews. If such is possible, it would further expose the falsehood of the Jewish claim to an exclusive status with the Lord-God in which they are recognized as His chosen people.

The Qur'ān confirmed that Allah Most High can bless any of His true servants by strengthening him with a *Rūh*, or spirit, from Him:

...أُولَٰئِكَ كَتَبَ فِي قُلُوبِهِمُ الْإِيمَانَ وَأَيَّدَهُم بِرُوحٍ مِّنْهُ...

(Qur'ān, al-Mujādilah, 58:22)

As for the true believers, it is they in whose hearts Allah Most High has inscribed faith, and whom He has strengthened with a Spirit from Himself...

يُنَزِّلُ الْمَلَائِكَةَ بِالرُّوحِ مِنْ أَمْرِهِ عَلَىٰ مَن يَشَاءُ مِنْ عِبَادِهِ...

(Qur'ān, al-Nahl, 16:2)

Allah Most High causes the angels to descend with the Rūh or Spirit which is bestowed at His behest upon whomever He wills of His servants . . .

The Qur'ān makes yet another mention of the *Rūh* which comes down with the Angels on a certain night of the year (i.e., *Lailatul Qadr*, or the night of power) to perform whatever errand is assigned to them. Most commentators of the Qur'ān recognize this *Rūh* who comes down to the believers on that night to be the *Rūh Al-Qudus* or Holy Spirit:

تَنَزَّلُ الْمَلَائِكَةُ وَالرُّوحُ فِيهَا بِإِذْنِ رَبِّهِمْ مِنْ كُلِّ أَمْرٍ

(Qur'ān, al-Qadr, 97:4)

The angels and the Spirit descend during that night, by the permission of their Lord, with all decrees.

It was precisely this *Rūh Al-Qudus* which was sent to Mariam عليه السلام so that she, who was still a virgin, could miraculously conceive a child. The *Rūh*, which is an entirely spiritual being, was made to appear before her in the material form of a man:

فَاتَّخَذَتْ مِنْ دُونِهِمْ حِجَابًا فَأَرْسَلْنَا إِلَيْهَا رُوحَنَا فَتَمَثَّلَ لَهَا بَشَرًا سَوِيًّا

(Qur'ān, Mariam, 19:17)

Mariam, or Mary, kept herself in seclusion from her people, whereupon Allah Most High sent unto her His Rūh, who appeared to her in the shape of a well-made human being.

Our examination of the event of the creation of mankind at the beginning of history has thus allowed us to recognize that all human-beings are divinely-blessed with a *Rūh* that is breathed into them by the Lord-God Himself, and that selective human beings who have faith in their hearts and whose conduct is righteous can be chosen by Allah Most High, to be blessed to receive a visit from the 'Holy Spirit'. The beginning of history did not confer on the Jewish people any special Divine status through which they were recognized as a chosen people of the Lord-God to the exclusion of the rest of mankind!

When Allah Most High breathed His Rūh into the human being, He gave to every human being a divine capacity to create. That creative capacity finds concrete expression in man's creative intellect aided with internal intuitive spiritual insight through which he can forge new knowledge or thought and new ideas with which to extend the frontiers of knowledge. Unless the human mind or intellect flies with the wings of the *Rūh* it will not be able to penetrate and discover new knowledge in the scriptures—especially the last scripture or the Qur'ān, and will not be able to even understand and hence can never respond, to the trials of Dajjāl, the false Messiah, or Anti- Christ, in *Ākhir al-Zamān.*

In the previous chapter we found nothing in the Qur'ān supporting the view that Jews, who claim to be a chosen people of the Lord-God, are the only people into whom a Divine *Rūh* or spirit was breathed, and hence the only people so honored by the Lord-God and endowed with a Divine capacity to create. Now we find further evidence which exposes as false the Jewish belief that Jews are the chosen people of the Lord-God, since they declare their enmity against Angel Gabriel, who is the Holy Spirit and, as a consequence, have no access to the Holy Spirit.

Allah Most High strengthened Nabī Īsā, i.e., Jesus عليه السلام with the Holy Spirit, yet the Jews rejected him, and Allah sent the Holy Spirit to his mother Mariam so that she could conceive a baby while yet unmarried and untouched by any man, and the Jews responded by slandering her. Finally Allah sent the Holy Spirit to Nabī Muhammad صل الله عليه و سلم continuously for a period of twenty-three years and sent down upon him, through the Holy Spirit, the blessed Qur'ān, and yet the Jews rejected him and rejected the Qur'ān. Finally, Nabī Muhammad صل الله عليه و سلم is reported to have invoked the blessing of the *Rūh Al-Qudus* i.e., the Holy Spirit, on his companion, the poet Hassān Ibn Thābit (Bukhārī, Muslim, Abū Daūd, and Tirmīdhī). Hassan Ibn Thābit was an Arab, as was Nabī Muhammad صل الله عليه و سلم , and so they both belonged to that part of mankind whom the Jews refer to as *Ummiyūn*, hence an inferior gentile people. It should be clear from the prayer of the blessed Prophet on behalf of his companion Hassan Ibn Thābit, that the Prophet, also, rejected the Jewish belief that they were the chosen people of the Lord-God with a birth-right of superiority over the rest of mankind.

It is possible that the Jews knew from their own sources that the Messiah would be empowered with the Holy Spirit and it was for this reason that they posed that question to the Prophet. If this was so then we can expect that Dajjāl would have to demonstrate such miraculous powers as would be adequate to convince the Jews that he is indeed empowered by the Holy Spirit. We can therefore look forward to his scientific and technological revolution delivering many more gadgetries than would render even today's so-called smart phone less than really smart!

The Messiah is himself a Rūh or Spirit

The Qur'ān disclosed one more thing concerning the *Rūh* which must have rattled the Rabbis. Allah Most High declared of Jesus the son of the Virgin Mary that he was, himself a *Rūh*, or Spirit:

وَالَّتِي أَحْصَنَتْ فَرْجَهَا فَنَفَخْنَا فِيهَا مِنْ رُوحِنَا وَجَعَلْنَاهَا
وَابْنَهَا آيَةً لِلْعَالَمِينَ

(Qur'ān, al-Anbiyāh', 21:91)

And remember Mariam, or Mary, who guarded her chastity, whereupon Allah Most High breathed into her of His Rūh, or spirit, and caused her, together with her son, to become a Sign unto all people—to be read by those who can read Signs of Allah Most High.

Perhaps it was in consequence of what was disclosed in the Qur'ān, that Prophet Muhammad once described Jesus as *Rūhullah* or Allah's Spirit. It is therefore possible for us to deduce that the Rabbis had secret information concerning the Messiah that he would be a Spirit who would appear in human form, and this is precisely what happened when Jesus came to them with the claim to be the Messiah.

When Dajjāl appears therefore, we can conclude that he would seek to appear to the Jews as a Spirit in human form. The reality, however, would be the opposite, since Dajjāl would be just a *Jasad*, or a human body, with no *Rūh*, or Spirit.

فَإِذَا سَوَّيْتُهُ وَنَفَخْتُ فِيهِ مِنْ رُوحِي

(Qur'ān, al-Hijr, 15:28–29)

… So when Allah Most High has formed him fully, and breathed into him of His Divine Rūh, i.e., Divine Spirit …

CHAPTER FOUR

The Angels Prostrate before Ādam in Awwal al-Zamān

Why Prostration?

The *Rūh* or spirit, is life. It is a capacity or a force which is breathed into a thing. When the *Rūh* is breathed into a human being, the human *Nafs*, i.e., soul or self, can then be activated (for want of better language). Allah Most High breathed the *Rūh* into the first human being, i.e., Ādam عليه السلام .

However in a Hadīth recorded in *Sahīh Bukhārī* Prophet Muhammad صل الله عليه و سلم explained that it is an angel (rather than Allah Most High) who breathes the *Rūh* into the unborn fetus:

> *Verily, each of you is brought together in his mother's abdomen for forty days in the form of a drop of fluid. Then it is a clinging object for a similar period. Thereafter, it is a lump looking like it has been chewed for a similar period. The angel is then sent to him and he breathes into him the Rūh or spirit.*

Who or what is 'I'? Where is my personal identity?

'I' is my *Nafs* or self. It is my personal identity. 'I' is not my body of clay, nor is 'I', my *Rūh* or spirit. The Qur'ān has warned of the day when the human body will be given the capacity to speak, and would then give evidence against the *Nafs* or person to whom the body belonged. Consider the following ominous verses of the Qur'ān:

الْيَوْمَ نَخْتِمُ عَلَى أَفْوَاهِهِمْ وَتُكَلِّمُنَا أَيْدِيهِمْ وَتَشْهَدُ أَرْجُلُهُمْ بِمَا كَانُوا يَكْسِبُونَ

(Qur'ān, Yāsīn, 36:65)

On that Day Allah Most High will set a seal on their mouths, but their hands will speak unto Him, and their feet will bear witness to whatever they have earned in life.

حَتَّى إِذَا مَا جَاءُوهَا شَهِدَ عَلَيْهِمْ سَمْعُهُمْ وَأَبْصَارُهُمْ وَجُلُودُهُمْ بِمَا كَانُوا يَعْمَلُونَ ۝

وَقَالُوا لِجُلُودِهِمْ لِمَ شَهِدْتُمْ عَلَيْنَا قَالُوا أَنْطَقَنَا اللَّهُ الَّذِي أَنْطَقَ كُلَّ شَيْءٍ وَهُوَ خَلَقَكُمْ أَوَّلَ مَرَّةٍ وَإِلَيْهِ تُرْجَعُونَ ۝

وَمَا كُنْتُمْ تَسْتَتِرُونَ أَنْ يَشْهَدَ عَلَيْكُمْ سَمْعُكُمْ وَلَا أَبْصَارُكُمْ وَلَا جُلُودُكُمْ وَلَكِنْ ظَنَنْتُمْ أَنَّ اللَّهَ لَا يَعْلَمُ كَثِيرًا مِمَّا تَعْمَلُونَ ۝

(Qur'ān, Fussilāt, 41:20–22)

When they come close to the fire on Judgment Day, their hearing and their sight and their very skins will bear witness against them, speaking of what they were doing on earth. And they will ask their skins, Why did you bear witness against us?—and these will reply: Allah, who gives speech to all things, has given speech to us as well: for He it is who has created you in the first instance—and unto Him you are now brought back. And you did not try to hide your sins lest your hearing or your sight or your skins bear witness against you: nay, but you thought that Allah did not know much of what you were doing.

عَنْ أَبِي سَعِيدٍ الْخُدْرِيِّ، قَالَ قَالَ رَسُولُ اللَّهِ صلى الله عليه وسلم : اتَّقُوا فِرَاسَةَ الْمُؤْمِنِ فَإِنَّهُ يَنْظُرُ بِنُورِ اللَّهِ

The Prophet warned: Fear the Firāsah of the one who has faith, for he surely sees with Allah's Nūr, or light.

(Tirmīdhī, Kitāb Tafsīr al-Qur'ān)

The Qur'ān confirmed this capacity as follows:

إِنَّ فِي ذَلِكَ لَآيَاتٍ لِلْمُتَوَسِّمِينَ

(Qur'ān, al-Hijr, 15:75)

Surely in this are messages or portents for the Mutawassimīn, i.e., those who can read the Signs of Allah.

Thus the human being, by virtue of a Divine-endowment, now occupied an elevated position in creation that was second to none, and this was permanently engraved at the very beginning of history in the most dramatic event ever to have occurred in history, i.e., the Angels prostrating themselves before Nabī Ādam عليه السلام as an act of honor, and in recognition of that Divine spark with which every human being was now endowed. (See verses below).

The Qur'ān has declared that the material human being, created from humble clay, did not occupy the status of highest in creation. Indeed, the creation of the *Samawāt*, i.e., the parallel universes—or the other worlds of space and of time, and the earth or material universe, is recognized in the Qur'ān to be greater than the creation of human-kind:

لَخَلْقُ السَّمَاوَاتِ وَالْأَرْضِ أَكْبَرُ مِنْ خَلْقِ النَّاسِ وَلَكِنَّ أَكْثَرَ النَّاسِ لَا يَعْلَمُونَ

(Qur'ān, al-Ghāfir, 40:57)

Greater indeed than the creation of man, is the creation of the heavens and the earth: yet most men do not know of this.

Here now, are the verses of the Qur'ān which inform us of the most dramatic event that occurred in *Awwal al-Zamān,* i.e., at the beginning of history:

وَإِذْ قَالَ رَبُّكَ لِلْمَلَائِكَةِ إِنِّي خَالِقٌ بَشَرًا مِنْ صَلْصَالٍ مِنْ
حَمَإٍ مَسْنُونٍ

(Qur'ān, al-Hijr, 15:28)

Allah Most High said unto the angels: Behold, I am about to create mortal man out of potter's clay, out of mud molded into shape:

فَإِذَا سَوَّيْتُهُ وَنَفَخْتُ فِيهِ مِنْ رُوحِي فَقَعُوا لَهُ سَاجِدِينَ

(Qur'ān, al-Hijr, 15:29)

So when I have formed him fully, and breathed into him of My Rūh, i.e., Divine Spirit, fall down before him in prostration!

الَّذِي أَحْسَنَ كُلَّ شَيْءٍ خَلَقَهُ وَبَدَأَ خَلْقَ الْإِنْسَانِ مِنْ طِينٍ ۝
ثُمَّ جَعَلَ نَسْلَهُ مِنْ سُلَالَةٍ مِنْ مَاءٍ مَهِينٍ ۝
ثُمَّ سَوَّاهُ وَنَفَخَ فِيهِ مِنْ رُوحِهِ وَجَعَلَ لَكُمُ السَّمْعَ وَالْأَبْصَارَ
وَالْأَفْئِدَةَ قَلِيلًا مَا تَشْكُرُونَ

(Qur'ān, al-Sajdah, 32:7–9)

Allah Most High makes most excellent, everything that He creates. Thus, He begins the creation of man out of clay; then He causes him to be begotten out of the essence of a humble fluid; and then He formed or fashioned him in accordance with what he is meant to be, and breathed into him of His Rūh or Spirit, and consequently He endowed mankind with hearing, and sight, and hearts: yet how seldom are they grateful!

In consequence of the Divine *Rūh* or Spirit being breathed into him, the human being was endowed with both sensory perception as well as a rational faculty. But that was not all! In going on to disclose that the Divine *Rūh* or Spirit also bestowed on the human being a heart, the implication was that every human being was divinely endowed with a capacity to see—both externally and internally—and hence to possess both external sight and internal sight, to hear, both externally and internally, and to process externally acquired information and thus acquire knowledge with the rational mind, as well as to receive knowledge internally with the spiritual heart.

This gift was divinely-conferred on all human beings, and it raised their status to such an extent that the Qur'ān declared it to be an honor:

وَلَقَدْ كَرَّمْنَا بَنِي آدَمَ...

(Qur'ān, al-Isra', 17:70)

Indeed, Allah Most High has conferred honor and dignity on the progeny of Ādam, and hence on all human beings ...

The Qur'ān has thus delivered a beginning of history in which every human being, by virtue of being a human being, held an honored status in Allah's creation. Every human being was honored when he was given the divine capacity for knowledge, both externally-acquired and internally received. It was because of this epistemological gift to man that the Angels were ordered to bow down and prostrate before Nabī Ādam عليه السلام.

The link between this gift to man, and the End-time, can be readily perceived when we ponder over the Hadīth of Prophet Muhammad صل الله عليه و سلم that "Dajjāl sees with the left eye and that he is blind in the right eye—but your Lord-God is not one-eyed". Dajjāl, who is internally blind, is incapable of acquiring knowledge other than externally, i.e., through the scientific method of observation, experimentation and rational inquiry, and all those who follow Dajjāl suffer the same fate of internal blindness!

The claim of the Israelite people to a unique spiritual status with the Lord-God to the exclusion of all the rest of mankind, is thus manifestly false, since all of mankind were honored by the Angels when they prostrated themselves before Ādam عليه السلام . All of mankind, including the Israelite people, have originated from the same father—Ādam عليه السلام, and the Lord-God has Himself honored all the progeny of Ādam عليه السلام.

Is Prostration before a human being an act of worship?

We have described the prostration (*Sijdah*) of the Angels before Nabī Ādam عليه السلام as an act of respect and honor, but the claim can be made that it was an act of worship. Indeed the Qur'ān has ordered that prostration be made only to Allah Most High:

وَمِنْ آيَاتِهِ اللَّيْلُ وَالنَّهَارُ وَالشَّمْسُ وَالْقَمَرُ لَا تَسْجُدُوا
لِلشَّمْسِ وَلَا لِلْقَمَرِ وَاسْجُدُوا لِلَّهِ الَّذِي خَلَقَهُنَّ إِنْ كُنْتُمْ
إِيَّاهُ تَعْبُدُونَ

(Qur'ān, Fussilāt, 41:37)

Among Allah's signs are the night and the day, as well as the sun and the moon: do not prostrate before the sun, neither the moon, but prostrate yourselves in worship (only) before Allah, who has created them—if it is Him and only Him, whom you (really) worship.

The above verse of the Qur'ān has very clearly prohibited prostration before any but Allah Most High. How then, could Allah command the Angels to prostrate before Nabī Ādam عليه السلام? And how could Nabī Yaqūb, i.e., Jacob عليه السلام, bow down in prostration before his own son Nabī Yūsuf, i.e., Joseph عليه السلام?

The answer is that bowing and prostrating, at that early stage in the historical process, was an act through which one showed reverence, respect and honor for someone. It was not necessarily an act of adoration or worship. It was in this context that the Angels were ordered to prostrate before Nabī Ādam عليه السلام, and in this context as well that Nabī Yaqūb عليه السلام prostrated before his son, Nabī Yūsuf عليه السلام.

However, when the Qur'ān was revealed, the previous law permitting bowing and prostration before a human being as an act of respect and honor, was canceled or abrogated for all those who accepted the Qur'ān as the (revealed) Word of the One God.

It was for this reason that when the Prophet's cousin, Ja'far رضي الله عنه , and the refugee Muslim slaves or semi-slaves whom he accompanied to Abyssinia, were brought before the Orthodox Christian King (the Negus of Abyssinia), and the entire court bowed down before the King in respect, Ja'far and the rest of the Muslims did not bow down. While it was still permissible for the Christians to bow down or prostrate to honor their King, it was no longer permissible for Muslims to do so. The Muslims meant no disrespect to the King in restraining themselves from bowing down before a King in accordance with court protocol. Rather, they conducted themselves with fidelity to the religion of Islam as it had come from Nabī Muhammad صل الله عليه و سلم .

The Christian King was gifted with such amazing spiritual insight that he was able to both understand and appreciate that there was something sacred in the scene before his eyes, and he not only took no action against the Muslims for this highly visible breach of court protocol, but went on to refuse the Makkan request that the runaway slaves be repatriated to Makkah.

One can only imagine how Queen Victoria of Britain would have responded if a Muslim had refused to bend on one knee before the Queen, in accordance with British court protocol, when he presented himself to be honored with the highest honor bestowed by Britain, in consequence of which he was knighted and became, for example, a Sir Muhammad Iqbal.

If Jeremy Corbyn, a British politician who is the leader of Britain's Labour Party, today finds it beneath his dignity to bend his knee before the Queen of England, it defies understanding that so many Muslims bent their knees to receive Britain's highest national award.

One of the objections that Protestants had to Roman Catholic Christianity was the obligation which western Christianity had imposed on those who were to receive the Holy Communion that they had to kneel to receive it. Some Protestants considered such an act to be idolatrous. The Roman Catholics countered with the argument that kneeling in Holy Communion was an act of reverence rather than adoration.

Hinduism, also, has preserved this act of prostration as a form of humility, reverence and respect (rather than adoration or worship) since, to this day, a Hindu wife bends down and touches her husband's feet in order to show her humility, reverence and respect.

It is now time for us to turn to the most famous act of defiance in all of history, when Iblīs, or Satan, defied Allah Most High, and arrogantly refused to prostrate himself before Nabī Ādam عليه السلام . Iblīs was not akin to the Protestant in the sense of arguing that prostration is due only to Allah. Rather Iblīs suffered from the deadly disease of 'arrogance' since he believed that he was born (or created) superior to Ādam. He believed that he had a birth-right of superiority. Those who claim that they are the chosen people of the Lord-God with a birth-right of superiority over the rest of mankind, suffer from the same deadly disease. As a consequence Allah Most High created and fashioned Dajjāl, and then let him loose, so that they might be taught a lesson in humility in *Ākhir al-Zamān.*

This subject is addressed in the next chapter.

وَإِذْ قَالَ رَبُّكَ لِلْمَلَائِكَةِ إِنِّي جَاعِلٌ فِي الْأَرْضِ خَلِيفَةً...

(Qur'ān, al-Baqarah, 2:30)

And Lo! Thy Lord-God said unto the Angels: Behold, I am going to establish upon earth one who shall be a Khalīfah, i.e., who would govern or rule . . .

CHAPTER FIVE

ARROGANCE IN AWWAL AL-ZAMĀN

A Khalīfah (or Ruler) on Earth

The Qur'ān has disclosed in the verse above, that Allah Most High addressed the Angels in *Awwal al-Zamān* and informed them that He was going to place on earth one who would be a *Khalīfah*, i.e., he would rule or govern on earth (*Qur'ān, al-Baqarah, 2:30*). This declaration constitutes the foundation on which the entire edifice of Islamic political philosophy, as well as Islam's model of a State, is built.

The Qur'ān went on to disclose that when Allah Most High appoints a *Khalīfah* on earth, his function would be to govern or rule with *Al-Haq* i.e., Divinely-revealed 'Truth', and hence to establish a Holy *Khilāfah* State or Pax-Dei, which would enforce Allah's Law as the Supreme Law. The modern West, created by Dajjāl, effectively denies any State the freedom with which to establish Allah's Law as the Supreme Law. All States must belong to the United Nations Organization and, as a consequence of membership in that organization, must accede to the UN Charter which has, in effect, imposed the UN Charter, and the resolutions of the UN Security Council, as the

Supreme Law. The modern West also demonizes the *Khilāfah* State as a theocratic State, and indoctrinates all of mankind to so despise and reject a theocratic State as to banish it to the museums of history.

In its place the West has delivered to the world the modern republican State in which the supreme law is the law of the State rather than Allah's law. A republican State, such as Pakistan, cannot be a *Khilāfah* State, since the highest law in a republican State is always the law of the State, and not Allah's Law. Dr. Muhammad Iqbal appears not to have been aware of this elementary fact when he wrote the following in his Magnum Opus, 'The Reconstruction of Religious Thought in Islam':

> *The republican form of government is not only thoroughly consistent with the spirit of Islam, but has also become a necessity in view of the new forces that are set free in the world of Islam.*
>
> Essay entitled:
> The Principle of Movement in the Structure of Islam

A republican form of government requires the prior establishment of a Republic, and the 'new forces' to which Dr. Iqbal referred above were, of course, the modern secular republican State which was created by Dajjāl, and was introduced to the world through Dajjāl's modern western civilization.

When viewed from the perspective of the less-than-dismal scholarship that still exists in the world of Islam on the subject of Dajjāl (who is the subject of this book), one cannot but respond with a summary dismissal of the expected objections and sarcastic comments that the above statement concerning the republican State will inevitably provoke from secular scholarship in and out of Pakistan.

Muslim India's *Khilāfat* Movement, with all its defects and deficiencies, represented the last effort on the part of Muslim India as well as the rest of the world of Islam, to remain faithful to the political philosophy and model of a State which was located in the Qur'ān. Britain, on the other hand, wanted to embrace all of British India, Hindu as well as Muslim, and then the rest of the world, with the new model of a republican State which had emerged in Dajjāl's western civilization. One misguided sentence (quoted above) from India's most illustrious Islamic scholar was sufficient to nail a final nail into the coffin of Islam's *Khilāfah* State, and pave the way for the birth of a republican State of Pakistan, and for the subsequent embrace of the rest of the world of Islam in Dajjāl's secular world-order of republican States. For this alone, Dr. Iqbal richly deserved the knighthood which Britain conferred on him—in consequence of which he became Sir Muhammad Iqbal.

(Readers may wish to read my essay entitled: *Can Muslims Vote in Elections of the Modern Secular State?*)

They may also wish to view my lecture entitled 'Iqbal Pakistan and the *Khilāfah* State' available on the Internet.

The Qur'ān went on to warn that those, such as the Republican secular State, who rule over the earth or any part thereof, and do not do so with *Al-Haq*, i.e., Truth, would face an awful doom on the Day of Reckoning. This will be because any rule, other than that based on *Al-Haq*, would lead the ruler (and hence the people as well) away from *Sabīl Allah*, i.e., the Divine Way or Path:

يَا دَاوُودُ إِنَّا جَعَلْنَاكَ خَلِيفَةً فِي الْأَرْضِ فَاحْكُم بَيْنَ النَّاسِ بِالْحَقِّ وَلَا تَتَّبِعِ الْهَوَىٰ فَيُضِلَّكَ عَن سَبِيلِ اللَّهِ إِنَّ الَّذِينَ يَضِلُّونَ عَن سَبِيلِ اللَّهِ لَهُمْ عَذَابٌ شَدِيدٌ بِمَا نَسُوا يَوْمَ الْحِسَابِ

(Qur'ān, Sād, 38:26)

And it was said unto him: O David! Lo! We have set thee as a ruler in the earth; therefore govern or rule over mankind with al-Haq, i.e., Truth, and follow not your own secular agenda, for such would lead you away from the way or path of Allah. Lo! Those who depart from the way or path of Allah have an awful doom, in consequence of having forgotten the Day of Accounts, i.e., Judgment Day.

If a *Khilāfah* State, or Pax-Dei, is to be established, and if it is to survive, then it must have power to resist those who will seek to attack and destroy it. Hence, when Nabī Daūd عليه السلام established the Holy State of Israel, Allah Most High also blessed it with power, thus clearly confirming that such a Holy State must have the power with which to establish itself as Pax-Dei:

وَشَدَدْنَا مُلْكَهُ وَآتَيْنَاهُ الْحِكْمَةَ وَفَصْلَ الْخِطَابِ

(Qur'ān, Sād, 38:20)

And Allah Most High strengthened his Kingdom, hence Pax Dei, and bestowed upon him wisdom and sagacity in judgment.

A *Khilāfah* State would thus have an obligation to build military power to the maximum extent that it can be built. The Qur'ān explains, however, that such power is to be used to deter aggression, and not to commit aggression or to establish a hegemonic dominance over others:

وَأَعِدُّوا لَهُمْ مَا اسْتَطَعْتُمْ مِنْ قُوَّةٍ وَمِنْ رِبَاطِ الْخَيْلِ تُرْهِبُونَ بِهِ عَدُوَّ اللَّهِ وَعَدُوَّكُمْ وَآخَرِينَ مِنْ دُونِهِمْ لَا تَعْلَمُونَهُمُ اللَّهُ يَعْلَمُهُمْ وَمَا تُنْفِقُوا مِنْ شَيْءٍ فِي سَبِيلِ اللَّهِ يُوَفَّ إِلَيْكُمْ وَأَنْتُمْ لَا تُظْلَمُونَ

(Qur'ān, al-Anfāl, 8:60)

Hence, make ready against them whatever military force and war mounts you are able to muster, so that you might deter thereby the enemies of Allah, who are your enemies as well, and others besides them of whom you may be unaware, but of whom Allah is aware; and whatever you may expend in Allah's cause shall be repaid to you in full, and you shall not be wronged.

We can see quite clearly that if Korea had not faithfully followed this command of the Qur'ān, it would have already become a client-State of the present Zionist Judeo-Christian world-order—which is the fate that has already befallen the southern part of the Korean peninsula. Dajjāl's modern West not only succeeded in embracing all of mankind in a United Nations Organization with a Security Council dominated by the oppressors of the modern world, i.e., Zionist western Judeo-Christian alliance, but also forced upon the world a Nuclear Non Proliferation Treaty (NNPT) which prohibits member States from building the power that the Qur'ān has demanded. If India had not demonstrated integrity in resisting membership in NNPT, it is certain that the so-called Islamic Republic of Pakistan would have acquiesced with docility to NNPT membership.

Whenever a *Khilāfah* State is established, and it struggles to build power in conformity with Allah's command, Divine assistance will always come to such a State, as it came to Solomon's Holy Israel:

وَاذْكُرُوا إِذْ جَعَلَكُمْ خُلَفَاءَ مِنْ بَعْدِ قَوْمِ نُوحٍ وَزَادَكُمْ فِي
الْخَلْقِ بَسْطَةً فَاذْكُرُوا آلَاءَ اللَّهِ لَعَلَّكُمْ تُفْلِحُونَ

(Qur'ān, al-'Arāf, 7:69)

. . . and remember how Allah Most High made you rulers on earth after Noah's folk, and gave you growth of stature; and remember all the bounties of your Lord, that you might be successful.

The Qur'ān reminded the Israelites that Allah responded to their plight of suffering by extricating them from that distress, and replacing it with rule on earth (through a *Khilāfah* State):

أَمَّنْ يُجِيبُ الْمُضْطَرَّ إِذَا دَعَاهُ وَيَكْشِفُ السُّوءَ وَيَجْعَلُكُمْ
خُلَفَاءَ الْأَرْضِ أَإِلَٰهٌ مَعَ اللَّهِ قَلِيلًا مَا تَذَكَّرُونَ

(Qur'ān, al-Naml, 27:62)

Is not He best who responds to those who are wronged when he such a person cries out unto Him and he removes the evil, and has made you rulers on earth? Is there any God beside Allah? Little do they reflect!

The above verses of the Qur'ān disclosed that it was by Allah's leave that the Israelites remained on earth as rulers for long years. But at no time were they able to restore Holy Israel as Pax-Dei. This was because Nabī Dāud's son, Nabī Sulaimān, عليه السلام, prayed that his Holy State of Israel could not belong to anyone after him, i.e., none could succeed in restoring Holy Israel after him. He made this prayer after he was shown the vision of a *Jasad* sitting on his throne:

وَلَقَدْ فَتَنَّا سُلَيْمَانَ وَأَلْقَيْنَا عَلَى كُرْسِيِّهِ جَسَدًا ثُمَّ أَنَابَ

(Qur'ān, Sād, 38:34)

Allah Most High caused distress to Solomon by placing upon his throne a Jasad, or body without a soul; and thereupon he turned to Allah in prayer.

The prayer was made because he recognized the *Jasad* to be Dajjāl, and he knew that Dajjāl would attempt to rule over Holy Israel. Hence he prayed as follows:

قَالَ رَبِّ اغْفِرْ لِي وَهَبْ لِي مُلْكًا لَا يَنْبَغِي لِأَحَدٍ مِنْ بَعْدِي إِنَّكَ أَنْتَ الْوَهَّابُ

(Qur'ān, Sād, 38:35)

Solomon prayed: O my Lord-God, forgive me my sins, and bestow upon me a kingdom which cannot belong to anyone after me. Verily, You are the one who bestows such!

Allah Most High obviously answered his prayer since Holy Israel collapsed after Solomon's death and has never since been successfully restored. Hence Dajjāl's present effort to restore Holy Israel in order to convince the Jews that he is the true Messiah, is bound to fail.

The Angels Respond to a Khilāfah State on Earth

The response of the Angels to the Divine announcement that a *Khalīfah*, or ruler, would be placed on earth, was to bluntly question it in overt disagreement! The Angels already knew that the subject of the establishment of rule, and of a ruling State, on earth, would result in *Fasād*, i.e., that which corrupts to an extent that can destroy, and the shedding of blood. The only source from whom they could have acquired such knowledge was the Lord-God Himself.

The dissenting view of the Angels was based on the argument that their constant worship of the Lord-God, while celebrating His Praise and glorifying His Holy Name, qualified them, instead, to rule:

قَالُوا أَتَجْعَلُ فِيهَا مَنْ يُفْسِدُ فِيهَا وَيَسْفِكُ الدِّمَاءَ وَنَحْنُ نُسَبِّحُ بِحَمْدِكَ وَنُقَدِّسُ لَكَ

(Qur'ān, al-Baqarah, 2:30)

The Angels asked Allah Most High: Will You place on earth such as will commit Fasād thereon i.e., engage in corruption which can destroy, and shed blood— whereas it is we who extol Thy limitless glory, and praise Thee, and hallow Thy name?

The enigmatic Divine response to the Angels was the declaration:

...قَالَ إِنِّي أَعْلَمُ مَا لَا تَعْلَمُونَ

(Qur'ān, al-Baqarah, 2:30)

Allah answered: Verily, I know that which you do not know.

Hence, while the Angels knew that the quest for establishing rule over the earth would result in destructive corruption and in bloodshed, they did not have complete knowledge of the subject that justified the Divine announcement. They did not have knowledge of two events which were about to occur at this time, i.e., the beginning of history, which were connected to the end of history, and which offered an eschatological justification for the Divine announcement.

Allah Most High then proceeded to confer knowledge directly on this ruler, i.e., into Ādam عليه السلام who would establish his rule on earth. He could do so since He had already breathed His Divine *Rūh* into him in such wise that he could receive knowledge both externally and internally or spiritually:

وَعَلَّمَ آدَمَ الْأَسْمَاءَ كُلَّهَا ثُمَّ عَرَضَهُمْ عَلَى الْمَلَائِكَةِ فَقَالَ أَنْبِئُونِي بِأَسْمَاءِ هَؤُلَاءِ إِنْ كُنْتُمْ صَادِقِينَ ۝
قَالُوا سُبْحَانَكَ لَا عِلْمَ لَنَا إِلَّا مَا عَلَّمْتَنَا إِنَّكَ أَنْتَ الْعَلِيمُ الْحَكِيمُ

(Qur'ān, al-Baqarah, 2:31–32)

And Allah Most High taught Ādam the knowledge of the names of all things pertaining to the subject of rule on earth; then He brought them within the ken of the angels and said: Declare unto Me the names of these things, if you are to be truthful in respect of your knowledge of the subject of rule on earth. They replied: Limitless are You in Your glory! No knowledge have we save that which You have imparted unto us. Verily, You alone are all-knowing, truly wise.

The implication of the above was that rule on earth could be established successfully only by those who received such knowledge directly from the Lord-God which would qualify them to rule. That knowledge is of course, located in the divinely-revealed scriptures. This appears to be one of the reasons why Allah Most High responded to the question posed by the Angels with the declaration: I know that which you do not know! Hence whoever does not turn to the Qur'ān for guidance and for Law, is not qualified to rule over Muslims.

Allah Most High then asked Nabī Ādam عليه السلام to respond to the question, and he did so:

قَالَ يَا آدَمُ أَنْبِئْهُمْ بِأَسْمَائِهِمْ فَلَمَّا أَنْبَأَهُمْ بِأَسْمَائِهِمْ قَالَ أَلَمْ أَقُلْ لَكُمْ إِنِّي أَعْلَمُ غَيْبَ السَّمَاوَاتِ وَالْأَرْضِ وَأَعْلَمُ مَا تُبْدُونَ وَمَا كُنْتُمْ تَكْتُمُونَ

(Qur'ān, al-Baqarah, 2:33)

Allah Most High then said to Ādam: Oh Ādam, convey unto them the names of these things. And as soon as Ādam had conveyed unto them their names, Allah said: Did I not say unto you, Verily, I alone know the hidden reality of the heavens and the earth, and know all that you bring into the open and all that you would conceal?

The conclusion to which we arrive from the above is that mankind was placed on earth for the over-riding imperative of establishing rule over the earth, and that such can be accomplished only by those who act faithfully in accordance with knowledge which has come to them from Allah Most High, and pursue no other agenda while establishing their rule.

Those who rule otherwise will face an awful doom on Judgment Day. We recognize this mission of ruling on earth on the basis of Truth, to be the *Amānah*, or Trust, that Allah offered to mankind, and which they accepted.

The Amānah or Trust was a mission to rule justly (in accordance with Truth)

The very first event to have occurred in human history following the creation of the human being and of the Divine *Rūh* being breathed into him, was Allah's offer of an *Amānah*, or trust, that was made to all of creation—including the mountains—but which they all refused to accept out of fear, and which only mankind accepted. In accepting this *Amānah*, or trust, however, some of mankind have misused it while acting either unjustly or foolishly with it. Does the Qur'ān identify any of those who betrayed the *Amānah*?

إِنَّا عَرَضْنَا الْأَمَانَةَ عَلَى السَّمَاوَاتِ وَالْأَرْضِ وَالْجِبَالِ فَأَبَيْنَ
أَنْ يَحْمِلْنَهَا وَأَشْفَقْنَ مِنْهَا وَحَمَلَهَا الْإِنْسَانُ إِنَّهُ كَانَ ظَلُومًا
جَهُولًا

(Qur'ān, al-Ahzāb, 33:72)

Lo! Allah Most High offered the trust unto the heavens and the earth and the hills, but they shrank from bearing it and were afraid of it. And man assumed it. Lo! man hath proved a tyrant and an ignorant fool.

The *Amānah*, or trust, which was divinely bestowed, and which was accepted by mankind, had to be something which, when misused, could lead to conduct which would be oppressive and wicked, or to a display of ignorance and stupidity, and it is the knowledge of precisely this betrayal of the Trust to rule with justice and Truth that the Angels had, and to which they referred, when they protested the Divine announcement that a *Khalīfah* would be placed on earth.

At the very heart of the *Amānah*, therefore, there had to be the offer of a free-will or a self-directed will with which a person could make a free choice to either accept or to reject, to obey or to disobey, to be grateful or to be ungrateful, to be just or unjust, etc. Thus the bestowal of the *Amānah* resulted in the emergence of a moral being who possessed the capacity for ethically acceptable conduct, as well as for spiritual insight. Dr. Iqbal identifies the *Amānah* with what he calls 'the trust of personality' (see essay on *'Knowledge and Religious Experience'* in his book: *The Reconstruction of Religious Thought in Islam*). There are many other distinguished scholars of Islam who hold the same view. Our differing view is based, however, on our study of Islamic eschatology.

The Jinn, who are a category of beings created from fire (while mankind was created from clay), also possessed a free will, and could choose to obey or disobey. However there is no evidence that they also possessed the capacity to receive knowledge internally, or directly from Allah Most High. There is no evidence that Allah's *Rūh* was breathed into them, hence the Jinn did not possess the spiritual insight which only human beings possessed.

The Angels had to be aware of the Jewish belief that they were the chosen people of the Lord-God, and they had to also be aware that this belief would lead them to conclude that they had an exclusive claim to morality since they believed that they, alone, are moral beings. Our view is that it was precisely this false Jewish belief in exclusivity as a chosen people which led the Angels to declare that it would lead to bloodshed and Fasād (that which corrupts and destroys) on earth.

The Qur'ān has exposed the falsehood of this Jewish claim to moral exclusivity. There are, says the Qur'ān, among the *Ahl Al-Kitāb*, i.e., people of the Torah, those who, if you were to place a *Qintār*, i.e., a treasure of about 1200 gold *Dīnār*, for safe-keeping with them, when you want your money returned, it would be returned to you. But if someone who was not from that group were to place even one *Dīnār* for safe-keeping, when he wanted his money returned, it would not be returned to him unless and until he struggled to get it back. The Qur'ān provided an explanation for this ethically repugnant double standard as follows:

وَمِنْ أَهْلِ الْكِتَابِ مَنْ إِنْ تَأْمَنْهُ بِقِنْطَارٍ يُؤَدِّهِ إِلَيْكَ وَمِنْهُمْ مَنْ إِنْ تَأْمَنْهُ بِدِينَارٍ لَا يُؤَدِّهِ إِلَيْكَ إِلَّا مَا دُمْتَ عَلَيْهِ قَائِمًا ذَٰلِكَ بِأَنَّهُمْ قَالُوا لَيْسَ عَلَيْنَا فِي الْأُمِّيِّينَ سَبِيلٌ وَيَقُولُونَ عَلَى اللَّهِ الْكَذِبَ وَهُمْ يَعْلَمُونَ

(Qur'ān, Āle 'Imrān, 3:75)

Among the followers of earlier revelation, i.e., the Torah, there is many a one who, if you entrust him with a Qintār, which is a treasure of about 1200 Dinars, will faithfully restore it to you; and there is among them many a one who, if you entrust him with a single Dīnār, i.e., a gold coin, will not restore it to you unless you keep standing over him demanding your money back. The reason for this is because they, the Jews, claim: We have no moral obligations to these Ummiyūn, i.e., Gentiles or non-Jews, but they tell a lie about Allah, being well aware that it is a lie.

Since they believed that the divinely-revealed Moral Law was applicable only to Jews, there was no sin on them if they were to rip-off, or exploit, the rest of mankind who were not Jews. It is remarkable that this same disease afflicted modern western civilization since the West has no sense of moral guilt at all in their exploitation and oppression of mankind through their endless wars of oppression and their bogus monetary and banking system which exploit, oppress and enslave all those who are targets.

Arrogance at the beginning of history and a false claim to a birth-right of superiority

After having announced to the Angels that He would place on earth one who would rule, and then after Nabī Ādam عليه السلام had explained to the Angels that part of the subject (of rule on earth) which they did not know, Allah Most Wise ordered the Angels to prostrate themselves before him, i.e., Nabī Ādam عليه السلام .

The Qur'ān then disclosed that they all obeyed the Divine command except Iblīs, i.e., Satan:

وَإِذْ قُلْنَا لِلْمَلَائِكَةِ اسْجُدُوا لِآدَمَ فَسَجَدُوا إِلَّا إِبْلِيسَ أَبَى
وَاسْتَكْبَرَ وَكَانَ مِنَ الْكَافِرِينَ

(Qur'ān, al-Baqarah, 2:34)

Allah ordered the angels to prostrate themselves before Ādam! They all prostrated themselves, except Iblīs, who refused and gloried in his arrogance: and thus he became one of those who deny the truth.

Angels cannot disobey (*Qur'ān, Al-Tahrīm*, 66:6), and since Iblīs disobeyed, he could not have been an Angel. In fact he was a Jinn (*Qur'ān, Al-Kahf,* 18:50). The reason which he gave for his refusal to so prostrate himself, was his (false) belief in his birthright of superiority over Nabī Ādam عليه السلام .

In consequence of this false belief in a birth-right of superiority, he could not tolerate anyone possessing more knowledge than he had, nor in ruling over him anywhere in the universe. Rather he was convinced that his (false) belief in his superior birth-right gave to him the right to rule over all. Hence he could not bow down in prostration to this divinely-educated and divinely-appointed *Khalīfah* or ruler.

قَالَ مَا مَنَعَكَ أَلَّا تَسْجُدَ إِذْ أَمَرْتُكَ قَالَ أَنَا خَيْرٌ مِنْهُ
خَلَقْتَنِي مِنْ نَارٍ وَخَلَقْتَهُ مِنْ طِينٍ

(Qur'ān, al-'Arāf, 7:12)

And Allah said: What has kept you from prostrating yourself when I commanded you? Answered Iblīs: I am better than he: You created me out of fire, whereas him, You created out of clay.

The Qur'ān has here disclosed a beginning of history in which someone's false claim to a birth-right of a superior status led to his arrogant refusal to obey the Lord-God who commanded him to accept the superiority of someone else over him. This arrogance resulted in a divine curse on him, and his expulsion from heaven. The Lord-God then decreed that he would hence-forth be reduced to a lowly state:

قَالَ فَاهْبِطْ مِنْهَا فَمَا يَكُونُ لَكَ أَنْ تَتَكَبَّرَ فِيهَا فَاخْرُجْ
إِنَّكَ مِنَ الصَّاغِرِينَ

(Qur'ān, al-'Arāf, 7:13)

Allah said: Down with you, then, from this state—for it is not meet for you to show arrogance here! Go forth, then: verily, among the humiliated, disgraced, degraded shall you be!

The significant implication of the above, significant most of all in *Ākhir Al-Zamān* or the end of history, is that any people who consider themselves to have a birth-right of superiority over others will similarly be cursed by the Lord- God, and would be debarred from entering heaven. There is no place in heaven for those who display this particular form of arrogance. In addition, their arrogant claim to superiority would end in the humiliation and disgrace of a lowly status: "... verily, among the humiliated shall you be!"

The arrogant Jewish claim, which was brazenly adopted by Dajjāl's modern western civilization, that they are the chosen people of the Lord-God with a birthright of superiority over the rest of mankind, is hence false. Any Jew, Christian, Hindu (or even a Muslim) who makes such a claim of a birthright of superiority over others, will have a divine curse on him, and will eventually be brought down to a lowly status.

The Qur'ān has singled out the Jews for this false belief that they are the chosen people of the Lord-God, and challenged them as follows:

قُلْ يَا أَيُّهَا الَّذِينَ هَادُوا إِنْ زَعَمْتُمْ أَنَّكُمْ أَوْلِيَاءُ لِلَّهِ مِنْ دُونِ
النَّاسِ فَتَمَنَّوُا الْمَوْتَ إِنْ كُنْتُمْ صَادِقِينَ ۝
وَلَا يَتَمَنَّوْنَهُ أَبَدًا بِمَا قَدَّمَتْ أَيْدِيهِمْ وَاللَّهُ عَلِيمٌ بِالظَّالِمِينَ

(Qur'ān, al-Jumu'ah, 62:6-7)

Oh you who are Jews, if you believe that you are a chosen people of the Lord-God to the exclusion of the rest of mankind, then why do you not express a wish for death—if you are convinced of the truth of your claim? But No! They will never do such a thing since they are well aware of their conduct. And Allah Most High has knowledge of those whose conduct is wicked.

The Divine challenge presented to the Jew, applies equally to all others who consider themselves to possess a birthright of superiority over others.

The Jew may respond to argue that the Lord-God had made them an exceptional people by favoring them and bestowing blessings upon them more than on any other of mankind. The Qur'ān confirms that the Israelite people received more of the divinely-conferred blessings than all of the rest of mankind:

يَا بَنِي إِسْرَائِيلَ اذْكُرُوا نِعْمَتِيَ الَّتِي أَنْعَمْتُ عَلَيْكُمْ وَأَنِّي
فَضَّلْتُكُمْ عَلَى الْعَالَمِينَ

(Qur'ān, al-Baqarah, 2:47)

Oh People of Israel! Remember those blessings of Mine with which I graced you, and how, in conferring those blessings and favors, I favored you more than all other people.

وَإِذْ قَالَ مُوسَى لِقَوْمِهِ يَا قَوْمِ اذْكُرُوا نِعْمَةَ اللَّهِ عَلَيْكُمْ إِذْ

جَعَلَ فِيكُمْ أَنْبِيَاءَ وَجَعَلَكُمْ مُلُوكًا وَآتَاكُمْ مَا لَمْ يُؤْتِ أَحَدًا
مِنَ الْعَالَمِينَ

(Qur'ān, al-Māidah, 5:20)

And, Lo! Moses said unto his people: Oh my people! Remember the blessings which Allah bestowed upon you when he raised up Prophets among you, and made you rulers/Kings, and granted unto you favors such as He had not granted to anyone else in the world.

The implication of this great Divine bestowal of favors on the Israelite people was that if they betrayed the standard of righteous conduct, they would be judged and punished with greater punishment than all of mankind. The Qur'ān demolished their claim to being an exclusive or chosen people when it denounced the false claim that heaven was reserved for them:

وَقَالُوا لَنْ يَدْخُلَ الْجَنَّةَ إِلَّا مَنْ كَانَ هُودًا أَوْ نَصَارَى تِلْكَ
أَمَانِيُّهُمْ قُلْ هَاتُوا بُرْهَانَكُمْ إِنْ كُنْتُمْ صَادِقِينَ

(Qur'ān, al-Baqarah, 2:111)

Jews and Christians claim: None shall ever enter paradise unless he be a Jew or a Christian. Such are their wishful beliefs: Say: Produce an evidence for what you are claiming, if what you say is true!

The Parallel between the End and the Beginning of History

The Qur'ān has hinted of a parallel between the beginning and the end of history:

... كَمَا بَدَأَكُمْ تَعُودُونَ

(Qur'ān, al-'Arāf, 7:29)

. . . As it was when Allah Most High brought you into being in the first instance, so also you will return in the end.

Prophet Muhammad صل الله عليه و سلم declared that there was never a Prophet but that he warned his people about Dajjāl:

وَمَا مِنْ نَبِيٍّ إِلاَّ وَقَدْ أَنْذَرَهُ قَوْمَهُ

(Sahīh Bukhārī)

The implication is that Dajjāl is located at both the beginning and the end of history. In declaring that Allah is the First and He is the Last, and that He has knowledge of all things, the Qur'ān has therefore confirmed an eschatological drama to wit, that: as it was in the beginning of history, so will it be at the end of history. This drama will unfold in the end of history in such wise that the parallel with the beginning of history could be discerned by those who employ an epistemology which harmoniously integrates *Al-Zāhir*, i.e., the externally visible, with *Al-Bātin*, i.e., the internally discerned.

The study of the subject of Dajjāl requires an effort to identify relevant data which is located at the beginning of history, and to then locate the connection of that data with the end of history.

What is the view of Islam of that end of history that will be a parallel to the beginning of history depicted above?

The voice of Prophet Muhammad صل الله عليه و سلم is the most powerful in history to have prophesied the return of the Messiah, Jesus the son of Mary, peace and blessings of Allah Most High be upon them both—blessed virgin mother, and blessed son.

(A man named Mirza Ghulam Ahmad from India sought to identify himself with this prophecy of the return of the son of Mary, claiming that he fulfilled in himself the prophecy of that miraculous return; but this liar had an insurmountable problem since he was the son of a Punjabi woman, whereas the prophecy identified the return of one who would be the son of Mary. Even if his Punjabi mother could be renamed Mary, that would still not be enough to solve his problem since there is only one Virgin Mary in all of history. Whoever claims that Mary was not a virgin, would hold a view which would be in manifest conflict with the Qur'ān, and hence would not be recognized as a Muslim.)

The Qur'ān has confirmed that miraculous messianic return, but has wisely chosen to do so in its *Āyāt Mutashābihāt*, i.e., allegorical verses, which must be interpreted in order for their inner meaning to be discovered.

Prophet Muhammad صل الله عليه و سلم went on to prophesy that Jesus would return to the world as *Al-Hākim Al-Ādil*, i.e., a just ruler; hence this prophecy establishes the Islamic eschatological belief that history will end with the Pax-Dei with which it began:

وَالَّذِي نَفْسِي بِيَدِهِ لَيُوشِكَنَّ أَنْ يَنْزِلَ فِيكُمُ ابْنُ مَرْيَمَ حَكَمًا
مُقْسِطًا . . .

By Him in Whose Hands my soul is, the son of Mary will shortly descend among you as a just ruler . . .

(Sahīh Bukhārī)

The same prophecy is to be found elsewhere with a slightly different text:

اَ تَقُومُ السَّاعَةُ حَتَّى يَنْزِلَ عِيسَى ابْنُ مَرْيَمَ حَكَمًا مُقْسِطًا
وَإِمَامًا عَدْلاً

The Last Hour will not occur until Jesus the Son of Mary descends as a just ruler, i.e., over all of mankind, and as a just leader of individual believers.

(Sunan, Ibn Mājah)

However let us recall that the beginning of history also gave us another parallel 'end of history' when an effort is made to establish a bogus Pax-Dei by those who arrogantly consider themselves, like Iblīs, i.e., Satan, to be superior to the rest of mankind. They will also claim, like Iblīs, a birth-right of superiority since (according to them) they were born, or created superior! In other words, they will claim that the Lord-God chose them as the elect of all of mankind, i.e., His chosen people to the exclusion of all the rest of mankind. They will also make a claim to be the intellectual elite of mankind since, according to them, the Lord-God bestowed superior knowledge on them, as He did to Nabī Ādam عليه السلام . Hence they alone would be eligible to establish Pax-Dei.

Such conduct was not tolerated in heaven, and it led to the expulsion of Iblīs from heaven, and to a divine curse on him. The Lord-God also declared that such arrogance will end in humiliation and debasement. Hence the end of history which will parallel the beginning, will witness the divine destruction of an arrogant and bogus Pax-Dei, and the humiliation and debasement of those who attempt to establish it.

Another event in Awwal al-Zamān

A second event occurred at the beginning of history which provided further information on that false Pa-Dei which would appear at the end of history. Allah Most High told Ādam عليه السلام to dwell in heaven with his wife Hawwa, i.e., Eve, but prohibited them both from approaching a certain tree, for such would lead to *Dhulm*, i.e., wickedness, oppression, injustice:

وَقُلْنَا يَا آدَمُ اسْكُنْ أَنْتَ وَزَوْجُكَ الْجَنَّةَ وَكُلَا مِنْهَا رَغَدًا
حَيْثُ شِئْتُمَا وَلَا تَقْرَبَا هَذِهِ الشَّجَرَةَ فَتَكُونَا مِنَ الظَّالِمِينَ

(Qur'ān, al-Baqarah, 2:35)

Allah Most High said: Oh Ādam, dwell thou and thy wife in this garden of paradise, and eat freely thereof, both of you, whatever you may wish; but do not approach this tree, lest you become wicked.

What is the Forbidden Tree?

A tree has no free will, and hence cannot exhibit 'conduct'. It should therefore be quite apparent that the Lord-God has used the 'tree' as a symbol to represent something quite reprehensible.

We learn something about the symbol when Iblīs, i.e., Satan, sought to seduce them to approach the tree while claiming that they would become like unto Angels who live eternally, i.e., for a very long period of time. The objective which he was pursuing in disclosing this information to them was to inject into their spiritual heart a form of lust, i.e., the lust to live forever. Such lust, like its sexual counterpart, i.e., sexual lust, destroys spiritual innocence and reduces one to a state of (spiritual) nakedness:

فَوَسْوَسَ لَهُمَا الشَّيْطَانُ لِيُبْدِيَ لَهُمَا مَا وُورِيَ عَنْهُمَا مِنْ
سَوْآتِهِمَا وَقَالَ مَا نَهَاكُمَا رَبُّكُمَا عَنْ هَذِهِ الشَّجَرَةِ إِلَّا أَنْ
تَكُونَا مَلَكَيْنِ أَوْ تَكُونَا مِنَ الْخَالِدِينَ

(Qur'ān, al-An'ām, 7:20)

Satan whispered unto both Ādam and his wife Hawwa, or Eve, with a view to making them conscious of their nakedness, of which hitherto they had been unaware; and he said: Your Lord-God has but forbidden you this tree lest you two become as angels, or lest you live forever.

Iblīs went on to reveal more about the symbol of the forbidden tree when he disclosed that it was not only the tree of immortality, symbolizing 'eternal life' (angelic style), but also 'eternal rule'. His objective in disclosing this information to them was to inject into their spiritual heart another form of lust, i.e., the lust to rule forever or eternally. In order to achieve eternal rule they would have to establish a ruling State that would rule eternally. The lust for such eternal rule, like the lust to live forever, and sexual lust, destroys spiritual innocence and reduces one to a state of spiritual nakedness:

فَوَسْوَسَ إِلَيْهِ الشَّيْطَانُ قَالَ يَا آدَمُ هَلْ أَدُلُّكَ عَلَى شَجَرَةِ الْخُلْدِ وَمُلْكٍ لَا يَبْلَى

(Qur'ān, Tā Hā, 20:120)

Satan whispered unto (only) Ādam, saying: O Ādam! Shall I lead thee to the tree of life eternal; and thus to a kingdom that will never perish or decay?

Iblīs succeeded in deceiving them, in consequence of which they both tasted the tree, i.e., they allowed their hearts to lust for that which the tree symbolized. As soon as that lust entered their hearts, i.e., the lust to live and to rule eternally, they lost their spiritual innocence and became conscious of their nakedness. They then sought, symbolically so, to cover themselves with leaves from the trees of heaven:

فَدَلَّاهُمَا بِغُرُورٍ فَلَمَّا ذَاقَا الشَّجَرَةَ بَدَتْ لَهُمَا سَوْآتُهُمَا وَطَفِقَا يَخْصِفَانِ عَلَيْهِمَا مِنْ وَرَقِ الْجَنَّةِ وَنَادَاهُمَا رَبُّهُمَا أَلَمْ أَنْهَكُمَا عَنْ تِلْكُمَا الشَّجَرَةِ وَأَقُلْ لَكُمَا إِنَّ الشَّيْطَانَ لَكُمَا عَدُوٌّ مُبِينٌ

(Qur'ān, al-An'ām, 7:22)

And thus Satan led them on with deluding thoughts, guile and deception. But as soon as the two had tasted the fruit of the tree, they became conscious of their nakedness; and they began to cover themselves with pieced-together leaves from the garden. And their Lord-God called unto them: Did I not forbid that tree unto you and tell you, Verily, Satan is your open foe?

Since they lost their spiritual innocence, they no longer qualified to dwell in heaven. This is so because heaven is reserved for those whose hearts are Salīm, i.e., sound, healthy and innocent:

يَوْمَ لَا يَنْفَعُ مَالٌ وَلَا بَنُونَ ۝
إِلَّا مَنْ أَتَى اللَّهَ بِقَلْبٍ سَلِيمٍ

(Qur'ān, al-Shūra, 26:88–9)

On Judgment Day neither wealth nor children will be of any benefit, rather, only he will automatically qualify for heaven who comes before Allah Most High with a heart which is Salim, i.e., sound, healthy, and innocent, and hence free from the lust for life and the lust to rule.

We learn from the passage below that both Nabī Ādam, عليه السلام , and his wife were expelled from heaven and sent to reside on earth, as soon as they tasted the forbidden tree:

فَأَزَلَّهُمَا الشَّيْطَانُ عَنْهَا فَأَخْرَجَهُمَا مِمَّا كَانَا فِيهِ وَقُلْنَا اهْبِطُوا بَعْضُكُمْ لِبَعْضٍ عَدُوٌّ وَلَكُمْ فِي الْأَرْضِ مُسْتَقَرٌّ وَمَتَاعٌ إِلَى حِينٍ

(Qur'ān, al-Baqarah, 2:36)

But Satan caused them both to stumble therein, and thus brought about the loss of their erstwhile state of spiritual innocence. And so Allah Most High said: Down with you, and experience the plague of enmity and hostility for one another as the lust for life and for rule corrupts you; and on earth you shall have your abode and your livelihood for a while!

They responded by seeking Allah's forgiveness, and He, in turn, forgave them:

فَتَلَقَّى آدَمُ مِنْ رَبِّهِ كَلِمَاتٍ فَتَابَ عَلَيْهِ إِنَّهُ هُوَ التَّوَّابُ الرَّحِيمُ

(Qur'ān, al-Baqarah, 2:37)

Thereupon Ādam received words of guidance from his Lord-God, and

He accepted his repentance: for, verily, He alone is the Acceptor of Repentance, the Dispenser of Grace.

The order of expulsion from heaven was maintained despite that Divine forgiveness. However they were informed that adherence to Divine guidance which would come to mankind from time to time, was the necessary condition for life on earth, and for efforts to establish Pax-Dei that would be free from fear and grief:

قُلْنَا اهْبِطُوا مِنْهَا جَمِيعًا فَإِمَّا يَأْتِيَنَّكُم مِّنِّي هُدًى فَمَن تَبِعَ هُدَايَ فَلَا خَوْفٌ عَلَيْهِمْ وَلَا هُمْ يَحْزَنُونَ

(Qur'ān, al-Baqarah, 2:38)

For although Allah Most High did say, Down with you all from this heavenly state, there shall, none the less, most certainly come unto you guidance from Me: and those who follow My guidance need have no fear, and neither shall they grieve.

The same event is described in the Torah quite differently. We quote the Torah at length:

Now the serpent was craftier than any of the wild animals the Lord God had made. He said to the woman, "Did God really say, 'You must not eat from any tree in the garden'?"

The woman said to the serpent, "We may eat fruit from the trees in the garden, but God did say, 'You must not eat fruit from the tree that is in the middle of the garden, and you must not touch it, or you will die.'" "You will not certainly die," the serpent said to the woman. "For God knows that when you eat from it your eyes will be opened, and you will be like God, knowing good and evil."

When the woman saw that the fruit of the tree was good for food and pleasing to the eye, and also desirable for gaining wisdom, she took some and ate it. She also gave some to her husband, who was with her, and he ate it. Then the eyes of both of them were opened, and they realized they were naked; so they sewed fig leaves together and made coverings for themselves.

Then the man and his wife heard the sound of the Lord God as he was walking in the garden in the cool of the day, and they hid from the Lord God among the trees of the garden. But the Lord God called to the man, "Where are you?"

He answered, "I heard you in the garden, and I was afraid because I was naked; so I hid." and he said, "Who told you that you were naked? Have you eaten from the tree that I commanded you not to eat from?"

The man said, "The woman you put here with me— she gave me some fruit from the tree, and I ate it."

Then the Lord God said to the woman, "What is this you have done?" The woman said, "The serpent deceived me, and I ate."

So the Lord God said to the serpent: Because you have done this, cursed are you above all livestock, and all wild animals! You will crawl on your belly and you will eat dust all the days of your life. And I will put enmity between you and the woman, and between your offspring and hers. He will crush your head, and you will strike his heel.

To the woman he said: I will make your pains in childbearing very severe; with painful labor you will give birth to children. Your desire will be for your husband, and he will rule over you.

To Adam he said: Because you listened to your wife and ate fruit from the tree about which I commanded you, 'You must not eat from it,' Cursed is the ground because of you; through painful toil you will eat food from it all the days of your life. It will produce thorns and thistles for you, and you will eat the plants of the field. By the sweat of your brow you will eat your food until you return to the ground, since from it you were taken; for dust you are, and to dust you will return.

Adam named his wife Eve, because she would become the mother of all the living. The Lord God made garments of skin for Ādam and his wife and clothed them. And the Lord God said: The man has now become like one of us, knowing good and evil. He must not be allowed to reach out his hand and take also from the tree of life and eat, and live forever. So the Lord God banished him from the Garden of Eden to work the ground from which he had been taken. After he drove the man out, he placed on the east side of the Garden of Eden cherubim and a flaming sword flashing back and forth to guard the way to the tree of life.

Genesis: 3–4 NIV

This book concludes with a warning to those who lust for life, seeking to live for as long as possible, and who also lust to rule over others with eternal rule, that such are a morally and spiritually naked people whose nakedness will increasingly become clearly visible to all of mankind (who have eyes with which to see) as Truth is proclaimed in the world. This book, which introduces the subject of Dajjāl or the Anti-Christ, is written to assist readers to be able to see and to understand the reality of the world today in which events which are ominously unfolding, have a parallel in a forbidden tree in *Awwal Al-Zamān.*

The Qur'ān has exposed the Jewish lust for life:

وَلَتَجِدَنَّهُمْ أَحْرَصَ النَّاسِ عَلَى حَيَاةٍ وَمِنَ الَّذِينَ أَشْرَكُوا يَوَدُّ أَحَدُهُمْ لَوْ يُعَمَّرُ أَلْفَ سَنَةٍ وَمَا هُوَ بِمُزَحْزِحِهِ مِنَ الْعَذَابِ أَنْ يُعَمَّرَ وَاللَّهُ بَصِيرٌ بِمَا يَعْمَلُونَ

(Qur'ān, al-Baqarah, 2:96)

And thou wilt most certainly find that they, the Jews, cling to life more eagerly than any other people, even more than those who are bent on ascribing divinity to other beings beside Allah: every one of them would love to live a thousand years, although the grant of long life could not save him from punishment in the hereafter: for Allah sees all that they do.

There is also ample evidence of a Jewish lust to rule the world eternally which, also, is a part of the forbidden tree. Consider Rabbi Emanuel Rabinovich's declaration:

> *"We will openly reveal our identity with the races of Asia and Africa. I can state with assurance that the last generation of white children is now being born. Our Control Commissions will, in the interests of peace and wiping out inter-racial tensions, forbid the Whites to mate with Whites. The White Women must cohabit with members of the dark races, the White Men with black women. Thus the White Race will disappear, for the mixing of the dark with the White means the end of the White Man, and our most dangerous enemy will become only a memory. We shall embark upon an era of ten thousand years of peace and plenty, the Pax Judaica, and our race will rule undisputed over the world. Our superior intelligence will easily enable us to retain mastery over a world of dark peoples"*

Rabbi Emanuel Rabinovich's summation of the progress of his tribe, the Modern Tribe of Jews, toward their goal of the One World under Jewry.

Emergency Council of European Rabbis
in Budapest on January 12, 1952

We have attached the full text of his speech as an Appendix 3 to this book.

Conclusion

Our effort in this book to locate Dajjāl at the beginning of history has borne fruit. Had there been no arrogant Jewish belief that Jews are the elect of mankind, or the chosen people of the Lord-God, with a birth-right of superiority over all other human beings, there would have been no cause for Dajjāl. It was this false belief which led them to reject Jesus, the son of the Virgin Mary, as the promised Messiah; and which continues to drive their futile quest to re-establish Holy Israel, by hook or by crook, as the End-time ruling State of the world.

The Qur'ān has not only rejected this false Jewish claim to an exclusive status with the Lord-God, but has also provided us with the means with which to identify Dajjāl's false State of Israel with the forbidden tree of heaven.

The most important discovery of this book is, without doubt, our identifying Dajjāl as the Jasad of the Qur'ān.

Our study in the Qur'ān of the beginning of history also now allows us to recognize and identify a strange new actor who has mysteriously appeared on the stage of the world in the end-times.

History began with a display of arrogance when Satan refused to bow and prostrate before Ādam on the basis of a claim to a birth-right of superiority. History is ending with precisely that arrogance, as the new actor on the stage of the world proclaimed his birth-right of superiority over the rest of mankind and then proceeded to wage wars of naked aggression in order to establish his rule over mankind so that he could civilize the rest of mankind—including this writer.

History began with Ādam عليه السلام and his wife displaying a sense of shame when they became conscious of their nakedness. They then took the leaves of the trees of heaven and used them to cover their nakedness. History is ending with that shameless new actor dismantling and destroying the inherent sense of modesty and shame in the human being as he proceeds to uncover the human body until people appear naked before each other in public. This writer is a native of the Caribbean island of Trinidad where, but for body paint, people now dance naked in public in what is proudly proclaimed as a national festival of Carnival. Around that actor's world of tinsel-town today, the glittering shopping malls are littered with women competing with each other in making a public display of their sexual assets.

History began with a Divine warning against approaching a forbidden tree of lust. That lust appears in the form of sexual lust. It should be clear that sexual lust is taking over the world in the End-time. It is that mysterious actor who is driving the wagon of lust helter-skelter around the world today.

That lust also manifests itself in the lust for life—hence to live for as long as is possible. It is that mysterious new actor on the stage of the world who is assisting in wondrous medical ways in fulfilling the lust of mankind to now live as long as is possible, and hence to delay death for as long as is possible.

History began with a Divine warning not to approach a forbidden tree of lust to rule over others. History is ending with that new actor on the stage of the world displaying an unprecedented imperial lust to rule the world. That new actor possesses power unprecedented in human history and has already used that power through Gog and Magog to spread himself out in all directions as he took control of the world. He then proceeded to liberate the Holy Land for the Jews, to bring them back to the Holy Land to reclaim it as their own two thousand years after they had been expelled from it by Divine decree, and to restore in the Holy Land a State of Israel. That mysterious new actor is now preparing the way for Israel's Pax-Judaica to replace USA's Pax-Americana. This pioneering book on Islamic Eschatology has identified that strange and mysterious new actor who occupies center-stage in the world in the End-time, and brought modern western civilization into being, as Dajjāl the false Messiah.

We now end this first of our five books on Dajjāl, the false Messiah or Anti-Christ, with Divine advice to those who would seek knowledge and guidance from the Qur'ān. The Word of Allah Most Wise, below, is in Arabic, followed by our explanation, rather than translation, of the two verses:

وَكَذَٰلِكَ أَنزَلْنَاهُ قُرْآنًا عَرَبِيًّا وَصَرَّفْنَا فِيهِ مِنَ الْوَعِيدِ لَعَلَّهُمْ
يَتَّقُونَ أَوْ يُحْدِثُ لَهُمْ ذِكْرًا

فَتَعَالَى اللَّهُ الْمَلِكُ الْحَقُّ وَلَا تَعْجَلْ بِالْقُرْآنِ مِنْ قَبْلِ أَنْ
يُقْضَى إِلَيْكَ وَحْيُهُ وَقُلْ رَبِّ زِدْنِي عِلْمًا

(Qur'ān, Tā Hā, 20:113-4)

Thus have We sent it down as a Qur'ān in Arabic – hence to be recited in Arabic and studied in Arabic, and We have explained therein matters concerning which We have warned (and the warning concerning Dajjāl is the gravest of all) in order that they may be conscious of Allah and fear Him, and also that it may be a means through which they remember Him. High above all is Allah. He is the Supreme Sovereign. He is the Truth! Hence be not in haste with this Qur'ān (either in reciting it, or in studying it to locate knowledge and guidance therein) before its inspired transmission to you is completed, but say, "O my Lord! Grant me more knowledge (of this Qur'ān)."

Appendix One

Qur'ān, Sūrah Al-Māidah: 5:51

Being a commentary by Hasbullah Shafi'iy to Maulānā Imran N. Hosein's interpretation of the verse.

Introduction

وَهَذَا كِتَابٌ أَنْزَلْنَاهُ مُبَارَكٌ فَاتَّبِعُوهُ وَاتَّقُوا لَعَلَّكُمْ تُرْحَمُونَ

(Quran, 6:155, 21:50)

The Qur'ān is a book which contains Barakah

إِنَّا أَنْزَلْنَاهُ فِي لَيْلَةٍ مُبَارَكَةٍ إِنَّا كُنَّا مُنْذِرِينَ

(Quran, 44:3)

The Qur'ān was sent down on a night of Barakah

Sayyiduna 'Umar رضي الله عنه in his six-line description of the Qur'ān that we are unable to discuss here except one particular word that is relevant to our subject, most aptly said that the Qur'ān is *Barakah*. Now, this is not a simple word at all. This word may be registered amongst the most frequently used vocabulary of any Muslim from any part of the world, but only that the meaning of this word is simply untranslatable into any other language, at least not into English. The meaning of this word can only be understood and explained by an event.

Sayyiduna Abū Hurayrah رضي اللہ عنہ gripped by the pangs of hunger, was waiting in *Masjid An-Nabawi* for someone to come who could understand his state and feed him. Embarrassed to ask directly for food, he had asked both *Sayyiduna* Abū Bakr and *Sayyiduna* 'Umar (رضي الله عنهم), to teach him something from the book of Allah, meaning to take him home as a guest. Not realizing his state, both of them had passed by him. The poor companion of the Prophet صل الله عليه و سلم had to continue hoping for someone else to come and take him home as a guest.

> *There came the Messenger of Allah(صل الله عليه و سلم) the dearest of all to the poor. Abū Hurayrah narrates, "Then Abul-Qasim passed, and he smiled when he saw me (knowing his state), and said:*
>
> *'Abu Hurayrah?' I said: 'I am here O Messenger of Allah!' He said: 'Come along.' He continued and I followed him, he entered his house, so I sought permission to enter, and he permitted me. He found a bowl of milk and said: 'Where did this milk come from?' It was said: 'It was a gift to us from so and so.'*
>
> *So, the Messenger of Allah said: 'O Abu Hurayrah' I said: 'I am here O Messenger of Allah!' He said: 'Go to the people of As-Suffah and invite them.' Now, they were the guests of the people of Islam, they had no people or wealth to rely upon. Whenever some charity was brought to him (صل الله عليه و سلم), he would send it to them without using any of it. And when a gift was given to him, he would send for them to participate and share with him in it. I became troubled about that, and I said (to myself): 'What good will this bowl be among the people of As-Suffah and I am the one bringing it to them?' Then he ordered me to circulate it among them (so I wondered) what of it would reach me from it, and I hoped that I would get from it what would satisfy me. But I would certainly not neglect to obey Allah and obey His Messenger, so I went to them and invited them. When they entered upon him they sat down. He said: 'Abu Hurayrah, take the bowl and give it to them.' I took the bowl and gave it to one man who drank his fill and returned it to me, and I gave it to the next and he did the*

same. I went on doing this till the bowl reached the Messenger of Allah (صل الله عليه و سلم). By that time all had taken their fill. He took the bowl, put it on his hand, looked at me, smiled and said, "Aba Hirr." I said, "At your service, O Messenger of Allah." He said, "Now you and I are left." I said, "That is true, O Messenger of Allah." He said, "Sit down and drink." I drank, but he went on saying, "Drink some more." I said, "By Him Who has sent you with the Truth, I have no room for it." He said, "Then give it to me," so I gave him the bowl. He praised Allah, uttered the Name of Allah and drank the remainder.

[Bukhārī, Tirmīdhī]

It is said that there were about eighty of them on that day at the blessed home of the Messenger of Allah. This is a recorded miracle of the Prophet witnessed and experienced by all the eighty Companions of *As-Suffah*. That blessed container passed around and all of them drank from it and Abū Hurayrah too drank from it to his fill. Yet there was more milk in it.

By Allah, if the entire Madīna was there that day at the Prophet's house, all of them would have drank from it and milk would still have remained in the bowl. This is *Barakah*. So is the Qur'ān. The Qur'ān remains one Book but does flow infinitely. In fact, every verse of the Qur'ān remains one, but meanings flow infinitely because it is from Allah Who is the Infinite.

There is not a single exegete (*Mufassir*) of the Qur'ān who would have dared say that he had already exhausted the full commentaries, interpretations and meanings of the Qur'ān and that therefore nothing else could be added to them. That would reflect the meanings of the Qur'ān as finite. How in that case could hundreds of thousands of *Tafāsīr* have been published so far on the meanings of the Qur'ān? History has it that the library of Libya alone once had preserved 20,000 commentaries of the Quran. No one of the 20,000 different authors ever claimed that no one could add on to the commentary he had himself written and then put a full stop to the science of *Tafsīr*.

New knowledge comes out from the Qur'ān and what meanings flow out from the 'spring' of the Qur'ān—that is the Spring of Allah's *Kalām*—has no limit. It continues and will continue forever till the Last Day.

Having established that, we now turn to Maulānā Imran N. Hosein's commentary to the 51st verse of *Sūrah al-Māidah*.

It does not befit Islamic scholarship for someone to say that Maulānā Hosein cannot add on to the existing commentaries on this verse and it further demands that readers approach his commentary with the meaning of *Barakah* in mind when it comes to the interpretation of the Qur'ān because the Qur'ān is ever fresh. It must explain every age, and Time is constantly in change.

The Verse

يَا أَيُّهَا الَّذِينَ آمَنُوا لَا تَتَّخِذُوا الْيَهُودَ وَالنَّصَارَى أَوْلِيَاءَ بَعْضُهُمْ أَوْلِيَاءُ بَعْضٍ وَمَنْ يَتَوَلَّهُمْ مِنْكُمْ فَإِنَّهُ مِنْهُمْ إِنَّ اللَّهَ لَا يَهْدِي الْقَوْمَ الظَّالِمِينَ

Translations

Before discussing the problems in the various published translations of the verse, it is necessary first to look into the literal translation of the verse without added parentheses:

> *O you who have Imān! Do not take the Yahūd and the Nasārā as Awliyā. They are Awliyā of each other (or, 'Some of them are Awliyā of others'). Whosoever turns to them from among you, would then become part of them. Certainly Allah does not guide the Dzālimīn.*

Our attention here is firstly directed to the word *Awliyā* and the following phrase in the verse, "they are *Awliyā* of each other," and then secondly to the overall meaning of the verse.

Various translators of the Qur'ān have translated this verse with only slight variations in the choice of words but not in the meaning it has been understood to convey. All of the translations that I have checked unanimously mention the same meaning of the verse prohibiting alliance and friendship with the Jews and the Christians because (by implication, as do most of the classical commentators have pointed out) they are friends, helpers, guardians, comrades, allies, confidants, and protectors (different choice of words for translating the word Awliyā) of each other. It is important to note here that in all of the existing English translations of this verse, there is an implied "because" before the phrase 'they are *Auliyā* of each other' for which reason it seems, from these translations, that Allah has prohibited alliance and friendship with them. Abdullah Yūsuf Ali, Pickthall, Asad, Maudūdī, Daryabādi (whose commentary on the verse will be quoted later), Arberry, Muhsin Khan, Zafrullah Khan, Syed Abdul Latīf, Maulānā Muhammad Ali, Shaikh Abdalhaqq and Aisha Bewley, and a number of others, have all translated the verse in the same manner with only variations in the choice of words when translating the word '*Auliyā*'. There seems to be no exception to this. The overall meaning of the verse implied in all of these translations is that the believers should not take the Jews and the Christians as *Awliyā* because these two parties are *Awliyā* of each other.

The translation of Amatul Rahman Omar and Abdul Mannan Omar has a slight variation that deserves some attention:

> *O you who believe! Do not take these Jews and the Christians for allies. They are allies of one to another (when against you), and whoso from amongst you takes them for allies, is indeed one of them. Verily Allah does not guide the unjust people to attain their goal. [Emphasis mine].*

Though the addition of the word 'these' may appear to signify that the translator has considered a definite group amongst the Jews and Christians—therefore not generally all of them—and though she further puts such a prohibition conditional in parentheses ("when against you") it does not still satisfactorily address the problem. Here the implication of the overall verse is: "Do not take these Jews and the Christians as your *Awliyā* because when they turn against you they will become *Awliyā* of each other..."

Some Tamil translations, including that of Maulānā S.S. 'Abdul Qādir Sāhib have, "... (Amongst them) some are *Awliyā* of others (in coming together against you, i.e. Muslims) ..." This therefore should mean some of them, not all, are enemies. But in translating the first phrase of the verse, there is no such distinction made. Instead, they too translate (in Tamil) as, "Do not take the Jews and the Christians as *Awliyā* ..." as if implying all Jews and Christians. However, in the next phrase, they indicate that some of them are *Awliyā* of others, not all, as if implying that enmity from their quarters will come from one faction of them, those who ally with each other, not all. This could have been made clearer in the first phrase itself as it was done in the second. Nevertheless, this Tamil translation is better than all that we find in English.

If the prohibition is based on the condition of the Jews and Christians turning against the Muslims, then the translation should read: "You who have *Īmān*, do not take (those) Jews and Christians (who turn against you) as *Awliyā*, (because when they turn against you, they will become) *Awliyā* of each other ..." This however shuts the possibility of alliance with all Jews and Christians because we may never know who will turn against the believers and who will not.

Here is Maulānā Imran Hosein's explanatory translation that is clearer and which differs quite largely in meaning from the rest:

> *Oh you who have faith, do not take (such) Jews and (such) Christians as your Awliyā (friends and allies) who (themselves) are Awliyā (friends and allies) of each other. And whoever amongst you turn to them for friendship and alliance, would belong to them (and therefore not to us). Surely Allah does not provide guidance to a people who commit Dhulm.*

The first point to note here is that this translation does not nullify all other previous translations of the verse. Rather, it adds on to the meanings of the verse; it has in fact opened a new dimension in understanding the verse according to our times; it sheds new guiding light for a political and communal response to the modern world situation that Muslim communities around the world find themselves in.

The differences in meaning between Maulānā Hosein's translation and others are:

1. Here the prohibition of taking the Jews and the Christians as Awliyā does not apply to all Jews and Christians, while in all other translations, the prohibition applies to all Jews and all Christians.

2. Not all Jews and Christians are *Awliyā* of each other as history testifies. There has been strong enmity between these two religious communities in the world. In fact Jews and Christians have never been *Awliyā* of each other except only until a certain period in

history from which moment onwards this new strange alliance has persisted till today, and daily grows stronger. In the last 100 years this alliance/friendship (*Wilāyah*) has intensified with certain clear objectives within the ranks of this particular alliance. Not only that, even within the Christian world, there persists till today a violent enmity, particularly between Western (Catholic and Protestant) and Eastern (Orthodox) Christendom. This historical evidence is reflected here but not so in all other translations.

3. The prohibition only applies to those Jews and Christians who have formed an alliance amongst themselves. It is this particular community that Allah has prohibited us from taking as our *Awliyā*. This difference is also comprehensible in Maulānā Hosein's translation compared to all others.

4. Since this *Wilāyah* between the Jews and the Christians did not occur in the time of the Prophet (صلى الله عليه و سلم) and since it did not occur for some centuries after the Prophet, this verse in fact was a foretelling at the time of revelation that there will come a time in the future (which we now have the records of history to testify) when this would happen and at that time when this will be fulfilled, we should bring this verse of the Qur'ān to attention and refrain from taking that particular group as our *Awliyā* no matter what the circumstances demand. This translation we present here sheds new light into the meanings of the verse as a sign of the Hour mentioned in the Qur'ān.

None of the above is reflected in any of the translations that have been published so far. None of the above have been dealt with in any *Tafsīr* that has been published so far except a few that have very briefly touched on some of the above points, though not clearly, but at least in passing.

The clear reasons, for such a translation that Maulānā Hosein has rendered, are the following:

1. Due to the daily unfolding signs of the Last Day or Islamic Eschatology pertaining to the end of history, or *'Ilmu Ākhir al-*

Zamān—knowledge of the end times— and due to what events have unfolded in the last few centuries that alarmingly indicate the appearance of Dajjāl the false messiah in our spatiotemporal dimension, and the sequence of events that would lead to the culmination of Nabī 'Īsa عليه السلام ruling the world from the throne of Nabī Dāud عليه السلام as, in the words of the Messenger of Allah صل الله عليه و سلم *Hakaman Muqsitan* and *Imāman 'Adlan*—a Just Arbiter and Leader—this particular verse shines as a warning for believers to pay particular attention to those amongst the Jews and Christians who would be Dajjāl's foot soldiers and who would facilitate Dajjāl's mission on earth. These Jews and Christians, who have joined hands putting aside their own political, social and theological differences to prepare the grounds for the world order of Dajjāl, have themselves betrayed their own people and religion. It is this very verse of *Sūrah al-Māidah* that has always indicated the appearance of such a group of people from among the Jews and Christians who would become allies of each other in especially assisting Dajjāl, who on his part will come to deceive both Jews and Christians to believe in him as the true messiah they had been all the while waiting for, in his mission on earth and demonstrate the apparent return of the golden age of the Prophets Dāud and Sulaimān عليهما السلام. It is *'Ilmu Ākhir al-Zamān* that throws new light on the verse and demands a new explanation to the verse. To be straightforward, this verse is the only clearest verse in the Qur'ān, which has foretold of the essentially European and Zionist Judeo-Christian alliance.

2. The Jews and Christians have never been allies, friends, protectors of each other ever since the advent of Nabī 'Īsā عليه السلام and the consequent attempt of the Jews to crucify him. The Christians have never forgiven the Jews for this. The Jews have never lived under the Christians in peace. This is the testimony of history. If we translate what Allah has mentioned in this verse as "they are *Awliyā* of each other" it would be a contradiction to what has occurred in history for some two thousand years. The truth is, they have never been *Awliyā* of each other. We cannot afford to allow this contradiction with history due to our misinterpretation of

the Qur'ān. Furthermore, even within the ranks of Christendom, there has been great enmity. We cannot afford to overlook the impossibility of reconciliation and alliance between Eastern and Western Christendom at large.

3. The translation would contradict other verses of the Qur'ān. For example, the 113th verse of *Surah Al-Baqarah*:

The Jews say, "The Christians have nothing (true) to stand on," and the Christians say, "The Jews have nothing to stand on," although they both recite the Scripture. Thus those who have no knowledge (the Arab polytheists and others) speak the same as their words. But Allah will judge between them on the Day of Resurrection concerning that over which they used to differ.

This verse clearly establishes the conflict between the Jews and the Christians. How then could they be *Awliyā* of each other? The only exception to this is that during times of war against a common enemy, two parties may politically postpone their own conflicts in order to first defeat a more important enemy common to them. Has this occurred between the Jews and the Christians against the Muslims? No, not until a certain time in history and that too, not all of Jewry and Christendom allied and came together against the Muslims. Only a certain faction did so, and while they did so, there were other Jews and Christians who opposed the formation of such an alliance. Eastern Orthodox Christendom is an example of such opposition within the Christian world against this alliance.

If we do not accept Maulānā Hosein's translation of the verse and then read further down the same *Surah Al-Māidah,* we will come across two more contradicting verses:

A. Verse 57: O you who believe! Choose not for *Awliyā* such of those who received the Scripture before you (Jews and Christians in particular but may also refer to others who received revelation too), and of the disbelievers, as make a jest and sport of your religion. But keep your duty to Allah if you are true believers. (Parentheses mine)

B. Verse 69: Lo! Those who believe, and those who are Jews, and

Sabaeans, and Christians—Whosoever believes in Allah and the Last Day and does right— there shall no fear come upon them, neither shall they grieve.

How would Allah, Most High, first prohibit believers to take the Jews and Christians as *Awliyā* and then immediately thereafter within a matter of twenty verses down the same *Surah* go on to prohibit believers from taking as their *Awliyā* only those amongst the People of the Scripture (which is a term in the Qur'ān that jointly refers to both the Jews and the Christians) and the disbelievers who make a mockery and play of *Dīn al-Islām*? Does this mean that believers are allowed to take as *Awliyā* others among the Jews and the Christians who do not make of Islam a mockery and play? How would Allah, Most High, soon thereafter mention with honor that there are also amongst the Jews, Sabaeans, and Christians believers in Allah and the Last Day who will have no fear in the *Dunyah* or grieve on the Day of Judgment? Are we believers, then allowed to take these believers among their ranks as our *Awliyā*?

Similarly, Allah, Most High, declares later on in the 82nd verse of the same *Sūrah al-Māidah*:

You will find the most vehement of mankind in hostility to those who believe (to be) the Jews and the idolaters. And you will find the nearest of them in affection to those who believe (to be) those who say: Lo! We are Christians. That is because there are among them priests and monks, and because they are not proud.

If we are prohibited from taking all Jews and Christians as our *Awliyā* then we have before us yet another contradiction with the above verse. How could it be that Allah, Most High, declares those who say, "Lo! We are Christians", and especially the priests and monks among them who are not arrogant, to be the closest in affection to the Muslims? How could it be that while the Qur'ān clarifies that those who are closest in affection to the believers will be the Christians, it also prohibits alliance and friendship with them, political or otherwise?

Though there are other examples, the above mentioned are sufficient to clarify that the 51st verse of *Sūrah al-Māidah* under discussion here has been translated in a way that contradicts with some important verses of the Qur'ān, at least three of which are in the very same *Surah*.

4. Other verses of the Qur'ān state plainly and clearly that Muslim men are allowed to contract marriage with Jewish and Christian women; that the food of the Jews and Christians has been permitted to Muslims. If this verse prohibits Muslims from friendship and alliance with all Jews and all Christians, then it would be yet another contradiction with the permission to contract matrimony with their women and consuming their food. How could Muslims not take them as friends and allies and yet marry their women and break bread with them? It is not logically coherent, unless the word *Awliyā* does not mean friendship in this context but rather a political alliance and protectorate as a community of people beyond social interactions, to support which meaning we would need further proof from the Qur'ān and Hadith. The reason for the revelation of this verse (*Sabab al-Nuzūl*, which we will come to, shortly) does not support this view. Even so, such an alliance as a community, directly affects social interactions at the individual level. How could an individual belonging to a community that prohibits friendship and alliance with another community of people go to the latter and break bread with them and propose marriage to a woman from amongst them? How would they look at him? In that case, we may have to answer another question: Would a Muslim individual who is in a situation of seeking political protection from the Jews and Christians, but who consequently refrains from doing so in submission to the command of this verse, still be able to maintain social friendship with them that would allow him to propose marriage to one of their women or break bread with them?

5. Translating the verse as "Do not take the Jews and the Christians as your *Awliyā*" only implies all Jews and Christians unless indicated otherwise which none of the translations have done. Why can we not engage in such an alliance? We cannot, because as the next phrase indicates, they (the Jews and Christians) are *Awliyā* of each other, and therefore will, by direct implication, turn against us or

betray us. If we take this meaning, which is what all translations offer us, it will similarly contradict the eighth and ninth verses of *Sūrah al- Mumtahinah*, where Allah, Most High, clarifies:

Allah does not forbid you from those who do not fight you (which includes the Jews and the Christians) because of religion and do not expel you from your homes—from being righteous toward them and acting justly toward them. Indeed Allah loves those who act justly. Allah only forbids you from those who fight you because of religion and expel you from your homes and aid in your expulsion—(forbids) that you make allies of them. And whoever makes allies of them, then it is those who are the wrongdoers.
[Parentheses mine]

Hence according to this verse of the Qur'ān, it is clear that this *Wilāyah*—alliance, friendship, and dependence on their protection—is only forbidden with some of them—not all. It cannot be that this verse is not referring to the Jews and the Christians, because how is it that Allah, the Most Just, prohibits *Wilāyah* with the Jews and the Christians, and then when it concerns others who are not Jews and Christians, He only prohibits *Wilāyah* with those who are hostile and ready to fight while allowing it with others who are not hostile? It is not befitting Allah's Justice; it would be a grave error on our part to say so. If this is not shown in the translation of the main verse in discussion here, then there would be a clear contradiction because while one verse prohibits *Wilāyah* generally with the Jews and the Christians, another verse clearly points out who we can actually maintain good ties, friendship and alliance with.

Maulānā Hosein's translation in fact clarifies all the apparent contradictions with other verses of the Qur'ān, which otherwise we will not be able to explain. It also clarifies the seeming contradictions with history.

Now we turn to the *Tafāsīr* (commentaries) of this verse that both classical as well as modern scholars have offered us so far. We shall begin with the reasons for the revelation of this verse, because it is necessary to understand the context of its revelation, and then move on to the discussion on the meaning of the verse.

Asbāb al-Nuzūl

As far as the reasons for the revelation of this verse are concerned, we find three narrations in the classical *Tafāsīr*. From Tabari and Ibn 'Atiyya, we summarize the following three instances to be the reasons for revelation. In the *Tafsīr* of Ibn Kathīr, we find a fourth incident, which is very similar to the three in Tabari and Ibn 'Atiyya and hence may be omitted from our discussion.

It must first be borne in mind that according to *Sayyidah* 'Āisha رضي الله عنها , *Sūrah al-Māidah* was the last *Sūrah* to be revealed and that what is in this Sūrah holds the last say in terms of the lawful and the prohibited. Consequently, when we look at all the verses of the Qur'ān, which prohibit *Wilāyah* with those who are outside the fold of Islam—and these verses are numerous—we would quite easily understand that the verses in *Sūrah al-Māidah* repeating the prohibition should be taken as the final seal on the matter in case of any doubt in the prohibition, or, as throwing new light on the prohibition. Let us look at one verse in *Sūrah al-Taubah* to elaborate the matter. Though this *Āyah* was revealed much later than the 51st verse of *Sūrah al-Māidah,* it is necessary to discuss this here before we look at the *Sabab al-Nuzūl*:

> *O you who believe! Choose not your fathers nor your brothers for Awliyā if they take pleasure in disbelief (Kufr) rather than faith (Īmān). Whoever of you takes them for Awliyā, such are wrongdoers.*
>
> [Verse 23]

Now, the essential question to ask is: While Allah سبحانه و تعالى had already made it abundantly clear that a believer is prohibited from taking even his own brothers and fathers as his *Awliyā* if they were to take pleasure in Kufr rather than *Īmān*, that is, under a condition of enmity, why is there a need for yet another verse to repeat the prohibition vis-a-vis Jews and Christians who are anyway more distant than one's own brothers and fathers? Is it not understood that if one's very own brothers and fathers cannot be taken as *Awliyā* when they prefer Kufr to *Imān*, what more the Jews and the Christians? On the other hand, it is also necessary to ask: If the Jews and Christians are closer in faith to a Muslim than his own brothers and fathers can these Jews and Christians then be taken as *Awliyā*? The verse in discussion here, therefore must have been revealed to clarify something else more profound which is what Maulānā Hosein's explanatory translation has brought to light.

We may deduce from this that while Allah, Most High, had already made it abundantly clear who believers are allowed to take as their *Awliyā* and who not, this verse of *Sūrah al-Māidah* was revealed to indicate of a new Judeo-Christian alliance to come in the future that would draw clear lines to differentiate who among the Jews and Christians could be allies, friends and confidants of the believers and who categorically cannot be. If this verse were not revealed, we would not know of this unprecedented and strange alliance within the ranks of the People of the Scripture that believers as a polity would have to be especially wary of not to engage with in a political and economic relationship towards the end of history.

Secondly, it must be taken into serious consideration that Madīna had from the People of the Book, a Jewish community alone. As for the Christian community, though there were individuals present, they were as a community or polity, all mostly found in *Bilād Al-Shām*, or Greater Syria.

Now returning to the reasons for the revelation of the verse, we find the following:

1. It is reported from Al-Zuhri that after the victory of Badr, the Prophet صل اللهٓ عليه و سلم wanted to kill the Jewish captives from Banū Qaynuqā'. 'Ubādah Ibn Al-Sāmit رضي اللهٓ عنه came to the Prophet and said that he has many allies and protectors (*Awliyā*) from among the Jews. He then carried on to say that he now had turned away from them towards Allah and His Messenger صل اللهٓ عليه و سلم and had made himself free from depending on them for protection and help (*Wilāyah*). At that point, Abdullah ibn Ubayy Ibn Salūl, the *Munāfiq* (hypocrite), came similarly to the Messenger of Allah صل اللهٓ عليه و سلم and said that as for him, he feared that a change of fortune would befall him and therefore he could not afford to give

up his *Wilāyah* with the Jews, implying that in case the Jews gain the upper hand in their battle for power against the Muslims, his retaining them as his protectors and allies would only continue to benefit him. The Messenger of Allah, Allah bless him and grant him peace, then said: 'O Abu'l-Hubāb, that which you reserve to yourself of the guardianship of the Jews apart from 'Ubādah ibn Al-Sāmit is all yours and none of it is his'. In another narration, it is reported that the Prophet صل الله عليه و سلم said, "I have given them to you." Abdullah ibn Ubayy replied: 'I accept'. It was at this point that the verse was revealed from "O you who believe!" to "It is the party of Allah who will be victorious". Most of the classical *Tafāsīr* have recorded this as the reason for the revelation of the verse.

2. The second instance was narrated by Al-Sadiy to have occurred just after the battle of *Uhud*. The situation had become severe for a group of Muslims who had security reasons to fear that the non-believers who were hostile towards them may overpower them and put their survival at risk. Therefore two men came out and declared something similar to what Abdullah ibn Ubayy had done in the above instance. One of them said that he had chosen to maintain his *Wilāyah* with the *Yahūd* (in Madina) and another said that he had chosen to maintain his *Wilāyah* with the Christians in *Al-Shām*. The names of these two men are not mentioned in the narrations. At this point the verse descended prohibiting both of them from doing so. In this case the verse would mean that one should not take the Jews (in Madīna) as one's *Awliyā* or the Christians (in *Al-Shām*) as one's *Awliyā*, because they are *Awliyā* of each other, meaning, the Jews (in Madīna) are *Awliyā* of each other and the Christians (in *Al-Shām*) are *Awliyā* of each other. This further means that at the event of a Jewish or Christian conflict with the Muslims, even though those Muslims who were under the protection of the Jews in Madīna or Christians in *Al-Shām* had received a contractual promise of protection from the respective Jews and Christians, they would not be spared or reserved, but would suffer the same enmity from their (Jewish or Christian quarters) as would the rest of the Muslims.

3. The third reason is reported from 'Ikrimah to have occurred just after the battle of *Khandaq* (trench). The Jews of Banū Qurayzah who had breached their contract with the Muslims by not only conspiring with the Quraysh against the Muslims but also by fighting alongside the Quraysh against the Muslims, found themselves under siege by the Muslims at the end of the battle. The siege lasted for fifteen to twenty days at the end of which period they surrendered. While the Muslims were deciding in a *Shūra* (council) how to now deal with them—Banū Qurayzah—Abu Lubābah was consulted who gave the clear statement that they should be slaughtered. When Banū Qurayzah attempted to negotiate by requesting Sā'd Ibn Mu'ādh, who was their *Halīf* in Madīna on the side of the Muslims (a *Halīf* is someone under the protection of a tribe but not associated with them through kinship), to give the ruling with the hope that perhaps he would be lenient with them since they had once promised him protection and security, Sā'd gave the same ruling as Abū Lubābah that they should be slaughtered. It was at this moment that the verse descended prohibiting any alliance with them. Rasūlullah صل الله عليه و سلم then passed the verdict and they were killed. In this case as it was in the first instance, the verse was a command against the Jews in Madīna who had breached their contract with the Muslims. It is noteworthy that neither in the first instance nor in this third instance were there any Christians involved in the implication of the verse.

Which was the exact reason for revelation we do not know and it is not our immediate concern here to decide on this because on all three cases the Divine injunction was clearly prohibiting *Wilāyah* with both the Jews and the Christians (either jointly or separately). However, we may take the first instance to be the most quoted amongst all the four, and due to which, is the most accepted and confirmed by what we read in the verse, i.e. verse 52, that follows: "You will see those, in whose hearts is a disease, race to be with them (the disbelievers, *Yahūd* and *Nasāra*) saying, 'We fear that a turn in fortune may overtake us...'" This in fact refers to Abdullah ibn Ubayy who used the same words mentioned in the verse. The two verses were in fact revealed together.

Now we are able to turn to the classical commentaries on the verse proper since we have understood the context of its revelation.

Classical *Tafāsīr* on the verse

1. Prohibition is on taking them as one's *Awliyā*. Most of the discussion in the commentaries is on what it means to take them as *Awliyā*, what constitutes this and what is not included in taking them as *Awliyā*. What is not mentioned in the classical commentaries is whether are we allowed at all to take any from their ranks as *Awliyā* if this does not refer to all Jews and Christians, especially in case they are not hostile or rather friendly and trustable. All implications of most classical commentaries point to the prohibition of taking all of them, regardless of whether they are hostile or not, as *Awliyā*. Al-Nasafi, for example, states that this is due to the reason that Kufr (disbelieve) is one *Millah*, pointing to the Hadīth that bears these words. Prohibition therefore is general, referring to all Jews and Christians, for all times and unconditional because when it suits them they may easily conspire and turn against the Muslims even though they are against each other with clear hatred within their own ranks.

2. Verse is generally referring to the Muslims but beneath the general command it is in reality addressing the hypocrites (*Munafiqūn*) who are hidden amongst the Muslims. This can be seen in the context of the verse, which we will come to later. Imām Al-Qurtubi, Al-Shawkāni, and Al-Sāwi amongst others have mentioned this.

3. Only English translations and commentaries show that the prohibition is conditional—most probably based on some classical *Tafāsīr* which I am unable to locate—and therefore applies only in war or if the Jews and Christians are hostile to the Muslims. If they are not hostile, neutral or even friendly, no commentary has pointed out whether there is a possibility of alliance with them.

4. Ibn 'Atiyyah states that Ubayy ibn Ka'b and Abdullah ibn 'Abbās رضي الله عنهما read the verse in a different *Harf* (there were seven Ahruf that the Prophet صلى الله عليه و سلم said the Qur'ān was revealed in, all of which were destroyed during Sayyiduna Uthmān's رضي الله عنه time except for one which has reached us now). In this reading, the two *Sahābah* mentioned above read "*Arbāban*" instead of "*Awliyā*". *Arbāban* means lords and gods, or even masters to whom a slave submits. We may therefore say that *Awliyā* in this verse takes on a stronger meaning than protectors and friends. However, we do not have this reading anymore.

5. Prohibition does not apply to trade, marriage or such social dealings according to a clear statement of 'Abdullah Ibn Abbās رضي الله عنهما , who said: "Eat from what they slaughter and marry from their women for Allah, Most High, has said in His Book, 'O you who believe, do not take the Jews and the Christians as *Awliyā* ...' and one does not become part of them except through *Wilāyah*, (only) then would one become part of them." (Al-Tabari) This is how the companions of the Prophet understood the verse to mean. Such then would be a clear prohibition of a political *Wilāyah*, and that does not prohibit one from eating their food and marrying their women.

6. Most of the *Tafāsīr* state that the justification (*'illah*) of such a prohibition is the following phrase "*ba'duhum Awliyā-u ba'd*"—meaning the prohibition is because they are *Awliyā* of each other. This opens the room for discussion or raises the question that in case they (those the verse prohibits Muslims from entering into friendship and alliance) are not *Awliyā* of each other, would the prohibition then be nullified? This in fact confirms with Maulānā Hosein's interpretation of the verse. This is because if the *'illah* is that they are *Awliyā* of each other, then when such an *'illah* is absent, the prohibition should not be binding anymore. In that case, there is room for alliance with those who are not hostile to the Muslims and who are not *Awliyā* of each other. However, the classical commentaries do not mention what is the ruling in case

the *'illah* is absent.

7. The phrase "They are *Awliyā* of each other" does not mean Jews and Christians are *Awliyā* of each other because they have never been in such friendship and alliance. It rather means the Jews are *Awliyā* of each to other Jews and the Christians are *Awliyā* of each to other Christians. Therefore the verse refers to each of the two parties separately. Imām al-Sāwi said this clearly in his commentary: "(This is) a new sentence; and the meaning is that some within each party are *Awliyā* of others in that party, because between the Jews and the Christians is a mighty enmity." This too, adds strength to Maulānā Hosein's commentary to the verse because here the historical enmity between the Jews and the Christians is taken into account. However, those commentaries that are of this opinion stop there and continue to say that we are still prohibited from taking all Jews and all Christians as *Awliyā*.

8. If you do so, you become one of them, means you have left the fold of Islam—that is, *Murtad*, or joined their *Dīn*. Ibn Abbās said, "If you join them in their Dīn, you have entered their Kufr, if you join them in treaty, you have violated the (Divine) command."

9. No classical commentary, any one amongst all those which I have referred to, has mentioned in any slight manner if this verse is in any way a foretelling of a future, mysterious alliance that would unfold between Jews and Christians—who are by nature of their beliefs, practices and historical relations—two conflicting polities.

10. Journalist Asad made an error when he attempted to summarize the classical commentaries to this verse. He wrote in his commentary to the verse: "As regards the meaning of the "alliance" referred to here, see 3:28, and more particularly 4:139 and the corresponding note, which explains the reference to a believer's loss of his moral identity if he imitates the way of life, or—in Quranic terminology—"allies himself" with, non-Muslims." Despite a brief journalistic adventure with Mujāhid and Shahīd Omar Mukhtār, Asad had befriended 'Abd Al-Azīz Ibn Sa'ūd, the man who betrayed Allah and His Messenger

and the Muslim world, and had been influenced by the dubious Rashīd Ridā, as is evident in his commentary to the Qur'ān, and finally sat on a ministerial position in the secular nation state of the Islamic Republic of Pakistan. We should therefore not expect him to have had the capacity to read the political, economic and military implications of the verse. He reduced everything to a moral alliance since his friends had embraced the very Judeo-Christian alliance politically, economically and militarily. However, what needs to be clarified here is that the classical commentaries did not register such an interpretation of the verse even though Asad might have wanted his readers to believe so. It is clearly narrated (as quoted above) from our Master Abdullah ibn Abbas, may Allah be pleased with him and his father, that this is beyond a moral alliance since this does not refer to imitating their way of life which includes eating with them and marrying their women. Even if this verse were not revealed we would have still understood from other verses of the Quran not to embrace them in their *Dīn*. As is so wont of modern western secular thought, when everything is reduced to personal morality and morality blaming, then of course all other important communal matters could be forced out of the thinking process to finally make everything circulate around the moral self. In that way of thought, we will never be able to identify injustice and understand events accurately and consequently not be able to respond appropriately. When everything becomes a simple moral issue, then the US will continue to bomb the world and carry on their *fasād* and get away with it while we will be forced to continue pointing the finger at ourselves. This is certainly a modern distortion of classical scholarship.

In order to explain the modern world using Allah's *Kalām*, and not fall into such errors, we must engage in *Fikr*. Allah says in the Qur'ān that He sent down the Qur'ān for a people who think, who reflect, who ponder. He, Most High, said in *Sūrah An-Nahl*, verse 44: "...We have revealed unto you the Remembrance (Qur'ān) that you may explain to mankind that which has been revealed for them, and that they may engage themselves in thinking/reflection." *Fikr* is not only thinking, but thinking things through. In this case, we are forced due to our world situation and the political state of the Muslims vis-a-vis the Jews and the Christians, to think things through and not entirely rely on the classical *Tafāsīr* alone in seeking an explanation from the Qur'ān to understand the modern world. While thinking things through, we get fresh knowledge and instruction from the Qur'ān. Maulānā Hosein has done exactly this. In fact, Maulānā Hosein's interpretation of the verse in no way contradicts any of the classical *Tafāsīr* that conservative scholars hold on tightly to as if saying that what the scholars of the past have explained is enough and there is no need to interpret the Qur'ān anew. While doing that, they firstly restrict the knowledge of the Qur'ān to the past, and secondly, fail to explain the modern world according to the Qur'ān. How could they find what was expressed in the past to explain what is happening today?

Well, what exactly is it regarding the modern world situation that they fail to explain using the Qur'ān?

Before we answer that question, let us turn to two important modern commentaries of the Qur'ān—written within the last hundred years—that have thrown new light on the verse, both of them adding more strength to Maulānā Hosein's interpretation.

Two Modern Commentaries
—Prof. Hamka and Maulānā 'Abdul Mājid Daryabādī.

1. Professor Hamka's *Tafsīr Al-Azhar*, a commentary to the Qur'ān in Malay. (2) Maulānā Abdul Mājid Daryabādi's English commentary to the Qur'ān.

Professor Hamka's commentary paraphrased in my own words:

In 1964, Pope Paulus VI, declared an official Christian (Catholic in particular) forgiveness for the Jews; that they are free of their sins, one of it being their attempt to crucify Nabī Īsā عليه السلام.

This is none other than political forgiveness. It is the strength of the Jews, who have a lot of wealth, to work together with the Christians in fighting what they consider the threat of Islam. Immediately after that, in 1967, Arab countries were attacked by the Jews (Israel) for four days (referring to the Six Day War) and *Bait Al-Maqdis* was seized from the hands of the Muslims even though they—the Muslims—had control over *Bait Al-Maqdis* before this for 14 centuries. Perhaps during the time of *Rasūlullah* صل الله عليه و سلم this was not yet seen because in Madīna a large group of Jews were congregated as a community but the Christians were in *Al-Shām*. But due to the miracles of the Qur'ān, we see today what has happened in the passage of time and we see with crystal clarity how the Christians and the Jews collaborate in turning against the Muslims and Islam. The verse in fact says that the two religious communities that were enemies of each other will one day come together in facing their enemy—that is Islam, until the state of Israel will dominate the lands of Islam with the help of the Christian communities who are actually supposed to be more inclined to help the Muslims. This is because the Jews oppose the Christians not only by rejecting Nabī 'Īsā عليه السلام as a Prophet and Messiah, but also that he was an illegitimate child while Muslims affirm Nabī 'Īsā عليه السلام. This makes Muslims closer to Christians and therefore make Christians more inclined to help Muslims. However, what has occurred is the opposite.

2. Maulānā Abdul Mājid Daryabādī:
"The Jews and Christians have much in common, and can, and do, readily form a combination against Islam. As the most recent instance of their animosity against Islam, witness the Christian Britain's zealous sponsoring of 'Zionism' and 'Jewish home in Palestine.'"
Maulānā Daryabādī's commentary sharply points out that this verse refers to the Zionist efforts in establishing the State of Israel. Though written in the context of his time it is certainly more relevant to our time too.

Comparing both, it is Prof. Hamka's commentary that more strongly supports Maulānā Hosein's interpretation of the verse.

Now, in thinking things through, let us look at the context of the verse in *Sūrah al-Māidah*. It is important to read the verse together with what precedes it and what follows it.

Context

The passages throughout the *Sūrah* linked to our study here are verses 5–19, 32, 41–88, 110–120. In these passages, Allah, Most High, addresses the Jews, the Christians, the Muslims and the hypocrites. It is clear that while attempting to understand Maulānā Hosein's commentary on the verse, the whole *Sūrah* should be read. It should also be clear in one reading that:

1. Not all Jews and Christians are enemies of the Muslims.

2. The Qur'ān came to affirm the Torah and the Gospel and to complete Divine revelation for mankind through Prophet Muhammad صل اللهٓ عليه و سلم

3. There are amongst the Jews and the Christians those who are believers and therefore could be taken as *Awliyā*.

4. There is a door of alliance and integrated living with the Jews and Christians always open for the individual Muslim as well as the Muslim polity.

5. There are intermittent warnings issued to the hypocrites who are outwardly Muslim but who hide their denial of truth, and thereby always incline to the disbelievers in Nabī Muhammad صل اللهٓ عليه و سلم and the Qur'ān which includes Jews and Christians.

6. Nabī 'Īsā عليه السلام forms an important part of the subject since the *Sūrah* not only speaks of him in the middle but returns to his subject at the end. There are warnings to the Christians as much as there are praises of the Christians to the extent that Allah, Most High, in His divine wisdom, confirms that there are some amongst them whom believers will find to be closest in faith, which Christians, Muslims can therefore take as their *Awliyā*. The *Sūrah* is named after an event in the life of Nabī 'Īsā عليه السلام . This is also important to consider because Dajjāl whose role is to impersonate

the Messiah will rule the world from Jerusalem declaring himself to be the Messiah while a Judeo-Christian alliance is what will unite under him believing in him as the true Messiah and facilitating his coming to and establishment of power.

7. As much as Allah, Most High, has spoken of Nabī 'Īsā عليه السلام in this *Sūrah*, so much has He also spoken of Nabī Mūsa عليه السلام. As Nabī 'Īsā is for the Christians, so is Nabī Mūsa for the Jews. They did not fight with Nabī Mūsa to conquer the Holy Land by which they openly rebelled against Allah and His Messenger, but there would come a time when they would go and fight under the sway of the false Messiah (Dajjāl) with a Christian backing and the Christians too would go and fight under Dajjāl's sway with a Jewish backing (as it was the case during the Crusades) to take control of the Holy Land. This alliance revolving around controlling the Holy Land and the Levant is directly founded on this 51st verse of the *Sūrah*.

From the context of the verse therefore, we should be able to understand that the Euro-Zionist, Judeo-Christian alliance, in their attempt to rule the Holy Land and dominate the Levant, cannot include all Christians and all Jews. Those who initially constituted its ranks were small in number in comparison to the whole of the Judeo-Christian world and did not appear in history except about 500 years after the Qur'ān was revealed. That community of people gradually grew stronger and became superpowers of the world in the last hundred years. More importantly, the people of this alliance took control of the Holy Land, established the State of Israel and have now successfully raised it to the level of a nuclear superpower capable of defying any other power in the world. They have done all of this while a large number of Christians and a significant number of Jews not only loathed at them and refused to join them, but were even so much as victimized by them. The verses of *Sūrah Al-Māidah* read in context will prove beyond doubt that Muslims are not prohibited from allying with such victimized Jews and Christians who recognize injustice and who are courageously willing to defy the Judeo-Christian Zionist alliance. All of this becomes clear only in context. For that the whole *Sūrah* must be read.

The verses of the Qur'ān are interconnected. In *Sūrah Al- An'ām*, verse

114, Allah, Most Wise, describes the Qur'ān as *Mufassalan*—joint together and fully explained, meaning all the verses are well connected and explain each other. They are neither isolated nor does each stand alone. In order to think things through it is not correct to look at this verse alone. It is a requisite to connect it with other verses of the Qur'ān.

It would be more enlightening, as is always the case with the verses of the Qur'ān, if this verse is read as a finely arranged part of the entire *Sūrah of Al-Māidah.*

Does the Qur'ān explain the world today?

Let us now return to answer the question: What exactly is it regarding the modern world situation that Muslim scholars trapped in religious conservatism fail to explain using the Qur'ān?

In attempting to understand the modern world using the Book of Allah, Most Wise, one must have a grasp over the trails of history that has built up to the present world situation. If one has no idea of the modern world and where it is leading, one cannot turn to the Qur'ān to take fresh knowledge from it. The opposite is also true. If one does not turn to the Qur'ān to understand the modern world and take heed and warning on what is unfolding today and what is to come tomorrow, one will remain in the dark concerning them. All of this is to understand the modern world accurately and respond to it appropriately.

With that light, we must first remember that we are now looking at the Judeo-Christian world. There is a faction within this community of Jews and Christians who are waging war on Islam and there is another faction amongst them who have defied the former and have refused to join them in their hegemonic rule, and as a consequence have been subjected to economic and political victimization. In the words of German legalist, Carl Schmitt, there is no *justis-hostis* in the world today. In other words, for those who rule the world today there is no tolerable enemy; the enemy has no right to exist; he must be demonized and depoliticized; he must be eliminated.

Amongst those who are subjected to such victimization, are Christians and Jews too. Not all Christians and all Jews are hellbent on a hegemonic control over the world. Here is where we have to ask an important question: If Allah, Most Wise, has prohibited believers from taking as their *Awliyā* all Jews and all Christians, and even if this prohibition is conditional on the count that this refers only to those who are hostile to Islam and the Muslims, then how do we deal with those Jews and Christians who not only defy the perpetrators of this political and economic bullying, but who are similarly victimized together with the Muslims and who have willingly opened their doors to Islam and the Muslims? What will be our (Muslim) communal relationship with such people?

The perfect example of this happened in the very blessed lifetime of *Rasūlullah* صل الله عليه و سلم in the case of the Christian King, Najjashi, of Abyssinia. He was not part of the Qurayshi and Jewish hostility against Islam and the Muslims; he further offered his territory as a place of asylum that the Muslims could seek refuge in, and he finally defied the serpentine negotiations from the part of the Quraysh to hand over the Muslims to them. He continued to protect them until he died, long after the 51st verse of *Sūrah al-Māidah* was revealed. The Messenger of Allah, صل الله عليه و سلم, went to the extent of accepting him as a believer and offered the *Salāt Al-Janāzah* for him from Madīna when the King passed away in Abyssinia. The most important point to note here is that when this verse of the Qur'ān was revealed, the Prophet صل الله عليه و سلم did not demand the Muslims to give up the asylum they had sought in Abyssinia, which means to give up the *Wilāyah* under Christian Abyssinia, and return to Madīna. If what was meant in this verse is referring to all Jews and all Christians, the Prophet صل الله عليه و سلم would have called the Muslims to give up their homes in Abyssinia and return to Madīna. But Sayyiduna Ja'far رضي الله عنه, one of the most beloved companions of the Prophet صل الله عليه و سلم continued to remain in Abyssinia until just before the war of *Mu'tah*, which occurred more than five years after this verse was revealed.

Who are these people who have imposed their hegemony over the rest of the world? They are surely Christians and Jews who were themselves never allies of each other; they are Christians and Jews whose alliance in the trails of history commenced with their joint political and military objective to liberate the Holy Land from Muslim rule.

In fact, the story could begin as early as the first Crusades in which a Euro-Christian world was funded by Jews to gather enough military strength to conquer the Holy Land— Jerusalem—and establish a Jewish national home there. They did not succeed but briefly until Sultan Salahuddīn Ayyūbi courageously and brilliantly wrested control of Jerusalem again.

It is significant to register into our study the fact that while Europe in her Judeo-Christian effort fought wars with the Muslim world to conquer Jerusalem, they similarly perpetrated such abominable crimes on Eastern Orthodox Christians, who were part of the kingdom of Constantinople, that it would be utterly unjust on our part to include the victims of that crime in the same Judeo-Christian alliance that commenced a hostile religious struggle against the Muslims and Muslim lands. In fact the story could even begin with the Khazars—also known today as the thirteenth tribe of the Jews—who embraced Judaism overnight when they clinically surveyed the world for a religion to embrace. Or, we could come down in history to a later time when soon after colonialism and mercantilism had ravaged Muslim lands by a forceful storm as it were and replaced their rule, when they left the lands in the hands of the people, with what we today call the secular nation-state. These colonial powers were made up of the same Judeo-Christian alliance that commenced the Crusades.

However, such a historical narration would require another separate book to be written. What would suffice here is to look merely at what happened to Jerusalem—the blessed land where the three Abrahamic faiths had existed under Muslim rule for thirteen centuries—within the last hundred years.

When Fir'aun's body was discovered, something strange occurred in history that appeared to reveal the real intention behind the Zionist struggle to discover the body during the desperate excavation projects in Egypt. Some 30,000 Jews migrated to Jerusalem as a direct consequence of the discovery.

During these migrations, the Zionist movement was legally established and launched. Within two decades came the Balfour declaration—1917—which promised the Jews an independent national home in Palestine. Those who did so were part of the same Christian world that had commenced the Crusades with the same objective. It was Britain; Christian Britain. America and Europe hopped onto the wagon and constituted a joint alliance with their Jewish funders who were primarily European Jews. By this time, the hatred the Christians had for the Jews had already been done away with.

The Ottoman Empire was dismantled; the backbone of Christian Russia—or the Third Rome—was similarly broken and replaced with Communism.

It was this very same alliance that mysteriously shook hands with Joseph Stalin, the Jew, just before the commencement of the Cold War (in fact, even Lenin and Trotsky, who were as Jew as Stalin, themselves originated from the same ranks). At that moment, just when the Cold War commenced, the Jewish state of Israel was established and their independence declared as a follow up and success of the Balfour Declaration. That Cold War was a sham because those who were leading it were only two factions within the same ranks of Gog and Magog who liberated the Holy Land from Muslim rule, who shook hands when they wanted to and had no qualms about fighting each other like waves crashing onto each other when they deemed it necessary. In fact, they only threatened to crash but never did. Only that some men of admirable courage like Fidel Castro were unfortunately caught in between.

During the Cold War, the secular nation-state of Israel rose to power in the region and being armed to the teeth, ready for a display of her military strength was further supported by the North Atlantic Treaty Organization (NATO), which was already established by that time as a response to the Cold War sham. Then Pope Paulus VI declared a religio-political forgiveness for the Jews from the part of the Catholic world, as Prof. Hamka pointed out in his *Tafsīr* to the Quranic verse in discussion, thereby cementing the alliance further. The Protestants had no objection to it. They shook hands again. It was at this time that the Six-Day War commenced as a demonstration of the power that Israel—not baby Israel anymore—possessed.

The persecuted Orthodox Christians and the persecuted Orthodox Jews never joined this American-Euro-Israeli alliance. They were victimized as much as they were during the Crusades, and the victimization of them continued until recently when they were challenged by the nuclear, economic, political and military power that energy-rich Russia and her allies possess.

Here it is necessary to point out that a split occurred in the Christian world that drew a line between Western Christianity and Eastern Christianity, and it requires experts in the history of Christian polity, beyond the scope of this essay, to explain why geography had a part to play in this, so much so that Catholicism and Protestantism belonged to the geographical West and Orthodox Christianity belonged to the geographical East. African Christianity that always maintained friendly ties with the Muslim world was hijacked by this Western Christianity in the last hundred years, so much so that today we find brutal wars between Christians and Muslims in Africa utterly unbefitting African history. These conflicts are funded, fueled and even fanned by NATO in maintaining their strategic hegemony over the natural resources and lands of Africa, and that is population control too by implication. These forces are the same that belong to the ranks of the American-Euro-Israeli alliance.

For a complete study of the split that occurred in the Christian world, please refer to Graham E. Fuller's, A World Without Islam, which explains the subject in a succinct manner. Russia and the world of Orthodox Christianity are not on the side of that Judeo-Christian alliance, which gave to Israel her secular nation-state.

A new Cold War commenced with the Iraq War in the year 2003. Russia and her allies have ever since been treated like an untrustworthy and unwanted power in the United Nations who is the only other power capable of challenging the American-Euro-Israeli hegemony. The American-Euro-Israeli alliance has not been able to deal with Russia and her allies the way they would have wanted to. Furthermore, Russia and her allies today, since after the commencement of the Iraq War in 2003, have proven to be an ally that Muslims can turn to in these times, especially after Russia intervened in Syria and turned the tables.

Today fourteen years have passed after the Iraq War commenced. Fourteen years is enough time to test the waters for an effective political ally in challenging the political crimes that have been visited on the Muslims for a hundred years now. Those who are lusting to control the Levant today are biting their fingers in frustration because of a Sino-Russian political, economic and military presence in the region. They cannot anymore conduct their regime change activities in Syria without suffering serious consequences to their power. The balance of power has already tilted.

That means, we cannot anymore hold on to the view that the 51st verse of *Sūrah Al-Māidah* is referring to all Jews and all Christians. Those who say such a thing will have to remain politically and historically uneducated for as long as they continue to say so. They cannot then say that Allah, Most High, said so and hide behind the Qur'ān for prohibiting them from doing so, let alone putting the blame on Allah سُبْحَانَهُ وَتَعَالَىٰ Himself.

This ignorance of history, especially the political history of the world, even the political history of the first community of *Madīna Al-Munawwarah*, must be attributed to their own incompetency, at least academic incompetency if not incompetency in the capacity to think. Muslim scholarship in our days has failed in this regard and has no solution to the political problems of the Muslim world today. However, this meaning that Maulānā Hosein has given to the verse is not merely due to giving a solution to the political problems of the world today. It is in fact the only way to be coherent in our approach to the Qur'ān as a whole, to history and to the modern world situation. This is to understand the world accurately and to respond to challenges appropriately.

As for now, what we see in the world today is that America and her pool of allies dominate political and economic control over the world. America remains the ruling state in the world, and that means she has the capacity to defy any other political challenger. Israel on the other hand, has risen to a nuclear power capable of waging war against any other state; she defies her very protectors—the United Nations Security Council,

Britain and America and many other states in Europe. She is poised to become the ruling state in the world. It is this verse in *Sūrah Al-Māidah* that explains the powers that dominate the world today. It is precisely this political alliance that comprises of a mysterious Western Judeo- Christian pool of hell-bent perpetrators of *Fasād* in the lands and in particular the Holy Land, including the Muslim world, that Allah, Most Wise, has referred to here. These are those who have allied amongst themselves, while having been enemies in all of history before, to facilitate for something more ominous to yet unfold in the Holy Land not long from now. If we understand this verse to mean all Jews and all Christians, then we will never be able to explain the contradictions it will create with the rest of the Qur'ān; the political turmoil that the unsuspecting populations of the world is being churned in today; we will never understand the new Cold War that is unfolding before our very eyes; we will never understand and be able to explain history; we will never understand what is happening in the Holy

Land after two thousand years. Most importantly we will never be able to understand this mysterious Judeo-Christian alliance that controls the world today. This alliance will then remain forever a mystery to us. This verse in *Sūrah Al-Māidah* is the most important verse that explains all of this.

This verse in *Sūrah Al-Māidah* is the most important verse that explains what Allah, Most High, has mentioned in the opening verses of *Sūrah Al-Rūm* (31). He said that Rome will be victorious and "on that day, the believers will rejoice." Why would a Roman victory against her enemies be a reason for Muslims to rejoice? Why would Muslims rejoice over a Christian victory if Allah has forbidden Muslims to enter into any kind of alliance with all Jews and all Christians? It is this verse in *Sūrah Al-Māidah* that explains which part of the Judeo-Christian world we are allowed to enter into an alliance with and which part of that same Judeo-Christian world we are prohibited from allying with. This verse does describe to us in parallel which part of the Christian world will be closest in faith to the Muslims mentioned in verse 82 of the same *Sūrah Al-Māidah.*

Dajjāl and the destiny of Jerusalem

Let us now return to Israel and the Balfour Declaration before we conclude. It would not be justified to conclude this essay without including Dajjāl and his role towards the end of history. This verse of *Sūrah Al-Māidah* is certainly linked strongly to Dajjāl's role in impersonating the Messiah when he comes into our dimension of existence, primarily because of what we have witnessed of events unfolding in the last hundred years.

In order for Dajjāl to successfully deceive the world into believing in him as the Messiah who would, according to scriptural basis, rule the world from the throne of Nabī Dāud عليه السلام in Jerusalem, he would have to do a number of things:

1. Liberate the Holy Land from Muslim rule.
2. Establish the state and consequently kingdom of Israel.
3. Raise that power to the ruling state in the world.
4. Then appear and sit on the throne and declare that he is the prophesied Messiah and that the throne of David has returned.

Now, it is impossible for anyone to deny that it was precisely this Judeo-Christian alliance that we have discussed so far, that has successfully fulfilled numbers one and two above. If Dajjāl is to come and declare himself the Messiah, that cannot happen unless number three too comes to pass. It therefore only remains for us to witness Israel taking over from the United States of America as the ruling state in the world.

Whether India or China becomes the ruling the state in the world as it has been of much debate, cannot be the concern of those who study the modern world using the Qur'ān. It is Israel that we would have to pay particular attention to. More than two thousand years after Allah, Most Majestic is He, expelled the Jews from the Holy Land for the crime they committed against His Messenger, Nabī 'Īsā, عليه السلام, they returned to the Holy Land gradually over a matter of about three decades to reclaim it as their own. This occurred between the Balfour Declaration in 1917 and the establishment of the State of Israel in 1947. The reference to this has been mentioned in the Qur'ān in the 91st and 92nd verses of *Sūrah Al-Anbiyāh,* where Allah laid down clearly that it would be the function of Gog and Magog to cause the Jews to return to the Holy Land. From the testimony of history, what we witnessed in the world from 1917–47, it is clear that those who facilitated the return of the Jews to the Holy Land were precisely those very same Jews and Christians who allied amongst themselves in the very beginning effort of the First Crusades. Though they were not successful then, they eventually became successful in 1947. It should therefore be established from the clear and distinct link between the two verses (95 and 96) of *Sūrah Al-Anbiyāh* and the 51st verse of *Sūrah Al-Māidah* that Gog Magog is located in the very Judeo-Christian alliance that would cause the return of the Jews to the Holy Land and who would, as we witness clearly unfolding now before our very eyes—for those who have eyes to read the modern world using the Qur'ān—raise that state of Israel to become the ruling state in the world for Dajjāl to finally appear in our dimension of existence and declare himself the King of the Jews, the Promised Messiah.

If we fail to grasp the meaning behind the 51st verse of *Sūrah Al-Māidah* to be the very description of Gog and Magog, then we will remain blind to Allah's warning in the Qur'ān not to take them, this particular Judeo-

Christian alliance, or in other words Gog and Magog as our *Awliyā*. We will never understand who Gog and Magog are and we will never understand that after all that have already unfolded in the political world today, what remains is only Israel's rise to become the ruling state in the world. We will never understand that it is this Judeo-Christian alliance, in whose ranks will be Dajjāl's foot soldiers.

Conclusion

The problem with modern Islamic scholarship generally is that anything new that comes out from a credible scholar is rejected on the grounds that scholars of the past did not hold such views. This is what may be called religious conservatism.

Secondly, anything new that comes out from a credible scholar is rejected on the grounds that it contradicts the scholars of the past, while it actually may not. Why should it not be taken as something that adds on new knowledge to the scholarship of the past?

The essential question now is: Are we going to understand and attempt to explain the modern world using the Qur'ān or remain in the dark of what has happened in history and what is to unfold tomorrow because of our holding on obdurately to what the noble scholars of Islam had written down in the past, without allowing ourselves any room to think things through?

Consequently, we should also ask: Does the Qur'ān prohibit us from doing that?

We cannot afford to reserve knowledge of Allah's Book, Most Wise is He, to the noble scholars of the past. They could not have seen what would unfold in the years 1917–47 for example, simply because it did not happen in their time. Prof. Hamka saw what happened in his time and gave new meaning to the verse of *Sūrah Al-Māidah* according to what he saw. He did not put a full stop to the meanings of the verse there.

Similarly Maulānā Hosein has explained the same verse in a better light now about four decades after Prof. Hamka, quite simply because he was able to read all the world events that occurred thereafter using the Qur'ān.

Let us now read Maulānā Hosein's translation of the verse again after having gone through all of the analysis above that has led us to where we are now:

> *O you who have faith, do not take (such) Jews and (such) Christians as your Awliyā (friends and allies) who (themselves) are Awliyā (friends and allies) of each other. And whoever amongst you turn to them for friendship and alliance, would belong to them (and therefore not to us). Surely Allah does not provide guidance to a people who commit Dhulm.*

This therefore is a modern attempt to translate the verse in as coherent as possible a manner to all the other verses mentioned above in our analysis that it would otherwise clearly contradict. This translation explains our times; it explains *Ākhir Al-Zamān*. It is further an attempt to be as coherent as possible to the trails of history. It is also a credible attempt of a scholar of integrity and age who found it necessary to add on to the meanings of the verse that the noble scholars of the past had explained and interpreted. Lastly it must be noted that the Maulānā's intention, as some would wrongly have it so, is not to contradict the scholarship of the past. This does not contradict previous explanations provided by the noble scholars of the past; it does not nullify all other explanations of the verse that have been given before. It has rather added on to them.

Maulānā Hosein's interpretation of the verse broadens what is being misinterpreted as a moral alliance—in itself ambiguous—to political, economic and military dimensions; it also explains the times we are living in and clarifies the prohibition in our times violating which has caused in the Muslim world all the innumerable consequences of taking part in the *Dzulm* (wrongdoing, oppression and injustice) of the oppressor. Saudi Arabia's, Morocco's and Turkey's alliance with NATO are clear examples of this. This is clearly not a contradiction of the scholarly work of the past but an expansion of the meanings of the Qur'ān, most importantly from an eschatological perspective.

Lastly, when we bring to mind the meaning of *Barakah* in the Qur'ān, that the Qur'ān explains all times and that the Qur'ān offers new and fresh knowledge in every age, we would not look at Maulānā Hosein's explanation of the verse as something which contradicts the previous classical commentaries to the Qur'ān. We would only look at it with gratitude that a Muslim scholar, ripe of age, knowledge and experience, has added on fresh knowledge to the meanings of Allah's *Kalām*.

It now suffices to conclude that modern global events that occurred in the last hundred years have demanded this interpretation to come out from the Qur'ān and it had to be Maulānā Hosein whom Allah, Most High, had chosen to bring this forward to those who would now turn to the Qur'ān to understand the ominous events unfolding in our world before our eyes, especially in the Holy Land. This has only given a new direction and meaning to the application of this verse in these times, especially now that we are living in an important phase of *Ākhir al-Zamān*.

Appendix Two

Summary of Views on the Jasad by the Classical Commentators of the Qur'ān

By Hasbullah Shafi'iy

1. Many of the classical commentaries mention that *Jasad*, linguistically, is a human body inclusive of the head and flesh but without the *Rūh*. [*At-Tafsīr Al-Kabīr*, At- Tabarānī; *RūhAl-Bayān*, Ismā'īl Haqqī; *Majma'ul Bayān*, At-Tabarsī; *Anwār At-Tanzīl*, Baidāwī; *Al-Bahr Al-Muhīt*, Abu Hayyān; *Gharāib Al-Qur'ān*, Nizām Ad-Dīn An-Naisāpūrī; *Al-Bahr Al-Madīd*, Ibn 'Ajībah; *At-Tas-hīl*, Ibn Juzayy al-Gharnātī; *Rūh Al-Ma'ānī, Al-Alūsī*]

2. Most modern commentaries in English, Tamil and Malay have repeated most of the content mentioned in the classical commentaries. The only exception appears to be Maudūdi's commentary in which he mentions that the *Jasad* could possibly also refer to Nabī Sulaimān's عليه السلام son who ruled for a short time after his father as a "good-for-nothing" since it is linguistically compatible to name a weak ruler such. He then lost the kingdom soon after he assumed power. Most of the modern commentators of the Qur'ān like Prof. Hamkā seem to incline towards Imām Al-Rāzī's commentary (refer to No. 5 below).

Amongst the modern commentaries, Al-Sha'rāwī's (d.1418H) is worth mentioning. He says in his commentary to this verse that *Fitnah* is not something reprehensible, and that the origin of the word *Fitnah* is the smelting of gold to purify it: "Gold is mixed with other materials and we want it to be pure; so what do we do? We smelt the gold in fire so that impurities are removed from it until it becomes clean and pure from them. In like manner, *Fitnah* purifies mankind to clarify the good from the bad, and Allah had caused Sulaimān to go through *Fitnah* like he had caused his father Daūd to go through *Fitnah*." He further comments on *Jasad*, "(it is) a body and structure outwardly visible that does not contain in it a *Rūh*, and about which Allah says, "And Behold in due proportion I fashioned it and breathed into it..." (15:29) i.e. *Al-Jasad* ("it") and referring to which He, Most High, mentioned in the story of *Sāmiriyy* (*Al-Qur'ān*, 20:88): "Then he (*Sāmiriyy*) brought out (of the fire) before the (people) the *Jasad* of a calf that seemed to low..." meaning: the structure of a calf and its physical body, one that is clearly visible but without a *Rūh*."

3. Amongst all the narrations mentioned in the classical *Tafāsīr*, only one is a *Marfu' Hadīth* recorded in Al-Bukhārī and Muslim. Abu Hurayrah رضي الله عنه narrated that the Prophet Muhammad صل الله عليه و سلم said that Sulaimān عليه السلام went to all his wives on a particular night with the hope that all of them will conceive a child each and will bear him an army of horsemen who will fight in the path of Allah, just that he did not say *Inshā Allah,* therefore only one lady conceived and later she gave birth to a deformed and dead child. The Prophet then went on to say that if only he had said *Inshā Allah*, he would have received an army of horsemen who would have fought with him *Fī Sabīlillāh*. The *Mufassirūn* say that this dead child was placed on his throne and this could be the *Jasad*. However, the Prophet صل الله عليه و سلم did not mention that this is the incident referred to in the verse and that it was the dead child that was referred to as *Jasad* in the verse, which if it was, he would normally specify, hence all the commentators are unsure if this is the *Jasad* (the dead child) that was placed on his throne. Imam Al-Bukhārī too did not record this Hadīth in his book of *Tafsīr*. It therefore remains as an authentic incident that had happened in Nabī Sulaimān's life but we are unable to confirm this to be the incident referred to in the verse.

Al-Qushayrī, Al-Zamakhsharī, Abū Hayyān, Al-Tabarsī, Al-Rāzī,

Al-Qurtubī, Al-Baidāwī, Al-Māwardī, Al-Baghawī, Ibn 'Abd As-Salām, Al-Nasafī, Ismā'īl Haqqī, Ibn 'Ajībah, 'Abd al-Razzāq al-Kāshānī, Al-Alūsī and others have included this as a possible explanation of the verse in their commentaries.

4. All other narrations lead back to 'Abdullah Ibn 'Abbās رضي الله عنهم and some other *Tabi'īn* and *Tabi' At-Tabi'īn* but not to the Prophet; some to Ka'b al-Ahbār too. These narrations are mostly only compiled as "it has been narrated", "so-and-so said" and "it is said" but not as confirmed explanations of the event that is referred to in this verse of the Qur'ān. Thousands of commentaries were more often than not compilations of narrations and interpretations unless otherwise clearly stated by the *Mufassir*, or commentator of the Qur'ān. In this case, no *Mufassir* has clearly state that this is the incident referred to in the verse. They are in summary as follows:

A. Nabī Sulaimān conquered an island kingdom called Saidūn, killed the king who was a tyrant and married his daughter who embraced Islām but remained unhappy. Her name was Jarādah. Some say she did not embrace Islām. She longed for her father's company and missed his court, therefore requested Nabī Sulaimān to instruct the *Shayātīn*, i.e., Jinn who are Satans, to make for her a structure of her father. He did so and she soon started to prostrate to the image together with her maids in the palace in reminiscence of what she used to do in her king-father's presence. This carried on without the knowledge of the Prophet (according to some for forty days). Later he found out this had been happening and destroyed the image, burnt it and dispersed its ash in the air. *Jasad* in this narration therefore would refer to this image/idol of her father. Al-Zamakhsharī has this with the comment that Allah knows best about the soundness of this narration. Al-Qurtubī narrates this from Wahb Ibn Munabbih and also records another version which has it that Jarādah remained an idol-worshiper even after the marriage, brought an idol made of Ruby into the house of Nabī Sulaimān and had been worshiping it in secret for forty days without his knowledge until she eventually submitted in Islām. Al-Qushayrī, Al-Māwardī, Al-Baidāwī, Ibn 'Abd As-Salām, As-

Suyūtī, 'Abd Al-Razzāq Al-Kāshānī, Al-Baghawī (with an extended version of this story leading up to the loss of his ring to a *Shaitān*), Ibn 'Ajībah, Al-Jawziy, Al-Alūsī and others have narrated this. Ibn Juzayy Al-Gharnātī has also recorded this with a note that this report is weak because of its distant possibility that an idol could have been worshiped in the house of a Nabī, or Prophet, and also due to the distant possibility of a Nabī having instructed an idol to be made.

B. A child was born to Nabī Sulaimān عليه السلام. The *Shayātīn* feared that they will be forced to labor for the kingdom for another generation after the Prophet so they plotted to kill him or make him a handicap. Sulaimān عليه السلام feared that they would achieve it so he concealed him for safety in the clouds and the winds gave him the nourishment he needed but Allah caused the child to die, according to Ismā'īl Haqqī, due to his trusting the clouds and the wind and fear for the harms from the *Shayātīn*. This *Jasad*—dead body—was then placed on his throne. Al-Qurtubī has paraphrased this from Al-Sha'biyy saying that he was made to suffer the ill consequence because of his fear for the harm the *Shayātīn* could cause his child and that he did not realize this until the dead child fell on his throne. Al-Qushayrī, Az-Zamakhsharī, Al-Nasafī, Al-Baidāwī, Al-Māwardī, Ibn 'Abd As-Salām, Ibn 'Ajībah, and others have included this in their commentaries. Al-Alūsī has also recorded this but argues that this is a false report by the very apparent sequence of the verses that follow. He says that the wind was subjected to Nabī Sulaimān only after the *Fitnah* had occurred and therefore this could not have been true. He says this is a fabrication.

C. Al-Suyūtī in his Al-Durr Al-Manthūr has reproduced a Hadīth recorded in Al-Awsat of Al-Tabarānī with a weak chain from Abu Hurayrah that the Prophet صل الله عليه و سلم said, "A child was born to Sulaimān. He said to (one) *Shaitān*, "Will you conceal him from death?" They (the *Shayātīn*) said, "We will take him to the East." He said, "Death will reach him." They said, "Then to the West." He said, "It will reach him." They said, "To the seas." He said, "Death will reach him." They (then) said, "We shall place him in between the heavens and the earth." And then the angel of death descended and said, "I was commanded to take a soul; I looked for it in the seas, I looked for it in all the boundaries of the earth but I did not reach it, and while I was ascending I found him and so I took his soul." (The Prophet then carried on to say) His *Jasad* came and fell on the throne of Sulaimān عليه السلام. And that is the mentioning of Allah, 'We had certainly tested Sulaimān and we placed on his throne a *Jasad* and then he turned.'" Al-Tabarānī however did not record this in his *Tafsīr* to the verse even though he had compiled it in his collection of hadith. This Hadīth according to Ibn Kathīr, Al-Jawziy and Al- Suyūtī himself in another of his books, is a fabrication. It is said about this Hadith that no one doubts it is fabricated unless one entertains doubts (in the tenets of Imān) that the Prophets of Allah may peace be upon them are infallible.

D. Sa'īd Ibn Jubayr said that Nabī Sulaimān عليه السلام went to the lavatory and left his ring with his most reliable wife called Amīnah. A *Shaitān* took on his form and appeared before the lady and took the ring from her. The kingdom came under his control. Qatādah said that Sulaimān gave the ring to the *Shaitān* who then threw it into the sea. Sa'īd Ibn Al-Musayyab said he put the ring under his bed when going into the lavatory. A *Shaitān* took it and flung it into the sea. These three reports are recorded in the *Tafsīr* of Al-Jawziy well summarized from Al-Tabarī, Az-Zamakhsharī, Al-Qurtubī and others. Here the *Jasad* refers to the *Shaitān* who sat on the throne of Nabī Sulaimān in his form.

E. Mujāhid said that Nabī Sulaimān عليه السلام asked a *Shaitān*, "How do you cause *Fitnah* amongst people?" He said, "Give me your ring, and I'll inform you." When he gave him his ring, the *Shaitān* flung it into the sea. His kingdom left him and the *Shaitān*, or Satan, sat on the Prophet's throne (as the *Jasad* mentioned in the verse). The ring and the kingdom eventually came back to the Prophet. Al-Suyūtī in his *Al-Durr Al-Manthūr* and many others amongst the *Mufassirīn* have recorded this. Here too the *Jasad* refers to the *Shaitān*, or Satan, taking the form of Nabī Sulaimān and taking over his rule.

F. Nabī Daūd عليه السلام had another son who during Nabī Sulaimān rule rebelled against him and took his kingdom from him and stood as King in Nabī Sulaimān's place for a long period of time. When Allah wished to return the rule to Sulaimān, he made the usurper a lifeless body on the throne that had no movement, meaning, from a king obeyed and who had control over a vast dominion, Allah snatched his power and made him one who had absolutely no control over anything, even over himself and his own limbs. His own people turned against him and was eventually killed by them. Then Nabī Sulaimān عليه السلام regained control over his kingdom. Ash-Sha'rāwī has recorded this attributing it to the classical *Mufassirīn*.

G. Nabī Sulaimān عليه السلام had withdrawn from public life for three days and due to that Allah had placed a *Shaitān*, or Satan, on his throne as a punishment for his withdrawing from the people. Al-Rāzī and others have included this in their commentaries. The different possible names of the *Shaitān* are also mentioned in these narrations, namely, *Sakhr, Āsaf* or *Hubqīq*, as well as the reasons why Nabī Sulaimān was put on this Divine trial. For example, Al-Qurtubī narrates from Ka'b Al-Ahbār who said, "When he (Nabī Sulaimān) wronged the horses by killing them, his kingdom was taken from him for forty days", and that it is also said he had taken an oath not to marry anyone outside of Banū Isrāīl but he broke his oath therefore made to suffer the trial. They also state why and how he turned back to Allah.

"Then he turned to Allah in repentance", or "Then the kingdom/power/his rule returned to him". Ibn al- Jawziy writes that the former is the view of Qatādah and the latter that of Ad-Dahhāk. Ibn 'Abd As-Salām mentions the above two and a third: "... or (he "returned" meaning) he became free from his illness."

5. Al-Rāzī divides all opinions on the matter into two categories: (1) The opinion of those who have gathered stuffing and mere stories and (2) the opinion of those who have verified factual evidence. Under the former he has collected A, D, a combination of A and D, E, and G. He relates why the people of the latter category have chosen to reject the stories of the former category. Amongst these reasons are that *Shaitān*, or Satan, cannot take the form of a Nabī and that a Nabī will not allow an idol to be worshiped and even if that had happened without his knowledge, how would Allah have punished him for a deed done without his knowledge? Under the latter category, he has collected 3, B and a third interpretation which is that Nabī Sulaimān عليه السلام was struck by a severe illness that made him appear like a *Jasad* in his physical capacity and that was his trial based on the expression of the Arabs to describe a person who is severely ill; they call such a person a *Jism* (synonym for *Jasad* with a slight difference) without a *Rūh*. Carrying on the linguistic interpretation, he gives a fourth which is his own view:

"It is not dismissible to think that he could have been tested with the imposition of fear in him at one point in his rule, or trials caused by some of his officials and institutions that could have caused him fear/worry that weakened his power to the extent that made him like a *Jasad* in his rule at one point." He is of the opinion that Sulaimān عليه السلام himself appeared like a Jasad on his throne/in his rule. This then would mean that *Kursiyy*, i.e., throne or chair, in the verse would refer to his position of authority and Jasad would mean his weakened capacity to handle the troubles he faced from his own people.

6. Ibn 'Atiyyah says that the consensus is that the *Jasad* refers to a certain Jinn (mentioned in these narrations) because it had been appearing in the bodily form of Nabī Sulaimān while in reality it was not the Prophet whose form people saw. Al-Qādi Abu Muhammad said this is the most correct view and the clearest in meaning. This appears to be close to Maulānā Imran Hosein's interpretation except that the *Jasad* is Dajjāl, not a Jinn. Someone appearing like Nabī Sulaimān in *Jasad* is clearer in meaning than to say Sulaimān عليه السلام himself appeared as a *Jasad* in a metaphorical sense.

Appendix Three

Rabbi Rabinovich's Speech on January 12th, 1952

A report from Europe carried the following speech of Rabbi Emanuel Rabinovich before a special meeting of the Emergency Council of European Rabbis in Budapest, Hungary, January 12, 1952:

"Greetings, my children; You have been called her to recapitulate the principal steps of our new program. As you know, we had hoped to have twenty years between wars to consolidate the great gains which we made from World War II, but our increasing numbers in certain vital areas is arousing opposition to us, and we must now work with every means at our disposal to precipitate World War III within five years. [They did not precipitate World War III but they did instigate the Korean War when on June 25, 1950 they ordered the North Korean army to launch a surprise attack on South Korea. On June 26, the U.N. Security Council condemned the invasion as aggression and ordered withdrawal of the invading forces.

"Then on June 27, 1950, our Jewish American President Truman ordered air and naval units into action to enforce the U.N. order.

"Not achieving their full goals, they then instigated the overthrow of South Vietnam Ngo Dinh Diem, Premier under Bao Dai, who deposed the monarch in 1955 and established a republic with himself as President. Diem used strong U.S. backing to create an authoritarian regime, which soon grew into a full scale war, with Jewish pressure escalating U.S. involvement].

"The goal for which we have striven so concertedly FOR THREE THOUSAND YEARS is at last within our reach, and because its fulfillment is so apparent, it behooves us to increase our efforts and our caution tenfold. I can safely promise you that before ten years have passed, our race will take its rightful place in the world, with every Jew a king and every Gentile a slave.

(Applause from the gathering)

"You remember the success of our propaganda campaign during the 1930's, which aroused anti- American passions in Germany at the same time we were arousing anti-German passions in America, a campaign which culminated in the Second World War.

"A similar propaganda campaign is now being waged intensively throughout the world. A war fever is being worked up in Russia by an incessant anti-American barrage while a nation-wide anti-Communist scare is sweeping America.

"This campaign is forcing all the smaller nations to choose between the partnership of Russia or an alliance with the United States.

"Our most pressing problem at the moment is to inflame the lagging militaristic spirit of the Americans.

"The failure of the Universal Military Training Act was a great setback to our plans, but we are assured that a suitable measure will be rushed through Congress immediately after the 1952 elections.

"The Russians, as well as the Asiatic peoples, are well under control and offer no objections to war, but we must wait to secure the Americans. This we hope to do with the issue of ANTISEMITISM, which worked so well in uniting the Americans against Germany.

"We are counting heavily on reports of anti-Semitic outrages in Russia to whip up indignation in the United States and produce a front of solidarity against the Soviet power.

"Simultaneously, to demonstrate to Americans the reality of anti-Semitism, we will advance through new sources large sums of money to outspokenly anti- Semitic elements in America to increase their effectiveness, and

WE SHALL STAGE ANTISEMITIC OUTBREAKS IN SEVERAL OF THEIR LARGEST CITIES.

"This will serve the double purpose of exposing reactionary sectors in America, which then can be silenced, and of welding the United States into a devoted anti-Russian unit.

(Note: Protocol of Zion No. 9, para. 2, states that antisemitism is controlled by them. At the time of this speech they had already commenced their campaign of antisemitism in Czechoslovakia).

"Within five years, this program will achieve its objective, the Third World War, which will surpass in destruction all previous contests.

"Israel, of course, will remain neutral, and when both sides are devastated and exhausted, we will arbitrate, sending our Control Commissions into all wrecked countries. This war will end for all time our struggle against the Gentiles.

WE WILL OPENLY REVEAL OUR IDENTITY WITH THE RACES OF ASIA AND AFRICA.

I can state with assurance that the last generation of white children is now being born. Our Control Commissions will, in the interests of peace and wiping out interracial tensions.

FORBID THE WHITES TO MATE WITH WHITES.

The White Women must cohabit with members of the dark races, the White Men with black women.

THUS THE WHITE RACE WILL DISAPPEAR, FOR THE MIXING OF THE DARK WITH THE WHITE MEANS THE END OF THE WHITE MAN, AND OUR MOST DANGEROUS ENEMY WILL BECOME ONLY A MEMORY.

"We shall embark upon an era of ten thousand years of peace and plenty, the Pax-Judaica, and our race will rule undisputed over the world.

"Our superior intelligence will easily enable us to retain mastery over a world of dark peoples."

Question from the gathering: Rabbi Rabinovich, what about the various religions after the Third World War?

Rabinovich:

"There will be no more religions. Not only would the existence of a priest class remain a constant danger to our rule, but belief in an afterlife would give spiritual strength to irreconcilable elements in many countries, and enable them to resist us.

"We will, however, retain the rituals and customs of Judaism as the mark of our hereditary ruling caste, strengthening our racial laws so that no Jew will be allowed to marry outside our race, nor will any stranger be accepted by us.

(Note: Protocol of Zion No. 17 para. 2, states: 'Now that freedom of conscience has been declared everywhere (as a result of their efforts they have previously stated) only years divide us from the moment of THE COMPLETE WRECKING OF THAT [Hated] CHRISTIAN RELIGION. As to other religions, we shall have still less difficulty with them.')

"We may have to repeat the grim days of World War II, when we were forced to let the Hitlerite bandits sacrifice some of our people, in order that we may have adequate documentation and witnesses to legally justify our trial and execution of the leaders of America and Russia as war criminals, after we have dictated the peace.

"I am sure you will need little preparation for such a duty, for sacrifice has always been the watchword of our people, and the DEATH OF A FEW THOUSAND JEWS in exchange for world leadership is indeed a SMALL PRICE TO PAY.

"To convince you of the certainty of that leadership, let me point out to you how we have turned all of the inventions of the White Man into weapons against him. HIS PRINTING PRESSES AND RADIOS are the MOUTHPIECES OF OUR DESIRES, and his heavy industry manufactures the instruments which he sends out to arm Asia and Africa against him.

"Our interests in Washington are greatly extending the POINT FOUR PROGRAM (viz. COLOMBO PLAN) for developing industry in backward areas of the world, so that after the industrial plants and cities of Europe and America are destroyed by atomic warfare, the Whites can offer no resistance against the large masses of the dark races, who will maintain an unchallenged technological superiority.

"And so, with the vision of world victory before you, go back to your countries and intensify your good work, until that approaching day when Israeli will reveal herself in all her glorious destiny as the Light of the World."

(Note: Every statement made by Rabinovich is based on agenda contained in the "Protocols of Zion.")

http://antimatrix.org/Convert/Books/ZioNazi_Quotes/Rabbis.html

INDEX

H

I

J

K

ANSARI MEMORIAL SERIES

(BOOKS WRITTEN BY IMRAN N. HOSEIN)

1. The Prohibition of Ribā in the Qur'ān and Sunnah; 1997
2. The Importance of the Prohibition of Ribā in Islam; 1997
3. One Jamaat One Ameer: The Organization of a Muslim Community in the Age of Fitan; 1997
4. The Religion of Abraham and the State of Israel—A View from the Qur'ān; 1997.
5. The Strategic Importance of Isrā and Mirāj; 1997
6. The Strategic Importance of Dreams and Visions in Islam; 1997. Second edition 2014
7. The Caliphate the Hejaz and the Saudi-Wahhabi Nation-State; 1997. Second edition 2013
8. Fasting and Power; 1997. Second edition 2011
9. The Quranic Method of Curing Alcoholism and Drug Addiction; 2000
10. George Bernard Shaw and the Islamic Scholar; 2000

11. A Muslim Response to the 9/11 Attack on America; 2002

12. Jerusalem in the Qur'ān; 2002, Second edition 2002

13. Sūrah Al-Kahf Text Translation and Commentary; 2007

14. Sūrah Al-Kahf and the Modern Age; 2007

15. Signs of the Last Day in the Modern World; 2007

16. The Gold Dīnār and Silver Dirham—Islam and the Future of Money; 2007

17. The Islamic Travelogue; 2009

18. An Islamic View of Gog and Magog in the Modern World; 2009, Second edition 2011

19. Explaining Israel's Mysterious Imperial Agenda; 2011

20. Iqbal and Pakistan's Moment of Truth; 2011

21. Madīna Returns to Center-State in Ākhir Al-Zamān; 2012

22. In Search of Khidr's footprints in Ākhir Al-Zamān; 2014

23. From Jesus the True Messiah to Dajjāl the False Messiah; (not yet completed)

24. Methodology for Study of the Qur'ān; 2016

25. Dajjāl the Qur'ān and Awwal Al-Zamān (i.e., the beginning of History) 2017

Aleemiyah Memorial Series

1. Islam and Buddhism in the Modern Age; 1972

World Federation of Islamic Missions

1. The Quranic Foundations and Structure of Muslim Society in 2 Vols. By Maulānā Dr. Muhammad Fazlur Rahmān Ansārī. First published 1973. Malaysian Edition 2011

More Books on the subject of Islamic Eschatology published by Iron Heart Publishing:

1. The Three Questions
2. The Divinity of Time and Cosmology

Upcoming Titles:

3. The One-Eyed Impostor
4. Tyrants of the Modern Age
5. The Abyss of the New World
6. Of Jinn and Man
7. The Progeny of the Holy Land
8. On the Wings of Two Angels
9. To Jerusalem and Beyond
10. An Ally in Byzantium
11. The Importance of Islamic Eschatology
12. The Signs
13. A World of Deception

To order any of the above books please visit the publisher's website:

www.ironheartpublishing.com

Or visit the author's website

www.imranhosein.com

To order a complete set of all books autographed by the author to you, with date, place, etc., please send an email to:

info@ironheartpublishing.com

ALFA

ALFA

Derde Deva Randevu 3

Genel Yayın Yönetmeni: M. Faruk Bayrak
Genel Müdür: Vedat Bayrak
Yayın Yönetmeni: Mustafa Küpüşoğlu
Kitap Editörü: Seçkin Erdi

ISBN: 978-625-449-534-2

1-5. Basım: Mart 2022

Baskı ve cilt
Melisa Matbaacılık
Çiftehavuzlar Yolu, Acar Sanayi Sitesi, No: 8
Bayrampaşa - İstanbul
Tel: (0212) 674 97 23
Faks: (0212) 674 97 29
Sertifika no: 45099

Alfa Basım Yayım Dağıtım San. ve Tic. Ltd. Şti.
Alemdar Mahallesi, Ticarethane Sokak, No: 15, 34110
Cağaloğlu - İstanbul
Tel: (0212) 511 53 03
Faks: (0212) 519 33 00
www.alfakitap.com- info@alfakitap.com
Sertifika no: 43949

MURAT MENTEŞ'ten

DERDE DEVA RANDEVU

No 3

çizen HAKAN KARATAŞ

ALFA

TAKDİM

Okumak, iki ruh arasında âşıkane bir mülâkattır.
[CEMİL MERİÇ, *Bu Ülke,* 1916-1987]

Fikirler, uğrunda kavga edilecek değil, akşam yemeğinde rahatça tartışılabilecek nitelikte olmalıydı.
[BERTRAND RUSSELL, *Eğitim Üzerine,* 1872-1970]

Gönül sevdi benim günahım nedir / Yandım hasretine bunca senedir
Mecnun'un derdinden derdim fenadır / Izdırabın sonu yok mu cananım
[MAHZUNİ, 1940-2002]

“O müstesna okura bir izahta bulunalım, selam verelim, ha?”

“Tabii ki… Hem işte üçüncü cildi kotardık. Arkası da gelecek. Gücümüz yeterse 10-11 kitap çıkaracağız.”

“Haklısın, Hakan. Bu hususlara değinmek iyi olabilir.”

“Ne yazacaksın?”

“Net bir fikrim yok… *Derde Deva Randevu* serisinin aslında bir edebiyat ve düşünce ansiklopedisi olduğunu belirtsek mi?”

“İyi olur.”

“Eski Yunan’ın felsefe metinlerindeki gibi diyalog yöntemini kullandığımızı söylemiş miydik?”

“Hayır.”

“N’apsak?”

“Söyledin işte?”

“*DDR*’nin niteliklerini maddeler halinde listelemek tat verebilir?”

“Deneyelim, Murat.”

“Sen başla.”

“Bir: Yazarlarla görüşmeler kurguluyorsun.”

“Evet, gezegendeki tüm rahmetli üstatlarla direkt görüşüyorum!”

“İki: Onlara sorular yöneltiyorsun.”

“Üç… Cevapları eserlerinden seçtiğim ifadelerle oluşturuyorum.”

“Bu önemli bence. Okuyucu da yazarın dünyasında turluyor yani.”

“Öyle... Üstatların yaşadığı döneme, şehirlere gidiyoruz. Bir nevi zaman yolculuğu. Senin çizimlerin sayesinde, bu fantastik olay, görsel kanıtlara kavuşuyor.”

“Beş?”

“Diyalogların gerçek gibi algılanmasını sağlamak üzere bir konuşma akışı oluşturuyorum.”

“Altı… Çoğunlukla basit ve net sorular soruyorsun yazarlara.”

“E tabii. Kendim bir yazar değil, okur olarak çıkıyorum üstatların huzuruna. Dickens’a akıl vermeye, Sontag’la tartışmaya, Oğuz Atay’ı eleştirmeye filan kalkışmıyorum. Zira okuru temsil ediyorum bir bakıma.”

“Murat, bu zaman yolculukları, bir tür nezaket ziyareti, değil mi?”

“Haliyle…”

“Yedi?”

“Yazarların yaşadığı yerleri çiziyorsun sen. Dönemin atmosferini kuruyorsun. Bazı tarihleri belirtiyoruz. İşin belgesel yönü de var...”

“Düşününce, cidden acayip bir fikir. Her çılgının aklına gelmez yani?”

"İltifat ediyorsunuz Hakan Bey... Sekiz: Yazarın düşünce ve duygu dünyasını genel hatlarıyla ve bazı kritik detaylarıyla görünür kılmaya çalışıyoruz."

"Yazarlarla ilgili birtakım önyargıları sarsıyorsun da. Tomris Uyar bölümünde, onun özel hayatından hiç bahsetmemişsin mesela"

"Valla, Hakan, her ne kadar okur konumunda dursam da, bir yazarın anlaşılmasını sağlamak için, onu mümkün mertebe doğru anlamış olmam gerekiyor."

"Bu da hassas bir sorumluluk."

"Simone Weil der ki 'Bir insana dikkat etmek, onun için dua etmektir.' Duayı, ötekinin 'iyiliğini istemek' olarak düşün."

"Haaa, biz de bir bakıma üstatlar için dua etmiş oluyoruz."

"Şöyle de düşünülebilir: 'Dikkate değer' biri olmak ile dikkatini neye veya kime yönelteceğini bilebilmek arasında sıkı bir bağ var, dostum. Dikkat süresinin kısaldığı, dikkatin çabuk dağıldığı, milyonlarca insanın dikkat çekmeye çabaladığı bir dönemdeyiz. Dikkat hem çok ihtiyaç duyulan bir şey hem de nadir bulunuyor."

"Doğru anlamış mıyım, Murat, kimse, kimse için dua etmiyor artık..."

"Azaldı, diyelim. Çünkü bir başkasının iyiliğini isteyecek kadar sakin olamıyoruz. Hız çağındayız. Fazla hızlanınca da dikkat parçalanıyor, anlam seyreliyor."

"*DDR*'ye dönersek... Dokuzuncu madde: Bu kitap aslında edebiyat ve düşünce dünyasına bir köprü kuruyor. Okur dilediği gibi gelip geçsin diye. Bir nevi amme hizmeti!"

"Güzel söyledin Hakan. Bu kadarı yeterli sanırım."

"Sen de bir madde ekle, on'a tamamlansın."

"Hımmm... On: *Derde Deva Randevu*'da aslında herkesin dertli olduğu açığa çıkıyor. Hayyam da dertli, Susan Sontag da. Fatma Aliye hüzünlü, Zweig elemli. Dickens endişeli, Oğuz Atay tedirgin. Keyifli görünen Asimov bile karamsar aslında. Dolayısıyla, aramızdaki farklılıkları düşmanlığa dönüştürmek... ancak kavrayış zaafının sonucu olabilir. Merhamet penceresinden bakabilirsek hem kendi derdimizi paylaşabiliriz, hem başkalarına faydamız dokunur. Çok da akıl verir, ahlak aşılar gibi konuşmak istemem. Her birimiz kendimizce iyiyi, doğruyu, güzeli arıyoruz. *DDR*, bu arayışı desteklemek için var. Okurun yoluna, ufkuna ışık düşürürse, ne âlâ...

"Umarım öyle olur, Murat."

ÖNSÖZ KISA OLDU. BİRŞEYLER EKLESEN YA?
DAHA NE EKLEYEYEYİM HAKAN?
NEREDEN BİLEYİM. YAZAR SENSİN.
KİTAPTAKİ YAZARLARDAN BAHSETSEK?
İYİ OLUR.

"Hayyam, Dickens, Fatma Aliye, Zweig, Abdülhak Şinasi, Asimov, Susan Sontag, Oğuz Atay ve Tomris Uyar..."

"Gene karışık bir liste... Kimi doğudan, kimi batıdan. 12. yüzyılda yaşamış olan da var 21. yüzyılı görmüş olan da..."

"Fakat böyle gerekiyor Hakan."

"Açıkla."

"Bilgi, düşünce, söz... insanlığın ortak değeridir."

"Ayrımcılığa koşullanmış biri, muhatabını anlayamaz ki."

"Güzel söyledin, Hakan. Anlamak, öğrenmenin de, bilmenin de şartı. Farklı kültürlerle, farklı yaklaşımlarla ne kadar çok temas edersek, zihnimiz o nispette genişler, gelişir."

"O nedenle mi Ömer Hayyam ile Susan Sontag'ı, Fatma Aliye ile Isaac Asimov'u, Stefan Zweig ile Tomris Uyar'ı aynı kitapta buluşturuyorsun?"

"Elbette. Bence hiçbirimiz göründüğümüz kadar katı bir dünya görüşüne sahip değiliz. Her birimiz, bazı konularda muhafazakar, bazı konularda devrimciyiz aslında. Oğuz Atay, Mehmet Akif'i çok sevdiğini söylerken samimi. Asimov, dindar dostlarıyla selamı kesmemiş. Ömer Hayyam bir yandan şüpheci, bir yandan inançlı işte..."

"Murat, ilk kitapta Fârâbî'yi okuyunca şaşırmıştım. Gayet modern fikirlere sahip, 1000 küsur yıl önce yaşamış bir İslam filozofu..."

"Orhan Veli de divan şiirine hayrandı, hatırlarsan."

"Demek ki biz birçok yazarı yanlış tanıyoruz."

"Sanatçıları konumlayamıyoruz. Bu ciddi bir mesele. Fatma Aliye'nin hem gelenekleri önemseyen hem ilerici bir entelektüel olmasını havsalamız almıyor. Sanat ve düşünce insanlarını sağa sola çekişt'rip duruyoruz.

"Ayıp aslında. Aynı zamanda kayıp."

"Maalesef. Bir toplum, dâhi evlatlarını anlamaya bakmalı. Onları birtakım ideolojilerin maskotu haline getirip sonra da alkışlar eş iğinde bir kafese kapatmak... acıklı yani."

"Abdülhak Şinasi Hisar, yeterince tanınmıyor sanki. Onu neden kitaba dahil ettin?"

"Harika bir yazar çünkü. 1963'te vefat ettiği halde, 19. yüzyıl yazarı gibi algılanıyor. Ciddi görünür, fakat muziptir. Karamsar fakat çok zekidir. İlginç olduğu aşikar. *DDR*, kimi okurların Üstat Hisar'ı keşfetmesine vesile olursa, ne mutlu."

Sana bir şey söyleyeyim mi Murat... ben de aslında Abdülhak Şinasi Hisar'ı bu kitap sayesinde fark ettim. Hikayesini çizerken, adama kanım kaynadı.

Onun konuşma balonlarını yazarken hem memnuniyet duydum hem de mahcup oldum. Dolayısıyla okurun duygularını anlıyorum az çok."

"Derler ki 'Hayat, keman çalmayı öğrenirken, sahnede keman resitali vermektir.' Bu işler böyle Hakan. Dünyadaki tüm kitapları okuyamıyoruz. Dikkate değer şeyler çoğaldıkça, dikkatten kaçan şeyler de otomatikman artmış oluyor."

"Amma acayip."

"Öyle valla."

"Ne gibi?"

"Figürleri, mekanları, hareketleri doğru yansıtmak yetmiyor. Estetik çözümler üretmek de gerek. Çizimler ile yazarın psikolojisi arasında daha çok uyum gözettim. En önemlisi, kapağı çizerken, Rembrandt'ın Galile Denizi'nde Fırtına tablosundan esinlendim."

"Aaa? Bunu fark etmedim... Neden böyle bir yola başvurdun?"

"Yelkenli teknenin şeklini, açısını doğru verebilmek için. 1600'lerin ilk yarısında yapılmış bir resim... 1990'da çalındı. Ve hâlâ kayıp... Biz de kimisi asırlar öncesinde yaşamış üstatlarla buluşuyoruz... Benim çizimim elbette bir 'taklit' değil. Büyük bir ressama uzaktan, saygıyla, sessizce bir selam vermek aslında."

"Her defasında, nasıl bu kadar iyi çizdiğine hayret ediyorum Hakan."

"Yorularak. Yeterince yorulursam, iyi bir sonuç çıkıyor."

"Büyük sanatçısın, gerçekten, sana imreniyorum."

"İmrenecek bir şey yok abi. Hayyam'ın dediği gibi 'Daima talebeyim.' Bu bir gerçek."

"Zweig söyleşisinin sonundaki portreyi nasıl çizdin, aklım almıyor."

"Ohooo, tamam... Ben de senin bunca alıntıyı nasıl olup da böyle akıcı konuşmalara dönüştürdüğünü çözemiyorum. Senaryoların da manyakça. Oğuz Atay'la müzik dinliyorsun. Fatma Aliye'yle bisiklete biniyorsun. Daha sayayım mı?"

"Birbirimizi övmeye son versek iyi olacak."

"Herhalde. Zweig ne diyor: 'Hakiki sanatçı, eserini övmez.' Kendini zaten övmez. Bitti."

"Eklemek istediğin bir şey?"

"Yok."

"Okura son bir şey söylemeyecek misin?"

"Valla ne diyeyim, iyi okumalar."

"O halde benden de iyi okumalar."

"Acaba şu anda bu satırı okuyan kişi nasıl biri?"

"Hakan, çok şey bilmek istiyorsun."

"İnsan merak ediyor."

"Senden benden genç biri bence."

"İyi tahmin."

"Bir şeyler yemek ister misin?"

"I-ıh."

"Bir kahve daha?"

"Olur."

ÖMER HAYYAM

NE MUTLU ADI SANI BİLİNMEYEN KİŞİYE

Ömer Hayyam hem bilgin hem dört dörtlük şairdir
Eşi yoktur üstadın benzeriyse çok nadir
Bir nebze cüretkardır, eh olacak o kadar
Onun rubaileri zamandan azadedir

GÜNAH SARHOŞUYUM BEN FAKAT AYIK TÖVBEKAR,
RAHMETİNDE UMUDUM, ŞANI YÜCE RABBİMİN.

Siz bir filozofsunuz, nerden çıktı "talebe?"
Olgun kişi herdaim hesap sorar kendine:
"Kime ne fayda sundum ve ne kattım kendime?"

Peki ya çiğ bir kimse ne yapar genellikle?
Yataktan kalkar kalkmaz başlar "Ben ben" demeye
Parasıyla puluyla durmadan övünmeye.

Durun tahmin edeyim: Umulmadık bir anda
Biri kapıyı çalar "Benim, Azrail!" diye?
Gene de bu vefasız dünyadan kopmamalı,
Hazır yaşıyor iken çıkarmalı tadını.
Sıra gelir miydi hiç senin de yaşamana,
Olsaydı eğer dünya insanlara vefalı?

An'ı yaşamak mıdır sırrı mutlu olmanın?
Bir yel vurur umutlar savrulur uçar gider
Sensiz bensiz kalır tüm sokaklar ve caddeler
Paran pulun nen varsa bugün ye, yoksa yarın
Ölüverirsin, açgöz düşmanların gelir yer.

İnsanca yaşamayı cimrilik mi engeller?
Mal mülk düşkünleri hiç rahat yüzü görmezler
Binbir derde düşer ve canlarından bezerler
Aptalca bir kaprisle her dem böbürlenir de
Sana bana bir tek gün selam bile vermezler.

Hasis efendilerin akıbeti nicedir?
Cimrilerin hakkından Hak elbet ergeç gelir
Cehennemin en dibi onlara rezervedir
Ne demişti ağzından ballar akan Muhammed:
"Cömert bir gayrimüslim cimri müminden yeğdir."

SEVER SAYARLAR MIYDI SİZİ ZAMANINIZDA?
FİLOZOFUM DİYE SIRF ÇATIP DURDULAR BANA,
BUNDAN BÜYÜK SAÇMALIK VAR MI ALLAH AŞKINA?

ANLAMADIM EFENDİM, BENİ MAZUR GÖRÜNÜZ, KİM NEDEN HÜCUM ETSİN, ŞAİR BİR FİLOZOFA?
DÜŞÜNMEMDEN ÖTÜRÜ: "BEN KİMİM, NEYİM, NERDEN DÜŞTÜM BÖYLE GAFİLLER GÜRUHU ARASINA?"

Devrinizde çoğulcu kişiler hiç yok muydu?
Sizde var mı ki hani aklı başında insan?
Kıymetli düşüncenin, fikrin peşinde koşan?
Herkes kendi zannının kulu kölesi olmuş
Var mı sahi doğruyu yanlışlardan ayıran?

Mutlu olmak mesele, bu yoldaş kıtlığında
Aptal olma dertlenme neşe sevinçle yaşa
Zulümler diyarında hakkı tutarak yaşa
Madem ki dünyamızın sonunda yokoluş var
Kendini kandırmayıp özgürleşerek yaşa.

Yaşayayım da üstat, bunaldım tek başına?
Bu toprakta dostun az olursa daha iyi
Ahaliyle uzaktan selamlaşıp geçmeli,
Aklı başına gelen her insan fark eder ki
Hançerliyor sırtından kim varsa güvendiği.

E siz de dertlisiniz, belli etmeseniz de?
Üstüne bastın dostum, ne yapalım, bu böyle…
Yazık ki pişmiş ekmek hep çiğlerin elinde

Yazık ki hep cimriler el koymuş çeşmelere
O cânım Türk dilberi hareli gözleriyle
İpten kazıktan kopmuş çakalların elinde.

Hazır "Dilber" demişken, gelelim aşk bahsine…
Ah gençlik şiirini başlatan mısradır aşk
Kalpte bir köşe değil, bütün kainattır aşk
Söylemeye ne hacet, hayatın manası aşk…

Aşk'ın şartları nedir?.. Sizin dileğiniz ne?
Ay gibi bir sevgili, yıl kadar uzun gece.

Maşuku anmak sanki sevindiriyor sizi?
Geçenlerde anlattım güllere sevgilimi
Bir baktım ki kuşlar da dinliyorlardı beni.

Güllere ve kuşlara anlattığınız nedir?
Nazlı sevgilim bana derdi derman edendir
"Çekil yolumdan sefil!" diye ferman edendir
Onun o nurlu yüzü kıblem olmuş bir kere
Kıbleye karşı beni her gün kurban edendir.

Kurban mı?! Kurban olmak uyuşuyor mu aşkla?
Nasıl ki mumun başı aleviyle bağlıysa
Benim de başım bağlı o güzelin aşkıyla.

Kim bu bahsettiğiniz vazgeçilmez sevgili?
İşin aslı, bilmem ki ah nasıl söylemeli
Canım burnuma geldi de cananım gelmedi.

Ne dersiniz o yâre çıkagelse tam şu an?
Aşkınla gireceğim bir gün kara toprağa
Aşkınla çıkacağım er geç kara topraktan!

Var mıdır aşka dair bir tavsiyeniz bize?
Aşk tavlasında hile hurdaya meyil verme
Her zarın hep-yek gelse, sürekli kaybetsen de.

Bu düpedüz ezaya davet etmek değil mi?
Leyla isteyen kişi, Mecnun'a dönüşmeli
Kendini hiçe sayıp dünyadan vazgeçmeli
Sevdiğinin kusuru karşısında körleşip
Acı sözlerineyse "Ben dilsizim" demeli.

Beden ile birlikte kalp de ihtiyarlar mı?
Maalesef, ne gezer, hiç de öyle olmadı,
Yaşlılıkta da kalbim aşk ağına takıldı
Sabır hırkamı zaman tuttu cart diye yırttı
Aklın yolundan beni narin yârim ayırdı.

Âşığın ahvalini kim anlar ki acaba?
Cebi boş gönlü dolu kişi anlar mesela
Dünyaya rest çekmeyi o iyi bilir zira.

Cebi boş olmak da zor, kendimden biliyorum…
Aklı olan paraya zerrece değer vermez
Lakin beş parasız da elin kahrı çekilmez.

Karnınız tok sırtınız pek miydi, tam tersi mi?
Dünya mutfağında bin bir türlü yemek pişer
Benim payımaysa mis gibi kokular düşer.

Alkolden ötürü mü biraz depresifsiniz?
Şarabı seviyorum çünkü kibri siliyor
Şarap içen cellatlar bile çocuklaşıyor.

Sizi kınayan çoktu… Makbul kimseler miydi?
Softalar adam olsa bana "Ayyaş" demezdi
Sarhoş etse her günah kimse ayık gezmezdi.

Vah… demek densizliğe vardırmışlardı işi?
Kabarık softa bana akıl öğretse iyi
Utanmadan Allah'a akıl verdiği vâki
Cennet tapusu onda sanki rahmet yetkisi!

Korkarım ki müskirat kötü gösterdi sizi?
Şeytan da şarap içmez, iyi biri mi yani?

Sarhoşluğun felsefi mesajı nedir bize?
Kendinden geç, sefil ol, en dibe vur ve delir.

Zihni dağıtan meyden bir fayda umulur mu?
Ferman padişahtaysa neşe ferahlık bizde
Ondan daha ayığız bu sarhoş halimizle
İnsan kanı içer o, biz ise üzüm suyu
İnsaflı konuş dostum, fenalık hangimizde?..
Sofular ikide bir dinden dem vuruyorlar…

Size "Zındık münafık sapık" falan diyorlar?
Yahu ben neysem oyum göründüğüm gibiyim
Onlarsa olduğundan başka görünüyorlar.

Bu bizim coğrafyada nasıl olmalı insan?
Şahsiyet kazanarak adını temiz tutsan
İyi kalplere girip mutluluğu arasan
"Din iman" diye diye kimseyi bunaltmasan
Hem şeker gibi tatlı olursun hem kahraman.

Beni bağışlayınız, sorum safi meraktan…
Oruç tutmadınız mı cidden hiç Ramazan'da?
Beni mübarek aydan habersiz filan sanma
Gamdan cefadan gece oluyordu gündüzüm
Sahura kalkıyordum ben de gün ortasında.

Yolunuz arada bir düşer miydi camiye?
Giderim elbet bazen kim gitmez ki camiye
Lakin ne abdest aldım namaza durdum ne de
Bir zamanlar bir kilim aşırmıştım camiden
O eskiyince gittim yenisin' yürütmeye

Ha ha ha âlemsiniz, sevgili Ömer Hayyam!
Şakalarınız kadar dualarınız da var…
Şu virane gönlümü onarsın Rahîm Allah
Yüreğimden kederi kaldırsın Kâdir Allah
Meyhaneyi yol tutan cılız ayaklarıma
Kadeh tutan elime acısın Gafûr Allah!

Allah'a yakın, dinden uzaksınız belki de?
Kalbin temiz pirüpak olmadığı müddetçe
Hacı hoca olmuşsun neye yarar bir söyle?
Sarık, sakal, seccade, cübbe, tesbih güzel de
Cenab-ı Hak kanar mı bu fos şekle şemale?

Haklısınız aslında, önemli olan kalptir...
Din ile dinsizliğin arası tek nefestir
Hayal ile gerçeğin arası tek nefestir
Aldığın her nefesin değerini bilesin
Hayatın tümü dostum aslında tek nefestir.

İki cihanı da pek umursamıyorsunuz?
Bıyığımı süpürge etmişim meyhaneye
Hayrı şerri unutup bırakmışım geride
İki dünyayı karpuz diye sunsalar bana
Metelik vermem dostum inan ikisine de.

Alkol konusunda hiç taviz vermiyorsunuz...
Yüzbin kere "Tövbe" der gene şarap içerim
Şanı hiç umursamam şerefe boş veririm
Kusurum' ayıplama benim güzel kardeşim
Sarhoş doğdum ben zaten, elbet sarhoş giderim.

Günah da sevap kadar neşe veriyor size...
Tamam evet anladım günahım çoktur benim
Ama dinsizler gibi umutsuz da değilim
Cennet olur, cehennem veya arada bir yer
Şarabımı içerim, başucumda sevgilim.

Saygı uyandıran bir tarzınız var gene de...
Bana şarap ve kızlar, sana cami ve tekke

Kesin cennetliksiniz, cehennemliğim bense
Kader bu, karışılmaz Yaradan'ın işine.

Sizi ne kızdırmayı isterim ne kırmayı
Sizden daha muteber olmadığım da kesin
Sorduğum suallerden ötürü incinmeyin
Netleşsin istiyorum sözünüzün anlamı.
Cenneti cehennemi gören var mı, hani, yok
O dünyadan haberler alıp getiren de yok
Madem bilmiyor kimse işin aslı faslını
Ne boşa ümit besle ne de boş boşuna kork.

Bilinemez değil mi, kimin kalbinde iman?
Bir elimizde kadeh bir elimizde *Kur'an*
Bir işimiz helaldir, diğer işimiz haram
Çarkı çengeli kırık şu üç günlük dünyada
Bizler ne tam kafiriz ne de tam bir Müslüman.

Bu sözlerden ötürü sizi öteler toplum?
Adımın geçimsize çıkmasından memnunum
"Softalar muhitinde otur" derseniz yokum.

Onlarda size menfi, katlanılmaz gelen ne?
Softalar hep gündüzü çevirirler geceye
Vururlar filozofa ve tüm düşünürlere
Halbuki biz Hudâ'nın hikmeti peşindeyiz
Onların aklı fikri abdest bozan şeylerde.

Sizde dervişane bir taraf var sanki, yok mu?
Ben zaten fukarayım, mal mülküm yok ki yahu
Gurbete düşmüş yolum, eş dostum yok ki yahu
Evliya hayatıdır bu benim yaşadığım
Demek ki bendenizim Hakk'ın sevgili kulu!..

Erdemler sözde değil eylemde mi olmalı?
Elbette! Her milletin var bin çeşit inancı
Mümin, kafir bilmem ben, tınmam helal haramı
Maksadım Hakk'ı bulmak, kabul etmem aracı.
Ben sorayım bu defa destur buyurursanız:
Günahsız bir Müslüman bulmak neden imkansız?

Bilmem ki... İnsanları haktan ne alıkoyar?
Gerçeği örtbas eder güç peşinde koşarlar
Ne yaşamayı bilir ne ölümü anlarlar

Peki ya yalancılar güce kavuşurlarsa?..
Padişahın sarayı yıkılmaz kalır sanma
Er geç bir tünek olur baykuş ve kuzgunlara...
Ben de mahsur kalmıştım zulümler diyarında
Mıhları gevşek çadır gibi çöktü sonunda
Sağlam görünüyordu sarsılmaz ve yıkılmaz
Yeri poyraza kaldı, o mübarek rüzgara...

Nasıl davranmak gerek zalimler sürüsüne?
Girme sakın o rezil güruhun hizmetine
Konma sinek misali, pisliklerin üstüne
Kuru ekmek yesen de haline şükret ahbap
Yüreğinin kanını iç gene boyun eğme!

Bir zalim gitse bile yenisi gelmiyor mu?
Ne diyorsunuz üstat bu zulüm nöbetine?
Görüyorum her yerde haksızlık olduğunu
Nemrutların sarayda köşkte oturduğunu
Sağa dönsem bir türlü sola dönsem türlü
Her yerde görüyorum kendi mutsuzluğumu.

Ne yapmak isterdiniz, hayalinizdeki ne?
Mümkün olsa dünyayı uçurumdan atardım
Nimeti külfetine tümden resti çekerdim
Dahası bu kepaze pespaye gezegende
Ne doğar ne yaşardım hatta ne de ölürdüm.

GELENEK BOŞ, TOPLUM KOF, DİN SOFTANIN ELİNDE
YALNIZLIKTAN ÇILDIRIP GİDECEĞİZ HERHALDE?
KAFANIN İÇİ BOŞSA, SEVGİ YOKSA KALBİNDE
UĞRAŞMA, EREMEZSİN, MANASTIRDA TEKKEDE!
TATTIYSAN FAKAT AŞKI, BİR KERECİK DE OLSA
YERİN CEHENNEMİN VE CENNETİN ÖTESİNDE.

CENNET İLE CEHENNEM, DÜNYADA MIDIR NEDİR?
DÜNYA GÖZÜMÜZDE BİR SİSLİ HÜLYADIR BİZİM,
CEYHUN NEHRİ KIPKIZIL GÖZYAŞIMIZDIR BİZİM,
CEHENNEM YOK YERE DERT ÇEKTİĞİMİZ ŞU GÜNLER,
CENNET GÜN ETTİĞİMİZ MUTLU GÜNLERDİR BİZİM.

Hayat berbat, değil mi, hiç umut yok aslında?
Olan olmuş birader gam yeme boş boşuna
Dünyayı kara zindan etme sakın başına
Dürüst yaşamaya bak, elinden tek gelen bu
Olup olacakları danışan var mı sana?

Pekala... neydi sizi şu hayattan soğutan?
"Kaderden şikayetçi değilim" desem yalan
Tescilli aptalları hep koruyup kollayan,
Madem ki aptallara veriliyor nimetler
Tamam, aptal olayım gitsin ben de o zaman!

Bir temenniniz var mı, tüm insanlık hakkında?
Ellerimiz birleşsin itimat ve dostlukla
Hiç işimiz kalmasın cehaletin tozuyla.

Cehaletten sıyrılmak yeterli mi acaba?
Okuryazar bir zatta vefa varsa ne âlâ
Çoğu girmekten kaçar vefa imtihanına.

Demek dünya muhteris kimselerin elinde?
Kendilerini bilgin bilge sanırlar bir de
Hem sonra biraderim, eşek eşeği sever…
Hayra alamet sana "Kötü" demeleri de.

Eşitlikten bihaber kimseye ne demeli?
Köle mi istiyorsun, kulun kölen olamam!
Köle mi satıyorsun, hayır, satın alamam!
İtaati sevmem ben, bunu anlıyor musun?
Özgürce yaşamaktan başka şeyden anlamam.

Herkes özgürlük ister şu üç günlük dünyada…
Aksine özgürlükten kaçar ve uzak durur
İnsanoğlu, nedense kendinden bile daha
Aptal birini bulur ve onun kulu olur.

Nedir sizce mertliğin sırrı, şifresi, kodu?
Gökyüzü gibi berrak ol yapma dedikodu.

Başka bir tavsiyeniz, sevgili ihtiyar kurt?
Çalma ve gülümse hep mazlumu, yoksulu tut.

Şöhret teselli vermiş olsa gerektir size?
Tesellinin t'sini bulmak bile mesele...
Ne mutlu adı sanı bilinmeyen kişiye
İpeklere kürklere bürünmeyen kişiye.

Kaçak mı yaşamalı cidden yani dünyada?
Ne mutlu bu dünyadan tez elden ayrılana
Hele ki hiç doğmayıp dünyaya gelmeyene!

Para konusunda bir ölçünüz var mı sizin?
Kula muhtaç olmamak... bana neden yetmesin?
Yükümü tek başına taşırım kabre değin.

Ölüm bir sigorta mı oluyor? Daha neler!..
Bu şartlarda bir kişi nasıl gülerek yaşar?
Ağlatamaz ki beni belalar felaketler
Mutluluk bayrağımı katiyen yırtamazlar.

Siz nasıl kaçındınız, gamdan, dertten, kederden?
Şan şeref külahını tutum yere çaldım ben.

Vazgeçmek yetmiyor ki güçten, mülkten şöhretten?
Tohumumuz fânilik suyuyla yeşermişken
Neşeli görünsek de dert çekeriz gizliden.

Dertler biter herhalde bir aşamadan sonra?
Eli ağır feleğin sillesini yeriz biz
Eli çabuk zaman bir vurunca seriliriz.

"İnsan son nefesine hazır olmalı imiş
Zira nasıl ölürse öyle dirilecekmiş..."
Biz kızlarla her gece gülüp eğleniyoruz
Bu halde dirilirsek doğrusu işimiz iş!

BENDEN BIR ISTEGINIZ, ARZUNUZ VAR MIDIR HIÇ?
BIR GÜN AHBAPLARINLA MEYHANEYE UĞRARSAN LÜTFEN BIR KADEHI DE BENIM ŞEREFIME IÇ.

CHARLES DICKENS

ŞANSSIZLARIN KUMARI

Charles Dickens [1812 – 1870]
Victoria Döneminin en sevilen, en etkili romancısı.
20'li yaşlarında uluslararası ilgi uyandırdı. Eserleri toplumsal ve politik yeniliklere yol açtı: Yetimhanelerin, okulların, mahkemelerin, hapishanelerin, fabrikaların… işleyişi ve koşulları iyileştirildi.
Romanlarını fasiküller halinde yayımladı. Böylece okurların reaksiyonlarına göre biçimledi hikayelerini.
Yarattığı karakterler gezegenimizdeki tüm edebiyatseverlerin hafızasına kazındı: Pip, Oliver Twist Fagin, David Copperfield, Uriah Heep, Scrooge, Nicholas Nickelby, Amy Dorrit, Martin Chuzzlewit… ve daha yüzlercesi.

SİZ.. CHARLES DICKENS'SINIZ ?!
BU SİZİN SANIRIM?
OH! ÇOK ÇOK TEŞEKKÜR EDERİM BEYEFENDİ.
Our* Mutual Friend
part I
C. Dickens
* Our Mutual Friend - Müşterek Dostumuz.

ÇOCUKLARA SAYGI

Oliver Twist, David Copperfield, *Antikacı Dükkanı*'ndaki Nell, *Büyük Umutlar*'daki Pip, *Kasvetli Ev*'deki Jo... Hep zor koşullarda büyüyen mazlum çocukları anlattınız...
Evet. Çünkü ben de onlardan biriydim. Babam borçlarından ötürü hapse atılınca, 11 yaşında ayakkabı boyası satılan bir depoda çalışmaya başladım. Sonra da ayak işlerine baktım.

Ah, bunu bilmiyordum...
Acı iyi bir öğretmendir... Bana çok şey öğretti. Eğdi beni, büktü ama daha iyi bir şekle soktu.

Vay canına?..
Çocukların, hayatın acılarıyla yüzyüze gelmeleri size de dehşetengiz ve hazin gelmiyor mu?

Haklısınız. Çocuklar kötü durumdaysa, her şey kötüye gidiyor demektir, Mr. Dickens.
Bence de… Çocuğun bulunduğu evde çocuktan daha değerli bir varlık yoktur.

Çocukların ölümünü en büyük felaket olarak niteliyorsunuz…
Kesinlikle. Bir çocuğun hastalık ve sefalet içinde ölüp gitmesi, tüm yöneticilerin, zenginlerin ve din-adamlarının vebalidir. Çocuklar ölüyorsa, tüm o şan, şöhret,

şatafat, şeref... tüm o hayırseverlikler, kahramanlıklar, misafirperverlikler adi birer yalan demektir. Hepsi yerin dibine batsın!

Böyle bir durumda toplum...
Sevinç, yoksulların yoldaş olarak benimsendiği toplumda yayılır. Kimsesiz bir çocuğa, soylu kimselere gösterilen saygıyı sunan toplum iyi bir istikbal inşa edebilir ancak.

Çocuklara saygı mı gösterilmeli?
Elbette. Çocuklar sevgi kadar saygıya da ihtiyaç duyar.

Yaşça küçük oldukları için onları küçümsüyoruz, ha?
Maalesef. Yalnızca çocuklara değil, zayıf olduğunu vehmettiğimiz herkesi küçümsüyoruz genellikle. En kötü, en çirkin yanımız insanları hor görmek olsa gerek.

ALÇAKLAR YÜKSELEMEZ

Çocuklara karşı işlenen suçların sorumluları arasında neden din-adamlarını da saydınız az önce?
Tanrı'nın hizmetinde olduklarını söyleyenlerin merhametsizliği katlanılır gibi değil. Hep ama hep sarayın müdavimi, kralın duacısı olmaları... tam bir rezillik!

Din görevlilerine fena içerlemişsiniz...
İtaat, yalakalık, dalkavuklukla alçaldıkça alçalanların cennete yükselmesi mümkün müdür?

Değildir, sanırım.
Azıcık düşünün, piskoposun kaftanını alırsanız ne kalır geriye? Şaşırtıcı derecede alelade bir adam! İpek kaftanı ve kokartlı şapkası gitti mi, tüm haşmetini kaybedecektir. Ve halk üzerinde hakimiyet kuramayacaktır.

Krala yalnızca din adamları veya dindarlar mı ram olur?
Yooo... Bayağı ruhlu kimselerin hepsi iktidar karşısında cezbeye kapılır.

***Nicolas Nickelby*'de zalim bir öğretmen olan Squeers vardı... Roman yayımlandığında birçok öğretmen size dava açtı. "Squeers'i yazarken beni model almış" diye... Ve siz de?..**
Bu durumdan çok memnun kaldım. Demek ki romanım gerçeklerle örtüşüyordu. Bir de... bana dava açan kötü öğretmenler besbelli salaktı. Yoksa neden "Burada bahsi geçen iğrenç insan bana çok benziyor" diye ortaya atılsınlar?

Öğretmenler arasında salaklar azınlıktadır sanırım...
Bence de. Salaklar sarayda çoğunluğu teşkil eder.

APTALLIKTAN, APTALCA YÖNTEMLERLE KAÇMAK

Yöneticileri mi salak buluyorsunuz? Neden? Ne tür bir salaklıktan söz ediyorsunuz?
Budalalığı kastediyorum... Fakirler yaşıyormuş, ölmüşmüş, saraylılar zerrece umursamıyorlar. Ama fakirler "Yaşasın kral!" diye bağırdığında, yöneticiler sevinirler; kendi büyüklüklerine inanırlar!

Yöneticiler ve zenginler neyi gözden kaçırıyor?
Korkudan ve bağımlılıktan doğan hürmetten hayır gelmeyeceğini.

Ve?..
Ve ne? Hepsi budala işte! Karnını halkın açlığı pahasına doyuranlar, işlerin ilelebet böyle güllük gülistanlık devam edeceğini vehmediyorlar.

Siyasi adaylık tekliflerini, budalalığa yakanızı kaptırmamak için mi reddettiniz?
Hah hah haaa! Belki de!.. Zira… aptallıktan korunmak için aptalca bir yöntem uygularız.

Neymiş o?
Aptal olmaktan değil, başkalarından daha aptal olmaktan sakınırız!

Romanlarınızda hep yoksulları anlattınız. Halbuki sizin devrinizde yoksullar okuma yazma bilmiyordu…
Öyle... Romanlarım mahrum ve mahzunlara bir sığınak, bir yurt olabilirse, bundan onur duyarım. Gerçi…

Gerçi, ne?
Yoksulluk yozlaştırır, ümitsizlik delirtir. Yoksul ve ümitsiz insanların adalet isteyecek kadar bile mecali yoktur. Edebiyatı neylesinler?

Müsterih olunuz üstat… Sizin eserleriniz, ülkenizde okulların, yetimhanelerin, mahkemelerin… iyi bir işleyişe kavuşmasına vazgeçilmez değerde katkılar getirdi.
Evet, galiba haklısınız bayım…

İNSAN SÜRÜSÜ, TOPLUM DEĞİLDİR

"Kapkara fukaralık bulutu gitgide kesifleşiyor..." yazmıştınız. Fukaralığın temel sebebi neydi sizce?
Parlamentodakilerin sorumsuzluğu. Yani kötü yönetim. Ve buna bağlı olarak halkın çıkarcılaşması. Hiç kimse yoksulları düşünmüyordu. Yoksulluğa son vermek kimsenin aklından geçmiyordu.

Bir toplum, yoksulluğu pekala ortadan kaldırabilir, öyle mi?
Öyle tabii. Toplum, her koyunun kendi bacağından asıldığı bir insan sürüsü değildir. Toplumsal yaşam, varlıklıdan yoksula, soyludan sıradan yurttaşa, tüm kesimlerden tüm bireylerin kader birliğidir.

Orta gelirliler, hatta zenginler yoksul düşmekten korkuyor sanki?

Maalesef. Böylece soylu umutlar uğruna çaba harcama gücünü kaybediyorlar.

Zenginlik hakkında ne düşünüyorsunuz?
Servet, insanlarla aramıza mesafe koyar. Para, çoğaldığı nispette, insanları birbirinden uzaklaştırır.

Zenginler kaçsa bile, onların kuyruğuna yapışan çok?
E, orası öyle. Çok zengin olursanız, sahtekarların yoğun ilgisinden kaçınamazsınız. Şahsiyet sahibi insanlar, zenginlere fazla sokulmazlar.

Tüm zenginler kötü müdür?
Kötü olan, fazla paradır. Ve sahibini en azından belli bakımlardan aşağı çeker. Sevgisiz ve cimri bir zengin ise…

N'olmuş ona?
Mutluluğu tadamaz.

KARANLIK BEDAVADIR

Bizi cimrilikten ne korur?

Müsriflikten koruyan şey: Görgü. Yani terbiye. Biliyor musunuz, cimriler karanlığı severler.

O niye?

Çünkü karanlık bedavadır!

Güzel espri. Paranın bir faydası veya anlamı yok mu?

Aksine, para sihirli bir ilaçtır.

A-ha?

Elinizdeki para, sizin dertlerinize deva olmayan fakat onunla başkalarının yaralarını iyileştirebileceğiniz bir merhemdir.

Tamahkar olmamak gerek, diyorsunuz…
Kâr hırsı, insanı soylu amaçlardan, ideallerden uzağa düşürür. Acılardan kaçsan da kurtulamazsın. Ve çok sevdiğin dünya, kabusun olur.

Kâr hırsı menfi bir şey ise, ticaret de…
Tüccarlık yarı-gerçek bir iştir. İnsanlığımızı asla tam manasıyla beslemez.

Ne yapmalı peki?
Tanrıdan ve kendi emeğinden başka hiçbir şeye güvenme dostum.

Bir de zenginler kibirli oluyor, değil mi?
Yooo? Yani… kibir denen günah, zenginler kadar, sıradan insanların ve hatta suçluların da payıdır.

ÖZGÜVENLİ KİŞİLER MÜTEVAZIDIR

Gösterişçilere ne dersiniz?
Kibir gibi o da zenginlik veya fakirlikle ilgili değil, görgüsüzlüğün tezahürüdür. Özgüvenli kimseler gösteriş yapmaz.

Özgüvenin başlıca kaynağı da...
Emeğiyle ve eseriyle var olmaktır. İhmalkarlığa meyletmemektir.

İhmalkarlığın sakıncası ne?
Zaman kaybettirir ve böylece aslında ömrü kısaltır.

Ooovvv, cidden fenaymış...
Fena ya... Çoğu kimsenin hayatı, kaçırılmış bir fırsattır. Malum, zaman hep akar, kimseyi beklemez.

“Zaman kimseyi beklemez” ve?..
Ve ölüm hiçbirimizi çok bekletmez. Sıramız çabucak gelir.

Ölümden ve trajik bir dezavantaj olarak ölümlülükten çokça söz ediyorsunuz… Ve galiba ölüme dair müspet bir söz söylemek kolay değil…
Aslında ölümün olumlu bir işlevi yok değil…

Nedir?
Kötülük, kötü kimsenin ölümüyle sona erer. Fakat iyi bir insan öldüğünde, iyilik yaşamaya devam eder.

Hiç böyle düşünmemiştim…
Ayrıca, ölüm bizi hayattan daha çok değiştirmez.

GURBET COĞRAFYASI

Sanayi çağının başlamasıyla meydana gelen değişiklikleri sizin eserlerinizden takip edebiliyoruz. Mesela *Kasvetli Ev* romanınızda at arabalarının yerini trenler alıyor... Hatta ulaşım hızının giderek artmasıyla daha da belirginleşen bir sorunu tespit etmiştiniz. Neydi o?
Demiryolları uzak şehirleri birbirine yaklaştırmıştı. Fakat insanları birbirinden gitgide daha çok uzaklaştırıyordu.

Sahi "Onca kalabalığa rağmen, bu nasıl bir yalnızlık!" yazdınız *İki Şehrin Hikayesi*'nde. "Kalabalıklar içinde yalnız olmak" tabiri size ait yani. Yıllar içinde küresel bir klişeye dönüştü...
Benim zamanımda dünya nüfusu 1 milyara ulaşmıştı. İngiltere nüfusu ise 25 milyonu buluyordu. Makineler hayatı tantanalı ve kaotik bir hale getirmişti. Sükûnet yok, hep bir acele var. Letafet yok, hep bir hararet var. Huzur yok, hep bir endişe var. Merhamet yok, hep bir öfke var. En kötüsü de zamanın önemi ve değeri yok! Şehirler kalabalıklaştıkça emniyetsizlik ve itimatsızlık herşeyi her şeyi gölgeliyordu. Gurbet coğrafyası genişlemişti...

Fakat yalnızlık insanı bir tek gurbette yakalamıyor, haksız mıyım?
Doğru... Gurbet kadar sıla da mahzun kılabilir insanı.

Emniyet ve itimadı ne tahrip veya imha eder?
Adaletsizlik. Adaletsiz memlekette her şey tersine döner. Katiller masumları yargılar. Masumiyet ıstıraba dönüşür.

Ve?
Adaletsizlik, temiz kalpleri kırar.

Üzülmek de işe yaramıyor. Sürdürülebilir bir hal değil sanki?
Orası öyle... Keder, kırık kemikleri onarmaz.

DUYGULARINLA HAREKET EDERSEN BAŞIN BELAYA GİRER

Bireysel ve toplumsal sorunları anlayabilmek ve ortadan kaldırabilmek için ne yapmak lazım?
Kanaatim o ki... her türlü kötülükle baş etmenin en sağlam yolu, iyi kitaplar okumaktır.

Tamam da bir avuç insanın kitap okuması, toplumun iyiye gitmesine yetmiyor ki?
Akıllı bir insan evvela kendi hayatını düzeltmeye bakar.

Toplum? Toplum ne olacak?
Toplum insanlardan oluşmuyor mu?

Oluşuyor?
Dar ufkunu genişletir, kötü düşüncelerden kurtulur, çarpık fikirlerini düzeltirsen, iyiye varan yolu yürüme tecrübesi kazanırsın. O zaman bir başkasına söyleyecek sözün olur.

Önce bilgilenmek gerekiyor, ha?
Tabii ki. Duygularınla hareket edersen başın belaya girer.

Duygularıyla hareket edenler ne yaparlar?
Etrafına ve insanlara bakıp her şeyin karanlık olduğunu haykırırlar. Haklıdırlar da. Ne var ki bu karanlık aslında onların kendi tasalı ruhlarının rengini yansıtır.

Ha?
Gerçekte ise hayat aydınlık ve güzeldir. Bunu görebilmek için sağlıklı gözler gerek.

DÜNYA, SIRADAN İNSANA NORMAL GÖRÜNÜR

Acaba? Binlerce sayfa boyunca toplumdaki kokuşmuşluğu, çürümüşlüğü anlatan sizden bunları duymak beni biraz şaşırttı doğrusu?
Ben "Dünya esasen iyi bir yerdir. Olayları akışına bırakırsak her şey kendiliğinden düzelir" mi dedim? Çaba sarfetmeden iyiliğe ermek muhal görünüyor bana.

Madem öyle Mister Dickens, neden böyle söy_
Lakin tüm belaların başkalarının başının altından çıktığını zannetmek, kendi kusurlarımızdan kaynaklanan sorunları görememek müthiş bir zayıflıktır.

Anlamama yardım edin lütfen. Adaletsizliklerle dolu bu dünya size normal mi görünüyor?
Kesinlikle hayır. Dünyanın hali ancak sıradan insana olağan görünür.

Çünkü?..
Etraflarında ne korkunç şeyler olup bittiğini öğrenmekten kaçınırlar. Gözleri görmez, kulakları duymaz.

Ya da...
Dar kafalılıkları sebebiyle olaylardan bir sonuca varmak yerine olayları fikirlerine uyduruverirler.

Böylece...
Kolay yoldan, mutlu olurlar.

Sonuç?
Birileri tarafından sürekli kandırılmanın zilletini, kendilerini kandırarak yumuşatırlar.

BİLGİ'NİN EŞLİK ETTİĞİ CESARET

"Adaletsiz bir dünyada, kolaya kaçan sıradan insanlar arasında, çaba sarfetmeden iyiliğe eremeyiz" diyorsunuz ve yapılacak en iyi işin "iyi

kitaplar okutmak" olduğunda ısrarcısınız. Doğru anlamış mıyım?
Evet, tam da bunu söylüyorum.

Göz önündeki kötülüğü düzeltmek için bir an önce harekete geçmek daha uygun değil mi? Çok bilgi bize ne sağlar ki?
Bilmek ve öğrenmeye devam etmek... bizi kuşku, endişe ve pişmanlığa yaklaştırır.

Kulağa enteresan geliyor...
Öğrendikçe, hazır kanılarından kuşkulanır, doğru davranma imkanını heba etmeme endişesi duyar ve hep "Daha iyisi olabilirdi" düşüncesiyle pişmanlığın yöresinde dolanırsın.

Başka?
Fark edersin ki itiraz da genellikle muhatabın inadını arttırıyor...

Dolayısıyla?
Bilgi'nin eşlik ettiği türde bir cesarete gereksinim duyarsın. Doğru davranmanı ve yanlıştan sakınmanı sağlayan bir cesarete.

Yavaş yavaş anlıyorum sanırım...
Biz İngilizler, vaktiyle, her şeyde en iyi olduğumuzdan şüphe etmenin bile vatana ihanet olduğuna inanıyorduk.

Acayipmiş...
Hazır düşüncelerle ve gerçeğin görünen kısmıyla yetinen kimse kolayca sapıtabilir.

SAVAŞ, MELEĞİ ŞEYTANA DÖNÜŞTÜRÜR

Sapıtmak derken?
Savaşa girmek mesela. Savaşla elde edilen sonucu iyi bir şey sanmak.

Sizce savaş nedir? Hak yolunda savaşılamaz mı?
Rica ederim, bunu duymamış olayım. Savaş, meleği şeytana dönüştürmektir. Hiçbir zafer, savaşı meşru kılamaz.

Kötülüğe karşı asıl mücadele, kötülerin aklının ermeyeceği bir seviye tutturmaktan geçiyor, öyle mi?
İşte bunu söylüyorum. Kaldı ki bu yol zannedildiğinden çok daha tehlikelidir.

Neden?
Çünkü sıradan insanlar gibi öngörülebilir ve basit davranışlar sergilemezseniz sizi kolay bağışlamazlar.

Kim bağışlamaz?
Hemen hiç kimse. Sizinle aynı safta yer alanlar da size müspet hisler beslemez. Sizi anlamazlar da zaten.

Niye anlamasınlar?
Kalben uzak kimseler, yakın olsalar bile birbirlerini anlamakta güçlük çekerler. Hem sonra bir sanat eserinin değerini tam manasıyla kavramak zordur.

Ne ilgisi var sanatla?
Çok bariz bir ilgisi var: Sahici insan, Tanrı'nın en soylu eseridir.

Bunu biraz açar mısınız üstat?
Nasıl ki bir heykel yavaş yavaş, yontula yontula şekilleniyorsa....

Eveeet, insan da yontulmamış kalmaktan sakınmalı...
Yani değişmeli. Başkalarını, hele tüm toplumu değiştirmeye yeltenmeden önce. Sorarım size, kendinizle ilgili neyi değiştirdiniz şu hayatta?

LİMANA YANAŞIRKEN BATAN GEMİ

Yontulup yontulmadığımı soruyorsunuz?
Sakıncası yoksa.

Bilemiyorum üstat... Hep aynıymışım gibi geliyor bana.
Bu normal. Bir insan her bakımdan değişse de özü aynı kalır.

Nasıl?
Değişen kişi kendini arıyor, kendini inşa ediyordur. Değişmekten geri duranların kişiliği yiter. Kendi kalmak, değişenlere özgüdür aslında.

Haaa?..
Böylece insan kendisinin yakın dostu olur. Değişmekten korkanlar, geri duranlar ise kendi kendinin düşmanı...

Değişen insanlar güvenilmez kabul ediliyor.
Ve dışlanıyorlar, değil mi?

Evet...
Dışlanma, en cesur insanı bile ürpertir ve kasvete sürükler.

Toplumu değiştirmek için kendimizi değiştirmemiz gerekiyor. Kendimizi değiştirince de dışlanıyoruz...
Hah hah haaa! N'aparsınız, hayat bu!

Olur mu öyle?.. Yani, bir çözüm yok mu?
Üstün nitelikli kişiler biçareliğin fevkindedir. Terk edilmek, iflas veya ihanet onları mahva sürüklemez.

Yaaa, demek o nedenle yapayalnız bıraktıkları kişilerin arkasından "Tuzu kuru" "Keyfi gıcır" filan diyorlar?
Üstüne bastınız. Tavsiyem, fazla dikkat çekmeyin ki kıskançlık ve dedikodu alıp yürümesin.

Aklıma takılan bir husus var efendim… Sizin tabirinizle "Sahici bir sanat eseri" katına 'yükselmemiş' bir kimse de pekala kendini "Kalabalıklar içinde yalnız" ne bileyim, kimsenin anlamadığı, herkesin vefasızlığına, ihanetine maruz kalan biri olarak görebilir? Böyle vehimlerle yaşayanlar yok mudur? Yöneticilerin budalalıkları gibi, muhaliflerin de budalalıkları var sanki?

Var elbet… Tam limana yaklaşırken batan bir gemiye benzer kimileri. Birçok meşhurun şöhretinin neden kaynaklandığı belli değildir. Gelgelelim aydının temel vasfı, kendi kusuruna, eksiğine, fazlalığına odaklanmasıdır. Ve aklını kullanan herkes bilir ki başkasında bir kusuru görmemizi en çok kolaylaştıran şey, o kusurun bizde de bulunmasıdır.

KAHROLURSAN SEVEMEZSİN

Bir de topluma ahlaklı olmayı vazedenler var...
Ahlaktan, kendini beğenmişler söz eder. Yani gerçek bir cazibeden mahrum kimseler. Dikkat ediniz, onlar tam da kendi melanetlerini başkalarının şahsında temizlemeye çalışmaktadırlar.

Ahlaksızlarla ilgili akılda tutmamız gereken şey...
Ahlaksızlık bazen de derinlerde gizli kalmış acılardan doğar.

A-ha? Onlara da mı yazık yani?
Aslına bakarsanız, evet. Murat Bey, şanssızların kumar oynadığı bir çağda yaşıyoruz.

Ve kumarda kazanmak şanslı olduğumuz anlamına gelmiyor aslında, ha?
İsabet buyurdunuz.

Şu dünyada hakiki bir iyiliğe ve şaşmaz bir doğruluğa yaklaşmak epey zor, ha?
Gene de… dünya, hayatı öğrenmek için gayet uygun bir yer.

Orası muhakkak! Bu koşullarda biz insanlar… Yani öylesine yuvarlanıp gidiyoruz anlaşılan?
Ne yazık ki. Çoğu kimse yeteri kadar iyilik etmez yahut edemez. Onlar, vicdanlarını, az kötülük ettiklerini düşünerek yatıştırırlar.

Diyelim aydınlandık. Bu, sizin de dediğiniz gibi, kendi hatalarımızla yüzleşmek ve geçmişimizin pek de parlak olmadığını anlamak demek. Fakat siz bir eserinizde [*Hayaletin Pazarlığı*] kötü anılarını sildiren adamın başının belaya girmesini anlatıyorsunuz?..
Evet. Geçmişte başımıza gelenler veya yapıp ettiklerimiz bugün bizi üzebilir, utandırabilir. Ama mazideki kendimizi hoşgörmeyi veya affetmeyi başarabilirsek, bugünkü kişiliğimizi kazanmamızın da öğretici bir anlamı olur.

"Kendinizi affedin." Mesajınız bu mu?
Kesinlikle. Bağışlamak bir insanı kurtarmaktır.

HAYAL KIRIKLIĞINA UĞRAMANIN SAKINCASI

Kendini bağışlamak da kendini kurtarmak demek.
E tabii. Mutsuz olmaya hakkımız olmadığı halde mutsuz olmanın âlemi var mı?

Benim dönemimde herkesin mutlu göründüğü sanal mecralar var. Buna ne dersiniz?
Mutlu görüneceğiz diye kendinizi zorladıkça içiniz büsbütün kararabilir.

Peki ya saygınlık? Bağışlanmaya muhtaç insan, nasıl saygın olabilir?

Sohbetimizin bir yerinde çocuklara sevgi kadar saygı da gösterilmesi gerektiğini söylemiştim.

"Saygınlık her şeyden çok başkalarına saygı göstermekle hak edilir" mi diyeceksiniz?
Tam da öyle diyeceğim. Hem sonra, saygınlığı korumak için gösterilen çaba, saygınlığı riske atar.

Hayat amma karmaşık. Peki ne tavsiye ediyorsunuz? Nasıl bir tutum benimsemeliyiz?
Aklınıza mukayyet olun ve neşelenin. Kimileri neşelenmeyi bilir, fakat akılları yoktur. Kimileri de akıllıdır, daha doğrusu kendini akıllı zannederler fakat neşe nedir bilmezler.

Ağlamayı yasaklıyor musunuz?
Hayır. Yeri geldiğinde gözyaşı da lazım. Ağlamak ciğerleri açar, çehreyi yıkar, insanın içini ferahlatıp sinirleri yumuşatır. Ağlamak gözün idmanıdır.

Hayal kırıklığından büsbütün kurtulamıyoruz değil mi?
Maalesef... Hayal kırıklığına uğramanın kötü yanı, sevme yeteneğimizi azaltmasıdır.

KÖR BİR GÖZCÜDÜR AŞK

Aşk'ın türlerinden bahsediyorsunuz. "Lüzumsuz" diye nitelediğiniz aşklar var. Gerçek aşk nedir?
Gerçek aşk… körü körüne bağlanmak, sevgiliye tam manasıyla boyun eğmektir. Aklın sesine, tüm dünyanın ikazlarına rağmen canını cellada tereddütsüz teslim etmektir.

Cellada mı?!..
Yani… Onu sevmenin hüsran olduğunu bilirsin, gene de sevgin zerrece azalmaz.

Aşk'ın gözü gerçekten de kör, değil mi?
Evet. Fakat buna rağmen aşk yaman bir gözcüdür.

Nasıl yani?
Bilmem?.. Bakınız dostum, çok derin sevgilerde ve çok derin anlaşmazlıklarda gizemler vardır. Bu girift ve hassas sırların mahiyetini anlamak zordur.

Aşk ve nefret bir madalyonun iki yüzü müdür?
Sanmam... Sevgi daima nefretten üstündür.

Sevenlere bir taktik veya öğüt vermek ister misiniz?
Kalbinizi açtığınız kişiye dudaklarınızı kapatmayın.

"Seviyorsan git konuş" mu diyorsunuz?
Evet, basitçe, öyle diyorum.

Aşkta tesadüflerin yeri ve önemi nedir?

Nerden bileyim?! Bildiğim şu: Tesadüfler çoğunlukla acayiptir.

Âşıklar evlenmeli mi?
Hımmm... Şöyle söyleyeyim sevgili dostum... Nikahlanmak, iki insanın kavga etmek için ruhsat almasından ibarettir çoğunlukla.

MASKELİ BALODA MAHSUR KALMAK

Yakınlık ile kavga arasındaki mesafe iki adımlık mı ne? Kötülükler daha kolay büyüyor galiba... Kimin aklından ne geçiyor bilemiyoruz da...
Başkalarının ne düşündüğünü bilen insanlar vardır...

Aaa?
İşte onların neredeyse tamamı kadındır.

En mühim değer doğruluktur ve kadınlar da doğruluğun, gerçeğin muhafızı mı sizce?
Kadınlar gerçeği yumuşatıp tatlandırma yetisine sahiptir. Dolayısıyla erkekler centilmenliği elden bırakmayarak durumu dengelemeliler.

Centilmenliğin ilk kuralı nedir?
Süreklilik. Bir centilmen, her zaman centilmendir. Normal şartlarda centilmence davranmak kolaydır. Gerçek bir centilmensen nezakete mahal bırakmayan durumlarda nazik olmalısın. Sadece kadınlara değil, tüm dünyaya olgun, yapıcı ve zarif yaklaşmalısın.

Örnek verebilir misiniz?
Ressamlar mesela, kadınları ve her şeyi güzelleştirerek çizerler. Dünya sende, olduğundan daha güzel yansımalı. Fotoğraf makinesi ise lüzumundan fazla doğru söylüyor.

Ehem... İleride, yani benim devrimde yalan söylemeyi fotoğraf makinesine de öğrettik. Fakat

acaba tek mesele katı gerçeği pembe, şekerli yalanlarla esnetmek mi?
Elbette hayır. İyilik içermeyen cazibe bir tuzaktır. Şatafatı zarafet sananlar, ömür boyu süren bir maskeli baloda mahsur kalır.

Oyuncak bir hapishanede kilitli kalmak gibi...
Öyle de denebilir. Velhasıl maddi çıkar beklentileriyle çıktığınız yolda manevi kazançlar elde edemezsiniz.

Doğru yaşamak için doğruluktan fazlasına ihtiyaç var, ha? İyi bir hayatın inşaat malzemelerini temin edebilmek epey güç görünüyor...
Hiçbir şeyi ihmal etmemek ve ihmalin kurbanı olmamak imkansızdır. Ama gene de hayatın güzelliklerini ortaya çıkarmak için çabalamaya değer.

VEDA HALKALARI

Centilmenliği tüm ömre yayabilmenin sırrı nedir?
Saygıyı hak etmeyen kimselere tepki göstermek için de olsa kaba, haince ve çirkin davranışlar sergilemeyin.

Suçlulara saygı mı gösterelim?
Kendinize saygı gösterin aziz dostum. Hırsızlık bir sanatsa, hırsız yakalamak bilimdir. Bilim insanı mikroplarla mücadele ederken mikropların değil bilimin yöntemlerini uygular. Hem suçlular er geç delirir. Onlara ayak uydurmakla iyi bir sonuca ulaşamazsınız.

Fazla kötü insan var...
Hıh... Kötü insanlar olmasaydı, iyi avukatlar olmazdı...

Victoria Çağı'nın en etkili yazarıydınız. Esaslı bir romancı olmanın yolu ne sizce?
Romancı olmak istiyorsanız... Kalbiniz asla katılaşmamalı,

asabınız hiç bozulmamalı ve dokunuşlarınız kimseyi incitmemeli.

İyi bir kitabı nasıl tanırız?
İyi kitaplar asla iç karartıcı olmaz.

Galiba okur da bir nebze hazırlıklı olmalı?
Muhakkak. İyi okur kitaba saygıyla yaklaşır. Kimileri ise kitabı eline, kitabın yazarı ona kötülük etmiş gibi bir tavırla alır. Çok konuştuk Mr. Menteş. Veda vakti geldi.

Veda mı? Hay Allah...
Sakin olunuz. Hayat, veda halkalarından oluşan bir zincirdir. Şimdi gitmem lazım. Beni cennetten çağırıyorlar...

FATMA ALİYE

HER KALP BİR BAŞKASINA AİTTİR

Fatma Aliye Topuz [1862-1936]
İlk kadın romancımız kabul edilir.
Georges Ohnet'nin *Volonte* adlı romanını *Meram* adıyla tercüme etti.
[Kitap mütercim adı yerine "Bir Hanım" yazılarak neşredildi.]
Ahmet Mithat Efendi, ondan övgüyle söz etti.
Ref'et, Udi, Enîn, Muhadarat gibi romanlar kaleme aldı.
Kadın sorunuyla ilgilendi. *Hanımlara Mahsus Gazete*'de yazdı.
Nisvan-ı İslam [1892], bir Osmanlı kadını tarafından yazılmış ve Batı dillerine çevrilen ilk kitaptır.
Aliye, bir dönem unutulsa da günümüzde yeniden keşfedildi ve eserleri okurla buluştu.

1905...
BİR BİLET UMULMADIK İNSANLARI SEYAHATTE BİRARAYA GETİRİVERİYOR.
FATMA ALİYE HANIM, ASLINDA SİZİ GÖRMEYİ ÜMİT EDİYORDUM... LAKİN BİR NEBZE MAHZUN GÖRÜNÜYORSUNUZ.

MUTLU OLMAK İNSANIN ELİNDE OLSA KİM BÖYLE BİR FIRSATI KAÇIRIR?
MUTLULUK ELİMİZDE DEĞİL Mİ?
HAYIR TABİİ Kİ. BAŞKALARINA BAĞLI.

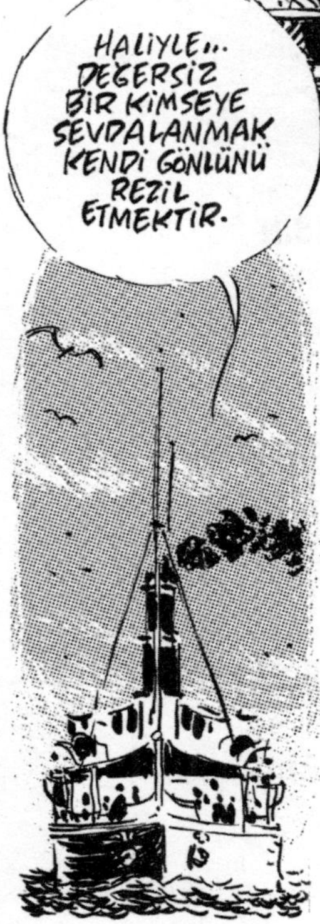

"Aşk, bir hastalık. Üstelik bulaşıcı" diyorsunuz. Nasıl bulaşıyor aşk?
Mektupla bulaşıyor mesela.

Sonra?
Toplumu saran bu korkunç aşk illeti, nice ailenin düzenini bozuyor. Uyumsuz evliliklere yol açıyor. Nasihat kâr etmiyor.

Tedavisi yok mu?
Bu illetin tek devası kavuşmak.

Eee, iyiymiş?
Nesi iyi? Kavuşunca, o âşıklar birbirine kayıtsızlaşıyor. Hayranlık, umursamazlığa; tutku, sorumsuzluğa; sevda, lüzumsuzluğa dönüşüyor.

O halde âşık olmaktan kaçınmayı bilmek lazım demektir? Önleyici tedavi gerekiyor yani?
Ah keşke... Zira aşk, diğer hastalıklardan daha önemsiz değil. Vereme çare bulan bilim insanları, belki aşka da çare bulur?

Birini gerçekten sevdiğimizi nereden anlarız?
Ayrı bir yerde ve mutlu olduğunuzda bile onu hatırlamanızdan.

Bir keresinde "Vuslat, aşkın sonu olamaz" yazmıştınız. Şimdi ise kavuşmayı menfi bir olay olarak nitelediniz?
Benimki bir temenniydi Murat Bey kardeşim. Asıl mesele şu ki...

Nedir?
Pişmanlık, âşıkları uzun süre takip eder.

Aşk'ın en tehlikeli yönü ne?
Aşk... gerçekleri örter.

SEVGİLİNİ, İŞ İŞTEN GEÇMEDEN TANIYAMAZSIN

Aşkta bizi hüsrandan ne korur?
Tesadüf.

Tesadüf mü?!
Evet. Hakikaten iyi birine rastlayıp rastlamadığınızı, iş işten geçmeden bilemezsiniz.

O halde işimiz zor, ha?
Gene de aşk bir delilik olmamalı.

Yani aşk, unutulması gereken bir hatıra silsilesine dönüşüyor...
Birçok yaşantı gibi... Geçmişi unutmak iyi de insan kendini unutmamalı.

Ne demek bu?
Kendi kendini sevmeyecek hale gelmektense ölmek daha iyidir.

Aşk acısı da tüm dertler gibi geçicidir... değil mi?
Öyle ümit edelim.

Yani?..
Hayat cidden acayiptir Murat Bey... Dert çekmeye tahammül ederiz de, gün gelir o dertleri anlatma zahmetine katlanamaz oluruz.

Bruce Lee "İnsanın en yakını kendisidir" diyor. Siz de aynı fikirde misiniz?
Bruce Lee bir bakıma haklıdır. Fakat gönül işleri mevzubahis olunca...

Evet?
Her kalp bir başka kalbe aittir. Ve kalpler birbirini arar.

"SEVİYORUM" KELİMESİ ASLA ESKİMEZ

Bir eserinizde "'Seviyorum' kelimesi ne acayiptir!" diyorsunuz. Nesi acayip?
Ne kadar çok söylenirse söylensin eskimez!

Neden eskimez?
Çünkü sevilmenin tadı vazgeçilmezdir.

E hani aşk hastalıktı? Ona karşı dikkatli olmak gerekiyordu?
Orası öyle... Lakin...

Lakin, ne?
Kalbin susuzluğu, vücudun susuzluğundan daha şiddetlidir.

'Seviyorum' kelimesinin hep yeni kalması ne gibi sonuçlar doğurur?
Bir bedbahtın saadetine, bir âşığın felâketine yol açabilir.

Aşkta sevinçler de hüsranlar da çok küçük şeylerle belirebiliyor galiba?
Özellikle de sevinçler. Sevgilinin yaşamasından, aldığı nefesten saadet duyarsın. Arada bir onun yüzünü görüyor, sesini işitiyorsun diye bahtiyar olursun.

Doğru düzgün bir aşk yaşamak muhal midir?
Aksine, pekala mümkündür.

Nasıl? Yani... ne yapmalıyız?
Gönlünüzü ve zihninizi dostluğun, sevginin, aşk'ın işaretlerini ve sırlarını kavrayacak şekilde terbiye etmelisiniz.

Terbiye derken?
Kültürden, görgüden bahsediyorum.

KALBİ KIRIK, KAFASI KARIŞIK OLMAK İYİDİR...

Görgüsüz kimse "Âşığım! Seviyorum" diye iddiada bulunmamalı... mı?
Orasını bir kenara bırakınız. Dediğim şu: Kalpten gelen ne varsa, beyinde tartılmalı.

Kültürlü bir sevgili olabilmek için...
Dikkatinizi kuvvetlendiriniz. Onu hikmet ve ibret aramada kullanınız.

Sevmeden yaşamak daha pratik sanki?
Bir şeyin içinde sevgi yoksa lezzet de yoktur.

Kıymetli Fatma Aliye Hanım... 21. asırda, hâlâ kalplerimiz kırık, kafalarımız karışık maalesef.
Tebrik ederim.

Şaka mı ediyorsunuz?
Bilakis... Kalbi kırık ve kafası karışık olmak, bence iyiye işarettir.

Çünkü?
Kalpsiz ve kafasız olmadığınızı kanıtlar.

İnsan âşık olunca ümit ile üzüntü arasında gidip geliyor…
Sevilen ise ümidini hiç kaybetmez, haksız mıyım?

Haklısınız da… Tüm aşklarda bir dengesizlik oluyor sanki?
Kimileri severse çok sever. Böyleleri tehlikededir. Zira o muhabbetin mukabilini sevdiğinin kalbinde bulamazsa bedbaht olurlar.

Tüm söylediklerinizden anlaşılıyor ki, terbiyeli, kültürlü de olsak, talihin ve tesadüflerin desteğine muhtacız. Şansın yoksa, normal bir hayat bile yaşayamazsın yani?
Aslında talihsizlik, çaresizlik değildir. Dahası, talihsizliği mutluluğa dönüştürmek pekala mümkündür.

Acaba?!
Düşünün, bir fırtınadan sağ salim kurtulduysanız, yaklaşan ikinci fırtınayı fark edersiniz. Her felaket aynı zamanda bir tatbikattır...

GÜZELLİĞİN VE YAKIŞIKLILIĞIN SON KULLANMA TARİHİ

Sevgilinin güzel veya yakışıklı olması önemli bir faktör müdür?
Birincisi, güzelliğin talihe hükmü geçmez.

İkincisi?
Evlilikte güzellik veya yakışıklılık asla mutluluğun kaynağı olamaz.

Yok be... Pardon, demek istediğim, güzellik öyle az buz bir şey değil. Sanırım siz bir entelektüel olduğunuz için böyle söylüyorsunuz.
Yanılıyorsunuz. Yaygın kabule göre güzel olmayan nice insanlar vardır ki birtakım güzel duygularla hislendiklerinde, yüce düşünceler düşündükleri zaman hoş ve güzel olurlar. Tavırlarına o anda düşündükleri ve hissettikleri şeylerin ışığı siner.

İsabet buyurdunuz. Sahiden öyle oluyor. Demek ki gerçek aşk... Bir dakika, gene de garantili bir aşk yaşamanın formülüne ulaşamadık?
Hakiki aşk pek enderdir. Lâkin ona uzananlar pek çoktur. Başlarına çöken belalı hevesi aşk zannedip divane olan pek çok zavallı genç vardır.

Aşk bir yanılsama bile olsa... Bize bir şeyler kazandırır... Mı acaba?
Her kimin elbisesi aşkın pençesi ile parçalanırsa o kimse hırstan da tamahtan da uzaklaşır, arınır.

FAKİRİN HALİNDEN FUKARA ANLAR

Yoksulluğu bir felaket olarak görür müsünüz?
Elbette.

Peki yoksulluk aynı zamanda bir tatbikat mıdır? Yararlı bir tarafı var mıdır?

Yoksulluk, insanı en net gösteren aynadır.

Ne? Ayna mıdır? Bağışlayınız fakat_
Temelde her birimiz sadece insanız... Zenginlik, insanın haricî bir kazanımı olabilir ancak.

Yoksulluk acı, acıklı değil mi?
Orası muhakkak. Çileği çok seven bir fakir, cebindeki üç kuruşla çilek yerine ekmek almak zorundadır. Bu bir gerçek.

Hah! Ben de onu diyorum. "Kimileri de mutluluk bahsinde kanaatkâr olmak mecburiyetindedir" yazmıştınız. Fakirler, her konuda kanaatkarlığa mecbur...
Hakkınız var. Bana sorarsanız işsizlik, kimsesizlikten beterdir. Buna mukabil bolluk içinde yaşamak da insanı her türlü kusurdan muaf kılmaz.

Mesela?..
Şımartılarak büyütülmüş kimseler, çok zeki ve bilgili olsalar bile halden anlamazlar pek.

Yani...
Fakirin halinden fukara anlar.

Ya da belki çok akıllı, kavrayış gücüne ve vicdani hassasiyete sahip kişiler...
Evet... Benim nazarımda akıllı kişi halkın dostudur.

Halkın da çoğunluğu fakir zaten efendim.
Bununla birlikte, anlayışsızlık, maalesef istisnai bir hal değil. Çoğu kimse size bakıp "Bir derdi var galiba" demez. Onun yerine "İtici biri" filan der.

Zenginlere ve fakirlere nasıl bakmalıyız sizce?
Zenginlerin gösterişinin gözlerimizi kamaştırdığından çok, fakirlerin ıstırapları yüreğimizi acıtmalıdır. Bu bir gurur meselesidir.

İKİ TÜR EVLİLİK VARDIR...

Diyelim pek akıllı biri değilim. Yahut aklımın başıma gelmesi zaman alıyor...

Tatlı dilli olun. Tatlı dil, sahibini erdemlere yaklaştırır ve alıştırır.

İlginç bir tavsiye...

Konuşması ölçülü ve düzgün insanlar makbuldür. Kötü söz, sahibini çirkinleştirir.

Zenginliğin haricî, dışsal olduğunu söylediniz. İçsel zenginlik de mi var sizce?

Elbette. O da bilgidir. Bilgi kaybolmaz ve çalınmaz bir servettir.

Fatma Aliye Hanım... Aşktan uzun uzun söz ettik. Sizce de münasipse, biraz da evlilikten konuşalım

isterim. Fakat zannetmeyiniz ki sizinle içtimai, felsefi ve siyasi konulara girmekten sakınıyorum. O bahisleri bilahare açarız, ne dersiniz?
Gayet münasip.

Kaç çeşit evlilik vardır?
İki.

Nedir bunlar?
Bazı evlilikler bir mutluluk sözleşmesi, bazıları ise bir geçim kontratıdır.

Hepsi bu mu?
Genel anlamda hepsi bu, evet. Öte yandan, her ev ayrı bir ülkedir. Her aile başka türlü yönetiliyor. Âdetleri, kuralları, kararları başkadır. Bazı evlerde özgürlük, eşitlik, barış vardır, bazısında yoktur ne yazık ki...

"NASİHATE İHTİYACIM YOK" DİYEN ADAM

Evlilikte sorunlar erkeklerden mi kaynaklanıyor? Yani... çoğunlukla?
Erkekler evliliğin ne olduğunu bilmeden evlenirler genellikle.

Erkek baba olunca toparlanıyor mu dersiniz?
Maalesef hayır. Babaların çoğu, çocuklarına örnek olmak şöyle dursun, nasihate muhtaç durumdadır.

Babaların nasihat almayı kabul edeceklerini sanmam pek.
Gelgelelim "Nasihate ihtiyacım yok" diyen kimsenin nasihate ihtiyacı vardır.

Evlenmek üzere olan erkek ve kadınların nasıl bir hazırlık yapması gerekir?
Her iki tarafın da yeni yuvaya hürmet, sevgi ve itimat getirmesi iyi olur.

Erkek, babalığı pek beceremiyor. Peki ya kadın, annelikte iyi mi dersiniz?
Gerçek şu ki annelik, babalıktan daha derinlerden doğan bir kaynak. Bir kadın kendi mutluluğunu feda edip mutluluk ümidini unutabilir. Fakat anneyse, evlatlarının istikbalini fedaya razı olamaz.

Eşler arasında geçimsizlik varsa...
Hiç kimse varlığını birilerinin kaprislerine adamaya mecbur değil. Kimsenin kimseden itaat ve fedakarlık beklemeye hakkı yok.

Aile içinde şiddet veya baskı olunca, çoğu kimse korkuya ve utanca yenik düşüyor ve başına gelenleri gizliyor...
İşte bu büyük bir yanlış. Yakınlarımızın suçları ve kabahatleri yüzünden utanmamalıyız...

DOSTUN YOKSA BAŞIN DERTTE DEMEKTİR

Aşkta, evlilikte, ailede... bir dostluk motifi olmalı, ha?
Kesinlikle öyle.

Dost kimdir?
Kederlendiğinizde size nazik bir dikkat ve yumuşak bir merakla yaklaşan kişi.

O takdirde, dostluk belki sevgililikten de önce geliyor?
Öyle de denebilir. İçinizi dökeceğiniz iyi ve cömert bir dostunuz yoksa dertlerinizden kurtulamazsınız.

Mizahı, espritüelliği önemser misiniz yoksa ciddiyetten mi yanasınız?
Mizah zaten ciddiyetin bir cüzüdür. Ve insanların yüzünü güldüren her söz önemsenmeye değerdir.

Bazen mizah da ters tepiyor. Tatlı dil bile işe yaramıyor. Konuşarak anlaşmakta zorlanıyoruz...
Yazık... Birbirimizin sözlerini mutlaka onaylamamıza lüzum var mı? Yanlış bir söz söylendiğinde itirazını açıklarsın. Hangimizin sözü hakikate yakınsa onu teslim ederiz. Teatide bulunmayı mümkün kılan terbiyeden mahrum kimseler ancak havadan sudan konuşabilirler. Yahut münakaşa ederler.

Münakaşayı, tartışmayı tatlıya bağlamak için neyi akılda tutmalıyız?
Tartışmalarda yenilgiyi kabul etmek, mertliğin büyük bir alametidir.

KÖTÜLERE BEĞENDİRME KENDİNİ

İki kere ikinin dört olduğu gibi bariz hakikatleri bile kabul etmeyenler var.

Yüreği murdar olmuş kimseler, iyi insanların sözlerini anlayamaz. Onlardan boş yere insaf ummayınız. Siz onların halini nasıl iğrenç buluyorsanız, onlar da sizi gülünç bulurlar. Gülünç! Onlara yalvaracak olursanız, hiddetlenirler. Şefkatten bahsederseniz, budala olduğunuzu düşünürler.

A-ha? Sizin gibi zarafet timsali bir hanımefendinin bu vahim gerçekleri böyle keskin ifadelerle dile dökmesine şaşırdım doğrusu?

Sizinle açık konuşabileceğimi düşündüm.

Neden? Ben bir yabancıyım nihayetinde?

Bazı şeyleri ancak bizi tanımayanlara anlatabiliriz. Bazı hallerimizi yalnızca yabancılar anlar.

Enteresan? Yani arkadaşlar, dostlar değil de yabancılar anlıyor öyle mi?
Yabancılığın imkanlarını gözardı etmeyiniz. Her tanışmada bir tazelik tadı vardır… Yoldaşlar; aynı dünya görüşüne, benzer düşüncelere sahip kimseler; birlikte hayal kuranlar… ayrı yollara giderler ve bir bakmışsın biri gülüyor, öteki ağlıyor.

Şu "yüreği murdar olmuş kimseler"… Kim onlar?
Menfi duygular kalbi zehirlenmiş kimseler. Onlar, kendi kibrini gurur, inadını sebat zannetmek hastalığına tutulmuşlardır…
Murat Bey, talih, kimilerini yüksek makama çıkarır, onlara her şeyin en iyisini sunar.

Fakat?
Fakat onlar şaşırtıcı bir biçimde adiliğe müpteladır.

Neden peki? Cehaletten mi?
Daha ziyade görgüsüzlükten. Konumları gereği, mükemmel insanlarla buluşmaları mümkünken, mide bulandırıcı tiplerle iş tutarlar. Böylelerine kendinizi beğendirmeye çalışırsanız insanlığınızı yitirirsiniz.

60 YAŞINDAKİ ÇOCUKLAR

Yani yüksek makamlardaki o kimseler de yanılgılara, yanılsamalara kapılıyor?..
Kahir ekseriyeti hem de… Dalkavukları dost sayanlar, riyakarca övgüleri gerçek sanırlar. Bu övgü sözlerinin de onlara kanmanın da ne kadar alçaltıcı olduğunu fark edemezler. Bununla birlikte, her türlü eleştiriyi, cezalandırılması gereken hakaretler olarak algılarlar.

Onları uyarmanın yolu yok mudur?
Yoktur dersem sözüme inanınız. Doğru sözü, eğri kimselere söylemek yanlıştır.

"Eğri kimse" derken?..
Olanca kudretine ve hiddetine rağmen, aslında gelişmemiş, çocuk kalmış kimseler... Böyleleri 60 yaşına da gelseler çocukturlar. Onlara gücenmek yerine acımalı.

Doğrusunu isterseniz tam anlayamadım.
Sizin ayıp saydığınız şeyleri kahramanlık sayan kimseler yok mu?

Var?
Onların övünerek anlattıklarını dinlerken yüzünüz kızarıyor mu?

Evet?
Rezillik bildiğiniz tavırları doğal buluyorlar, öyle mi?

Öyle?
Onlara alışmayın. Onlarla bir olmayın. Onlardan uzak durun.

KİBİR, YETERSİZ KİMSELERİN İNADIDIR

Peki onlara neden "çocuk kalmış" diyorsunuz? Çocuk kalmanın nesi sakıncalı?
Bilinci ve vicdanı gelişmemiş olmak. Sakınca burada... Şu da bir hakikat ki, vicdansız kimseler asla yüce bir hayat yaşayamaz.

Hay Allah...
Murat Bey, çok basit: Bir insan saygıya layık değilse, sevgiye de layık değildir.

Ve?
Muktedir suçlulara saygı duymak skandaldır.

Öylelerine kim, nasıl saygı duyar ki?
Büyük bildiği kimselerin suçları karşısında çoğu kimse evvela bocalar ve hatayı kendinde arar. Gerçeği fark

ettiğinde hâlâ onların emirlerine uyar, haksız hükümlerine boyun eğerse alçalır.

Güçlü suçlulara itaatin, hürmetin sonucu nedir?
Seçkin kişilerin kıymetinin bilinmemesi. Bu beni çok şaşırtıyor. Şahsiyet sahibi insanlara saygısızlık benim nazarımda bir hastalık krizidir.

Bazen de sevdiğimiz, güvendiğimiz insanlar tarafında hayal kırıklığına uğratılıyoruz...
Eee, bir insanın gönül kabında zehir varsa er geç taşar.

Kibre ne diyorsunuz?
Kibir, zorlama bir tutum gibi görünür bana. İnsanlar yetersizlikleri ve zayıflıklarını yüzlerine çarpan nice deliller arasında bulunmalarına rağmen, inat eder gibi kendilerini üstün sayıyorlar.

KALBİN KARARI, BEYNİN HÜKMÜ

Aşktan bahsederken "Kalpten gelen ne varsa, beyinde tartılmalı" dediniz ya...
Evet?

Galiba bu tüm duygular için geçerli, değil mi? Hislerimizin sağlamasını düşünceyle yapmalıyız...
Tabii ki. Ben kalbimden gelen heves ve arzunun tesiriyle hareket etmem. Onu beynimin hükmüne bırakırım. İşte orada kabul edilen şeyle hareket ederim. Uygun ve elverişli görülmeyeni yine geldiği yere yani kalbime iade ederim.

Gerçekten mi?
Hayır... Duygularımla savaşıyorum ve kaybeden hep ben oluyorum.

Aaa?..
Aşkın getirdiği acılar kalbimizi ezer geçer bazen. Kalbimizden beynimize varan yolları kapatır.

Peki, duygulara kapılmamak, zihni geliştirmek için…
Herkes bilir ki okumak icap eder. Pek az insan okumanın tadına varabiliyor fakat.

Bir de eser vermek iyi olur değil mi?
Size bir şey söyleyeyim: Bence emek, eserden de değerli. Bir ressamın en güzel resmine malik olmak isterseniz, şövalesi önünde, fırçası elinde olduğu ve işine dalmış bulunduğu anda fotoğrafını çekiniz.

Bir romancı olarak siz bir yandan da "halkın dostu" aynı zamanda öğretmeni idiniz, yanılıyor muyum?
Öyleyse ne mutlu... Zira öğretmenlik görevini layıkıyla yerine getirmek için öğrencilere şefkat ve sevgi duymak gereklidir. Sanatını sevmeyen kişi sanatçı olamayacağı gibi, öğrencilerini sevmeyen de iyi bir öğretmen olamaz.

Siz hep özel hocalardan ders aldınız. Okula gitmeden ileri seviyede Fransızca öğrendiniz. İmrenilecek şey doğrusu. Öte yandan eğitimi ve öğrenimi çok önemsiyorsunuz.
İlim yuvalarını önemsememek mümkün mü?.. Okulda kültür yani terbiye edinemezsek dünya ile zaman denen okullar bizi terbiye eder. Zamanın terbiyesine kalmak ise talihsizliktir.

Çünkü?
Geç kalırız. Zaman okulundan, ruhumuzu teslim etmek suretiyle mezun oluruz.

Ölüm hepimizin başında, ha?
Öyle... İnsan bu dünyaya ağlayarak gelir ve bu dünyadan inleyerek gider.

Başlıca dileğiniz, temenniniz nedir?
Bu vatanın kızlarının evlat sevgisiyle sevilmesi.

NE? NEDEN?
ÇÜNKÜ HER TEBESSÜM ANLAMLIDIR.
YANi?
SURAT ASMAYINIZ, SOMURTMAYINIZ.
HEPSi BU MU? BAŞKA NE YAPALIM?
KAiNATIN TADINI ÇIKARIN.

STEFAN ZWEIG

HAKİKİ SANATÇI, ESERİNİ ÖVMEZ

Stefan Zweig [1881-1942]
Kısa romanlarıyla [novella] tanınır. 60'tan fazla kitap yazdı.
Günümüz Türkiye'sinde en çok okunan yazar…
Edebiyat onun için düşünce ve duyguları somutlaştırma alanı, hayatı sorgulama imkanıydı.
İnsanı anlamak için psikolojiyle, hayatı kavramak için tarihle ilgilendi.
Balzac, Tolstoy, Dostoyevski, Dickens, Stendhal gibi birçok yazarın biyografisini yazdı. Bu metinlerde, yazarlara hem saygıyla hem de yoğun bir anlama arzusuyla yaklaşır ve dikkate değer çıkarımlarda bulunur.

Hitler bunca suçu nasıl işledi?
Devlet katına yalan ve aldatmayı taşıyarak. Hitler'den önce hükümdarlar, liderler yalan söylemezdi.

Bunlar akla hayale gelmeyecek türde yalanlar mıydı?
Hayır, aksine, yavan lakırdılardı.

Hitler'in yalanlarının başlıca amacı neydi?
Milyonlarca insanı kişiliksizleştirip kindarlaştırmak. Nefret, öfke, 'savaşma arzusu'... kısa süreli coşkulardır. Bunları sürekli kılabilmek için propagandaya başvuruldu. Düşmanlık içermeyen bir söz veya davranışın değeri kalmayıncaya dek.

KURBAN EDİLEN SUÇ ORTAĞI

Kitleyi şartlandırmak için propaganda yeterli midir?
Bunun yanısıra, iktidar sürekli kriz yaratıyordu.

Niçin?
Çünkü kriz döneminde halkı kışkırtmak kolaydır.

İnsanlar aldatıldıklarını neden anlamıyordu?
Bir dönem hakkında en az bilgiye sahip olanlar, o dönemde yaşayanlardır. En önemli olaylar dikkatlerinden kaçar.

İkna olmadım açıkçası, Sayın Zweig...
Her zaman heyecana kapılan insanlık, sabırlı ve adil kişilere itibar etmez. Sabit fikirlilere; kendi iktidarını tek doğru, kendi iradelerini kanun ilan etme cüreti gösterenlere boyun eğer.

Genelleme yapıyorsunuz... Diktatörlüğe hiçkimse karşı çıkmamış olamaz?
Çıktı elbet. Diktatöre karşı duran bilinçli kişilerin,

arkaya baktığında gördüğü şey insan türünün sonsuz korkaklığıydı.

Korkaklık mı?
Maalesef... Diktatörlüğün klişeleri vardır...

Nelermiş o klişeler?
Diktatörlükte insancıllık küçümsenir. Şiddet sürekli yükselir. Devlet suç örgütüne dönüşür. Toplumdaki tüm gruplar dağıtılır. İnsanlar devletin hem kurbanı hem suç ortağı haline gelir. Herkes durmadan birbirini suçlar. Sürüyle sürüklenmek en büyük erdem kabul edilir.

NAZİK VE SAĞLAM

Hitler devrinde toplum sürüleşmişti demek?
Evet... Kim kaygısını azıcık dile getirse, onun vatanseverliği sorgulanıyordu. Toplumu uyaranlar horlanıyordu. Savaş karşıtlarına hain damgası vuruluyordu. Yalanlarla güdülen halk, dalkavukça bir coşkuya kapılmıştı.

İktidarın en tehlikeli yönü ne sizce?
İktidarın her türü, insanı katılaştırır.

Ya zafer?
Her zafer ulusların ruhunda donukluğa sebep olur.

Doğru yaşamanın yolu güçsüz ve mağlup olmak mı yani?
Güçsüz yönlerini kabul eden, 'her zaman en önde, en üstte olma saplantısından' kurtulmuş kişiler insani bir ışıltı taşırlar ancak.

Ve?..
Zorbalar şiddete başvurur. Çünkü gerçekte kofturlar. Hakiki güçlüler ise nezaketle hareket eder. Zira kendi sağlamlıklarından emindirler.

BOMBALAR VE MERMİLER KÖTÜLÜĞÜ YOK EDEMEZ

II. Dünya Savaşı sizi derinden etkiledi. Savaş bitmeden intihar ettiniz...

Öyle oldu... Savaş; nefret, suç ve deliliğin toplamı. Asla hakkaniyetle bağdaşmaz.

Savaşın yüceltilmesinin sebebi ne peki?
Bir-iki nesil süren bir barıştan sonra, kitleler savaşı unuturlar. Savaş efsaneye dönüşür. Çok uzaklarda, geçmişte kaldığı için, kahramanca ve romantik bir şey haline gelir. Savaşı okul kitaplarında yazılanlardan ve galerilerdeki resimlerden tanırlar: Pırıl pırıl üniformalar içindeki süvariler, coşkulu zafer yürüyüşleri, anıtı dikilen mağrur kahramanlar... Savaş başladı mı cepheye giden acemi erler, annelerine "Noel'de evdeyiz!" diye gülerek el sallarlar.

Halbuki?..
Düşünün, dünyadaki kötülük bombalarla ve mermilerle ortadan kaldırılabilir mi? Savaş; zenginliği yoksulluğa, mutluluğu kahra, bolluğu açlığa çevirir. Paranın değer kaybetmesi, isyanlar, yurttaş özgürlüğünün yok olması, devlete kölelik, kahredici bir güvensizlik ve herkesin herkesi suçlaması...

KENDİNE KARŞI KAYITSIZ KİMSELER

Acayip bir soru soracağım, belki cevaplamayı seçersiniz: Kimler kolay kandırılır?

Cevabı biliyorum: Kendini daha güçlü, daha akıllı, daha güzel hissetmekten zevk alan kimseler.

Psikolojimiz bozuk. Bu bir gerçek...

Çaresizlik hissi, değersizlik duygusu, ve kendinden ümit kesmişlik... insanı kendine karşı dehşetengiz bir kayıtsızlığa sürükler.

Hepimiz şefkate muhtaç garibanlar mıyız? Yani son tahlilde?

İlginç bir yaklaşım... Belki de... Zira insan, birine iyilik etmek için bile ona ihtiyaç duyulmasına ihtiyaç duyar.

Kitleleri etkilemek, büyük bir dava uğruna coşkuyla mücadele etmek...

Ooo, hayır... "Kahraman" olarak bilinen tipleri gözüm hiç tutmamıştır.

Kahraman pozu kesenler var bir de...

Ah evet... Yurtseverliklerini ona buna hakaret ederek ucuz yoldan kanıtlamak isteyen beleşçiler.

Fakat kahramanlık aynı zamanda başarmak demek değil mi?
Sorun da bu ya. Başarılı kimseleri değil, ahlaki bakımdan doğru tutumu benimseyen kişileri ilgiye değer bulurum. Kendinden emin bir şekilde hedefine yürürken başkalarına acı çektiren insanlara itibar etmem.

HER TÜRLÜ CESARETİN KAYNAĞI

Nasıl mutlu olacağız dersiniz?
Harika hissetmek istiyorsanız, kolayca yapabileceğiniz bir şey var: Başkalarını sevindirin.

Bunu daha önce de duydum. Yeni bir şey söyleseniz?
Sahici mutluluk, farklı düşünmeye başlayıp yeni hassasiyetler kazandığımızda yaşadığımız aydınlanmayla gelir.

Vay canına... Yani mutlu olmak aslında bilmek ve düşünmekle ilgili...
Elbette. Ne yazık ki çoğu kimse mutluluğu bilgide değil boş hayallerde bulacağını zanneder.

Boş hayallere tembellikten ötürü kapılıyoruz sanırım.
Ve tembellik korkaklıktır.

Yani?
Tembeller korkaktır.

Bu durumda?...
Çalışkanlık seni cesur kılar.

Medeni cesareti mi kastediyorsunuz?
Her türlü cesareti kastediyorum.

Hayat hakkında epey reçeteniz var ha, Bay Zweig?
Hıh... Başkalarının dertleri söz konusu olunca gayet mantıklı ve nesnel oluveririz.

1933'TE NAZİLER İZİN KİTAPLARINIZI DA YAKTILAR. O ZAMAN NE HİSSETTİNİZ?

MURAT BEY, BİR ENTELLEKTÜEL İÇİN HAYATTA EN ZOR ŞEY.. DİRENME GÜCÜNÜ KAYBETMEKTİR.

Entelektüel demişken... İnsan neden düşünür?
Zaafları aşabilmek ve hayatımızda anlam biriktirebilmek için düşünürüz.

Gençler sanatla ve düşünceyle nasıl bağ kurmalı?
Gençlerin bir sanata veya sanatçıya pasifçe bağlanması, teslim olması doğru değildir. Çünkü gençliğin doğasında 'üretkenlik' yatar. Genç için mesela tiyatroyu sevmek, kendisini tiyatro sahnesinde hayal etmek demektir.

Bu alanlarda gençlere özgü bir avantajdan söz edilebilir mi?
Şurası kesin: Aceminin cesareti, bilginlerin tereddüt ettiği noktada, yaratıcı hamle yapma imkanı verir.

İyi bir entelektüel olmak, hayatı doğru yaşamak için...
Acele etmemek ve zamanı boşa harcamamak... Bu ikisini becerebiliyorsanız ne âlâ...

Daha net tavsiyelerde bulunsanız...
Mal mülk edinme. İnsanların kaderine müdahil olma. Karnını başkasının ekmeğiyle doyurma. Şehvete kapılma. Ve konfora alışma! Aklın varsa ve temiz kalmak istiyorsan, bunların hiçbirini yapma.

"İnsanlardan birşeyler istemek deliliktir. Vermek ve hizmet etmek ise bilgelik" diyorsunuz. Mal mülk edinmezsek kime ne verebiliriz Sayın Zweig?
Size basit ve kolay bir öneride bulunduğumu söylemedim ki? Hayatta en zor şeyler paranın gücüne riayet etmemek ve insanlar arasında tek bir düşman bile edinmeden yaşamaktır.

Akıllı olabilmek için bir nebze çılgın olmak lazım anlaşılan?
Aynen öyle. Fakat asıl çılgınlık nedir biliyor musunuz?

Nedir?
Kendimizi dünyanın insafına bırakmak.

ŞANSLILAR YETERİNCE ŞANSLI DEĞİL

Biraz da şans meselesi, ha?
Sanmam. Dikkat ederseniz, şanslılar bile yeterince şanslı değildir.

Aha? Ne olacak peki?
Bakınız, yaratıcılık diyarında tehlike bir lütfa, engel bir yardıma dönüşür. Çünkü bunlar insan ruhunun gizli güçlerini zorla ortaya çıkarırlar.

Ve tabii düzenli olarak kitap okumak gerekiyor, değil mi?
Kuşkusuz evet. Kitap okuyan insanlar, dünyayı başkalarının gözleriyle görebilir.

Bir insan kaç yaşında okumaya, düşünmeye yönelmeli?
Kaslarını ihmal eden kimse, bunu yıllar sonra telafi edebilir. Düşünsel gelişim ise zihinsel kavrayışın güçlü olduğu gençlik çağında başlamalıdır. Zihin açıklığını erken yaşta deneyimleyen kişi, sonraki yıllarda tüm dünyayı içine sığdırabilir.

Bir nevi süper güç!.. "Sıradan insanların huzurlu olmasının nedeni, düşünmemeleridir" diyor Romain Roland. Siz ne dersiniz?
Düşünmek hem hayatımızı tehlikeye sokar, hem de bize insanca yaşama imkanı sağlar.

Pekala... Diyelim dâhi bir genç var. Kendindeki deha belirtilerini fark edemez gibi geliyor bana. E kimseden şefkat de görmüyorsa, körelip gidebilir?
Deha sıra dışıdır. Dehaya yaklaşmak için sıranın, hizanın dışına çıkmak şarttır.

DÂHİNİN ÖZELLİKLERİ

Bize dâhiyi detaylı bir şekilde tanıtır mısınız?
Dâhilerin dünyevi hevesleri yok. Pratik değiller. Kurumsal eğitimin kalıplarına sığmazlar. Bilgilenme, öğrenme süreçleri farklıdır. Âşık olur fakat normal bir aile kuramazlar. Eserleri ve buluşları servet değerindedir fakat paraya önem vermezler. Standart bir işleri ve düzenli gelirleri yoktur. Bizim 'hayatın gerçekleri' dediğimiz şeye karşılık, onların başka bir gerçeklik ve hayat telakkileri vardır. Başıboş, aylak görünürler. Zira göçebe tabiatlıdırlar. Topluma ayak uyduramazlar. Sahip olmayı bilmezler. Tapulamaz, kiralarlar. Goethe gibi istisnalar haricinde, dâhiler bir meteor gibi yaşarlar.

"Meteor gibi yaşamak" ne demek? Yaşamayı bilmemek veya beceremememek mi?
Tam aksine… Kendi kaderini gözlemleyen, istikbali ve akıbeti üzerine kafa yoranların gerçek anlamda yaşadıklarına inanıyorum.

Halbuki çoğu kimse kurallara uyup çevresinin onayını aldı mı doğru yolda olduğunu, makbul

hatta büyük bir zat olduğunu düşünür?
Bir zamanlar bu dünyada Rembrandt, Beethoven, Dante'nin yaşamış olduğundan tümüyle habersiz birinin, kendini büyük bir insan sanmasından daha kolay ne var? Öte yandan…

Evet?
İnsanların, çağdaşları olan bir dâhinin veya bir şaheserin büyüklüğünü kavradıkları pek seyrek görülmüştür.

Ve?
Gelgelelim hayatımızın anlamı, bir 'çevrenin' hiç değilse bir başka insanın tasdikiyle belirir. Bir kişinin bizi karşılaması, bize mukayyet olması şart. Kimsenin umursamadığı biri olmak katlanılmazdır.

Dâhi olsak da olmasak da bize dikkatini lütfedecek birini bulmak pek kolay değil be üstat?
Maalesef… Kabul etmemiz gerekir ki çoğu kimse bizim içimizdeki bahçenin tarumar olmasını da, çiçek açmasını da umursamaz.

PANİĞE YOL AÇAN HÜZÜN

Âşık olunca akıl baştan gidiyor. Aşkta özenli ve dengeli davranmanın kuralı nedir?
Bir insanı sevmek, onun kıymetli zamanını boşa harcamamayı gerektirir.

Âşıklar kavuşunca aşk biter mi?
Tam tersi: Aşk'ın önemli kısmı kavuşmadan sonra başlar. Aşk bilgisi, 'beraber yaşamanın' bilgisidir.

Beraberliğin muhtevası nedir?
Beraberlikte dert ortaklığı vardır. Ve varoluşsal bir hüzün.

Pek de cazip değil açıkçası.
Evet... Kimileri bu hüzünden ötürü paniğe kapılır. Ve hayallerle dolu, ürpertili bir uzaklığı seçerler.

İnsanların çoğu uzaktan mı sever?
Öyle görünüyor. Uzaklığı, belirsizliği, merakı tercih ederler.

Çok sayıda insanla kısa süreli birliktelikler yaşayanlara ne dersiniz?

Bu tutum genelde erkeklerde görülür. Yalnızca kalın kafalı bir erkek, kadınlar konusunda "başarılı" olmaktan keyif duyar ve bununla böbürlenir. Gerçek bir erkek ise, hislerine karşılık veremediği kadının ona âşık olmasından korkar.

Ya kadınlar?

Eskiden genç kızlar, hayata tamamen yabancı bir eğitimle, her şeyden habersiz, utangaç ve güvensiz yetiştiriliyordu. O dönemin ahlak anlayışı, kadını haddinden fazla sakınırdı. Ancak bu genç kızlar 25-30 yaşlarına geldiklerinde hâlâ evlenmemiş iseler, acımasızca, korkunç bir karikatüre dönüştürülürdü. Mizah dergilerinde onlarla "kız kurusu" diye alay edilirdi.

Kadınların bir ömür genç ve güzel olmaları zımnen şart koşuluyor bir de...

Aslında kadınlar gençliğe özgü tazelikleri azaldığında bilgeleşiyorlar. Dolayısıyla bir kadının ömür boyu güzel, cazibeli ve etkileyici olması mümkün.

EN MUHTEŞEM DUYGU

Aşkta sadakat, dostlukta vefa… pek yok gibi…
Murat Bey siz de herkesin herkesi aldattığı hissine kapılmıyor musunuz?

Öyle… Fakat tüm ilişkilerimizi kusursuz kılmak da imkansız… değil mi?
Dürüstlükten uzaklaşmamak lazım gene de. Arzularının peşinden koşan kişi, gönülsüz bir sadakati muhafaza eden kimseden daha dürüst görünüyor bana.

Şu dingili kırık dünyada kimseye güvenemeyecek miyiz?
Hah hah haaa! İtimadın şartı samimiyettir. Fakat samimiyeti teşhis etmek zordur. Dolayısıyla birine tümüyle güvenmek, emniyette olmak anlamına gelmez.

Ne peki?
Riske girmek anlamına gelir.

En görkemli duygu ne sizce?
Gurur.

Neden?
Çünkü gurur kimseden asla bir şey istememiş olanların sırrıdır. Ve her türlü ihtişamdan daha önemlidir.

Kibre ne dersiniz?
Kibir, adiliğin kanıtıdır. Dahası, kibirli kimse çevresini tehlikeye sürükler.

Sevgiliyi denetleme ve baskılama meselesi aklıma takıldı. Çoğumuz düşüyoruz bu hataya. Neden?

KENDİNİ BULAN KİŞİ KAYBA UĞRAMAKTAN KORKMAZ

Fakat asıl mesele kendimizi anlayamamak veya yanlış anlamak sanki?

Doğru… İnsan kendini buldu mu birşeyleri yitirmekten korkmaz; yitirdiğinde üzülmez artık. Ve bir kez kendi içindeki insanı anlamış olan, diğer insanları anlar.

Hımmm?
Bir adam yaşam amacını buldu mu, amaç da adamını bulmuş olur.

Toplum gözünün önündeki dâhiyi veya başyapıtı göremez minvalinde konuştunuz ya... Birçok eser kaybolup gidiyor o halde?
Hayır. Dahiyane bir eser ilelebet gizli kalmaz. Görmezden gelinebilir, yasaklanabilir ve hatta unutulabilir. Ancak ondaki cevheri kimse söndüremez. Er ya da geç keşfedilir.

Eğitim ve öğrenimin, akademik unvanların değeri hakkında ne düşünüyorsunuz?
Sıradan biri için akademik faaliyet çok yararlı olabilir. Fakat yaratıcı kişiler için akademik kariyer pek gerekli görünmüyor bana. Hatta bu tür insanlarda engelleyici bir etkisi bile olabilir.

Engelleyici mi?
Okullar devletin yaklaşımları doğrultusunda eğitim verir. Ayrıca kurumsal standartlara bağlı kalır. Benim dönemimde mesela okulun gerçek hedefi bizi ilerletmek değil, geri planda bırakmak; benliğimizi geliştirmek değil, sisteme uymamızı sağlamak; enerjimizi yükseltmek değil, azaltmaktı.

BAZI ŞEYLERDEN VAZGEÇMEN ŞART

Öğrencilik insanın kişiliğini ve ruhunu tehlikeye sokabilir, öyle mi?!
Bu pekala mümkün. Mevcut düzeni, eleştirilecek yanı olmayan mükemmel bir şey sayarak ona saygı gösterecek; öğretmenlerin sözlerini hatasız, babaların sözünü karşı çıkılmaz, devletin kurumlarını mutlak ve sonsuza dek değişmez olarak görecek şekilde yetiştirilen öğrenciler... kişilik kazanamaz.

Abarttınız mı acaba?
Sanmıyorum. Öğrenci, müfredatta belirlenmiş beklentileri karşılayan bir makine değildir. İnsan sevgisi içermeyen bir öğrenim düzeneği, çocukların onurunu ve ümitlerini kırar ancak. Disiplin adı altında canlılıklarını azaltır. Yıllar geçer ve kimse çocuklara ne öğrenmek istediklerini bir kez bile sormaz. Çocuklar içten içe aradıkları, gelişimi destekleyici teşviki okulda bulamazlar.

Modern sanatçıyı da bahtsız buluyorsunuz...
Evet, insanı her türlü içsel birikimden vahşice alıkoyan günümüz yaşam biçiminde, kim kendini bütünüyle sanatına verebilir?

Kendini 'bütünüyle' sanata vermek... gerekli mi cidden?
Sanatınız sizin tüm hayatınıza sirayet etmeli... Örneğin hakiki yazar için yaratmaktan, hayal kurmaktan başka her türlü tutku bir sapmadır.

Şair, şair hayatı yaşamalı; ressam, ressam hayatı, öyle mi? Bu, fazla kısıtlı değil mi Sayın Zweig?
Bir insanın kendini sınırlamadan kişisel bir dünya kurması mümkün olmaz. Bazı şeylerden kaçınmak veya vazgeçmek, kişilik kazanmak için elzemdir.

İTİRAZ ETMEZSEN, RUHUN DONUKLAŞIR

Sanatın canlılığı ve yüceliği neye bağlı?
Sanat, tüm halkın yaşamının bir parçası olduğu yerde zirveye ulaşır.

Hakiki sanatçıların değişmez bir ortak özelliği var mı?
Hakiki sanatçı kendi yapıtlarını övmez.

Aaa? Kendini övmek aslında acemilik veya hamlık alameti demek?

Kesinlikle evet. Kader ölümsüzlerin arasına sokulmaya çalışan heveslilere acımaz.

Sanatçı veya filozof... mükemmel olmalı demek?
Hiç de bile, Murat Bey. Mükemmel insan yoktur. Dikkat edin, mükemmel, 'tamamlanmış' demektir. Halbuki insanın gelişimi sürmelidir.

Çelişkilerden kurtulmak da mümkün değil, ha?
Aksine, hayatımızdan çelişkileri kovmak kolaydır. Fakat bunu yaptığınızda canlılığınızı kaybedersiniz. Aynı şey, itirazlarınızdan vazgeçtiğinizde de olur. Ruhunuz donuklaşır.

Az önce şey dediniz ya... "Dâhilerin tümü iyi kalplidir..." Kimi dâhiler de fazla aykırı değil mi? Hatta itici?
Şunu unutmayın Bay Menteş: Vicdanımızı ve bilincimizi sarsan kişi, isterse bunu sertlikle yapmış olsun, bizim için çalışmış demektir.

ÇOK MUTSUZSAN, KOLAY MUTLU OLURSUN

Birçok kitabınızda insanı olgunlaştıran şeyin ıstırap olduğunu yazdınız. Neden?
Çünkü çabasız, miras olarak alınan lüksler, idraki zayıflatır. Bilinçsizce, gafilce; mutluluk getirmeyen bir refahın içinde bulursunuz kendinizi. Istırap, insana soru sordurur. Peşin konfora eşlik eden haz ise, yerinde saymaya, geri kalmaya sebep olur.

Söylediklerinizden anladığım şu: Mutlu olabilmek için evvela epey mutsuz olmak şart?
Mantıklı... Nitekim kendini iyi hissedenler, çevrelerinde olup bitenlerin pek farkına varamaz. Mutlu insanlar aslında kötü psikologlardır.

Cesaret kazanmak, olgunlaşmak için, çalışkan olmayı ve zorlukları göğüslemeyi öneriyorsunuz... Ya diğer erdemler?
İnsanlığımızı teşkil eden tüm erdemler... dikkat, gayret, ihtimam, cömertlik... aslında deha gerektirir. Yani ahlakın hakkını dâhiler verebilir.

Ahlakın başlıca faydası nedir?
Ahlaki açıdan belli bir düzeye ulaşmak bize olayları ve durumları net görme gücü verir.

Dâhi değilsek, çok çalışkan olamıyorsak ve hayatımız da azbuçuk rahat ise... ne yapabiliriz? Bilgiye, sanata, ahlaka giden yolu nasıl bulabiliriz?
Şefkatle. Müşfik olun. Mütebessim olun.

"Yargılamaktan, yaftalamaktan, yıkıcılıktan sakının" diyorsunuz?
Doğru. İnsan kendini de başkalarını da tek bir olaya, tek bir hale kilitlememeli. Bu, sık yapılan bir haksızlıktır. Fakat bunun da ötesine geçip hoşgörü ve yüceltmeyi teklif ediyorum. Zira toplumda müşfik bir tebessüm... nadir ve paha biçilmez değerdedir. Dehâ kadar değerli belki... Ayrıca...

Ayrıca ne?
İnsanları anlamaya çalışmak, onları yargılamaktan çok daha zevkli ve ufuk açıcıdır.

Güzel söylediniz... Bazen kendimize karşı da müşfik ve hoşgörülü olmamız gerekebiliyor...
Tabii ki. Gün gelir bilmediğimiz veya bilmek istemediğimiz şeyleri anlayıveririz. Dolayısıyla, gelecekte fikirlerimizin değişebileceği ihtimalini aklıda tutmalıyız. Bu, bize onurumuzu koruma imkanı veren bir temkinlilik sağlayabilir.

1942...

BAĞIŞLAYIN FAKAT ŞİZİN GİBİ BİRİNİN İNTİHAR ETMESİ BENİ ŞAŞIRTIYOR.

İNGİLİZ VATANDAŞI OLMUŞTUNUZ. VE BOL BOL SEYAHAT EDİYORDUNUZ.
İNSAN NE KADAR GEZSE, NEREYE GİTSE, DÖNEBİLECEĞİ BİR YURT İSTİYOR.

UMUTSUZLUK İNSANI HASSASLAŞTIRIYOR MURAT BEY.
İYİ AMA "TEHLİKE BÜYÜYÜNCE UMUT DA BÜYÜR" YAZMIŞTINIZ?
EVET... GELGELELİM HAYATIN SONA ERMESİ İÇİN İLLE DE CANIN ÇIKMASI GEREKMEZ.

"YOLUM YANLIŞMIŞ MEĞER" DİYENLER MEDENİDİR

Bir insanın hem aydınlanıp hem de umudunu koruması çok zor, anlaşılan?
Şunu söyleyecek cesaretin varsa, medenisin demektir: "Gittiğim yol, doğru bir yol değilmiş. Yanlış yönde ilerlemişim meğer."

Gerçi bizde fikir değiştirmek "döneklik" sayılıyor. Boşlukta asılı kalıyorsunuz.
Yazık… Düşüncelerini değiştirmesine izin verilmeyen zihin yok olur: Zihin olmaktan çıkar.

İnanç hakkındaki düşünceniz…
Bu hususta tek bir söz söylemekle yetineceğim: İnancın değeri asla görünüşte değildir.

Bağnazlık nedir?
Bizimle aynı görüşü benimsemeyenleri küçümsemek bağnazlıktır.

"Mutluluğu boş hayallerde aramaktan" söz ettiniz. Tüm hayaller boş olmasa gerek?
Değil elbet. Hayal gücü esasen idrakin hizmetindedir. Hayal gücü yüksek birinin, bir meseleyi anlaması ve gereken duyarlığı göstermesi için, her şeyin gözünün önünde olup bitmesi gerekmez.

Enteresanmış…
İnsanın hata yapmasının başlıca sebebi, hayal gücünden yoksun olmasıdır. Böyleleri, çoğu kimsenin aynı hatalara düşmesinden avuntu duyarlar.

Ya aptallar? Bir aptalı nasıl tanırız?
Hımmm... Aptallar düşüncelerini sert ve buyurgan bir ifadeyle ortaya koyarlar.

ABDÜLHAK ŞİNASİ HİSAR

ENTELEKTÜELLER DEDİKODU YAPMAZ

Abdülhak Şinasi Hisar [1887-1963]
Son derece özenli, zeki ve espritüel bir yazar. Üç romanı vardır: *Fahim Bey ve Biz, Ali Nizamî Bey'in Alafrangalığı ve Şeyhliği, Çamlıca'daki Eniştemiz.* Bu eserler nispeten kısa olduğu için, kimileri onun romancı olmadığını söyler. Bana göre rafine ve derinlikli kitaplarıyla, müstesna bir romancıdır. Abdülhak Şinasi Hisar hem hayatta hem de sanatta ölçülü ve iyi düşünülmüş bir modernleşmeden yanaydı.

ÜSTAT!
ABDÜLHAK ŞİNASİ BEY!
SENİ DUYMADI.

MÜSAADENİZLE ÜSTADIM.
KALSAYDINIZ AZİZ DOSTUM?
MERHABA SELİM BEY.
SELİM İLERİ
MAVİ KANATLARINLA YALNIZ BENİM OLSAYDIN

UMARIM ZAMANINIZ VARDIR EFENDİM?
AH MURAT BEYCİĞİM.. HAYAT ÖYLESİNE HIZLANDI Kİ, ZAMANIN GEÇTİĞİNİ FARK ETMEYE VAKTİMİZ YOK!
EN SEVDİĞİMİZ ÖLÜLERİMİZ DİRİLİP YANIMIZA GELSELER ONLARLA HASBIHALE ZAMANIMIZ OLMAYACAK.

"Sevdiğimiz ölülerimiz" dediniz ama insanları pek sevmediğiniz söyleniyor?
Kim demiş? Nazik ve herkesin iyiliğini isteyen kişileri gayet severim.

Gene de çoğu kimseyi pek beğenmiyorsunuz?..
Bu doğru…

Neden?
İnsanlar özgür değil. Dolayısıyla yüzeysel, kararsız, hilekar ve özgüvensizler.

Özgürlük olmazsa…
Fikir, izan, vicdan, tecrübe, terakki, ilim, sanat hiçbir şey olmaz.

FAZLA HOŞGÖRÜ, SEVGİYİ YOK EDER

Özgür olamamamızın sebebi ne?
Biz yasaklar ve korkularla yaşıyoruz. Bu yüzden fikirlerimizi beyan etmekten kaçınıyoruz. Giderek fikir üretmekten, düşünmekten de kaçınır olduk.

İleri, gelişkin bir toplum nedir, nasıldır?
Özgürlükle beslenmiş ve bilgiyle kuşanmış toplumdur.

Böyle toplumlar...
Tarih karşısında haklarını savunmayı da, mazeretlerini sunmayı da bilirler.

Toplumsal problemlerin çözülmesi, halledilmesi için ilk ne yapılmalı?
Münakaşayı bırakıp dertleşmeliyiz artık. Bizi insani hakikatlere ulaştıracak şeyler kardeşçe itimat, itiraf ve hoşgörüdür.

Güven, özeleştiri ve hoşgörüde denge tutturmak da gerekiyor fakat sanki?

Orası muhakkak. Her konuda herkese hoşgörülü olmak insanı sevgisiz kılar.

Şahsen ben, toplumdaki bozulmaya sebep olanlar, mevcut anormalliklerden faydalananlar ve içine düştüğümüz hali fark etmeyenler karşısında ne yapacağımı bilemiyorum...
Bu bahsettiğiniz üç grup da herkesi çıkarcı yani ahlaksız zannederler. Onların zannettiği gibi biri olmadığını göster. Senin anlaşılmaz bir olduğunu düşünmeleri iyidir. Zira hemen hiçbir zaman seni neysen o olarak göremezler.

En çok da entelektüeller, akademisyenler, yazarlar yanlış anlaşılıyor sanki?
Kaidesi mızıkçılık olan bir oyunu oynayanlar, yazarın da mızıkçı olduğunu sanırlar.

TAVUS GÖSTERİŞLİDİR FAKAT SOLUCAN YER

İnsan şikayet etmeye başladı mı duramıyor... Mızıkçılıktan çok öte meseleler var fakat galiba?
İnsanlar hakikati söylemekte tembeldirler. Birinin acı gerçeği söylemesi lazım. Hukuku hep kendi hakkımızı aramanın metodu olarak görürüz. Halbuki asıl mesele bizim kimseye haksızlık etmeden yaşamayı öğrenmemizdir. Kendi kişiliğimizi temiz tutma bilgisine ulaşmamızdır.

Kimseye haksızlık etmeden yaşamaya çalışmıyor muyuz?
Nerdeee?.. Bir yangın çıksın, kırk yağma başlar.

Bu bozuk düzen içinde yükselmeyi, zenginleşmeyi başaranlara ne dersiniz?
Tavus gösterişlidir fakat solucan yer.

İşimiz zor, ha?..
Öyle... Neye şaşıyorum biliyor musunuz Murat Beyciğim?

Neye üstat?

Yalaka olmayan kişilerin bile kendilerine yalakalık edilmesini sevmelerine.

Kendini beğenmişlik, egosantriklik, megalomani, böbürlenme, nasisizm, kibir... Bunlar aslında birer yük, birer engel... Yanılıyor muyum?
Gel de anlat... Kendi önemimize öyle inanıyoruz ki, gök gürlese üstümüze alınıyor, Mikail bizi tehdit ediyor sanıyoruz!

BAĞNAZLARIN İKİYÜZLÜLÜĞÜ MEŞHURDUR

Toplumdan söz ederken birçok hastalığa aynı dönemde yakalanmış bir hastayı tarif ediyor gibisiniz?
Ne yapalım ki bu böyle. Muhakeme zayıf, ahlak düşük, hafıza yok...

Sizin gibi nazik, ihtimamlı ve toleranslı bir beyefendinin cemiyete dair bu tür menfi intibalar edinmesi enteresan...
Sorunları inkar ederek doğruya yaklaşamayız Murat Bey...

Evet...
Hiç şaşmayan bir intizam ile işlediğini gördüğümüz beşeri bir kanun vardır...

Neymiş?
Nerede zekâ umarsak orada ahmaklıkla karşılaşırız. Nerede sadakat beklersek orada ihanete uğrarız. Nerede kibarlık ararsak orada bayağılığa rastlarız. Kime dostluk gösterirsek ondan husumet görürüz.

Bildiğim kadarıyla siz şikayetten, şikayetçilerden de pek hazzetmiyorsunuz...
Tenkit ile kara çalma, tespit ile çamur atma apayrı şeyler. Kişisel ve afaki görüşlerini herkesi ilgilendiren kesin bilgiler gibi sunanlar aslında insanları sömürme sevdasındadırlar.

Siz iyiye gidişi mümkün kılmak niyetiyle tespitlerde bulunuyorsunuz, öyle mi?
Ümidim o cihette… Tek tek insanları suçlamak istemem. Kaldı ki başkalarının ahlaksız olduğunu söyleyen kimsenin ahlaka ihanet etmiş olma ihtimali pek kuvvetlidir.

Ve?
Bağnazların ikiyüzlülüğü meşhurdur.

-EDEBİYATTAN BAHSEDELİM… ROMAN NEDİR?

ROMAN: RUHUN LEZİZ GIDASI

Sizce metni önemli kılan nedir?

Bir eserin ehemmiyetli tarafı, başkasının yazamayacağı kısmıdır.

"Başkasının yazamayacağı" derken benzersizliği, orijinalliği mi kastediyorsunuz, yoksa ifade gücünü mü?

Daha ziyade anlatımdaki yetkinliği kastediyorum. Yazar hiç kimseye benzememeli. Fakat metin hiçbir şeye benzemezse olmaz.

Çoğu kimse romanı eğlenmek için okunan, sonra da unutulan bir anlatı olarak görüyor. Romanın başka hiçbir yerden temin edilemeyecek bir faydası var mıdır?
Roman göz önünde olmayan gerçekleri araştırır. Roman kimseyi incitmeden insanı kurcalar. İnsanın bilinçaltına iner, aklından geçenleri duyar ve duyurur.

Romanı entelektüelin beslenme çantasında muhakkak bulunması gereken bir gıda olarak görüyorsunuz demek?
Romanın besleyici niteliğini fark etmemek büyük kayıptır. Zira roman edebî türlerin hepsinden tatlar barındıran, leziz bir gıdadır.

"Besleyici ve leziz" derken, romanların hem düşünce hem duygu eşliğinde okunmasından mı söz ediyorsunuz?
Evet. Çocukken okuduğumuz romanların kahramanlarını ömür boyu hatırlarız.

Gençlikte okunan kitaplar?
Gençken okuduğumuz kitaplar bizi çok etkiler ve onların yazarlarını üstat kabul ederiz.

Kitap okurlarının belirgin bir özelliği var mı? Okuyan birini nasıl tanırız?
İyi kitaplar okuyan kişiler, günlük laflamalardan, dedikodulardan hoşlanmaz. Ve kendi zamanını yabancılara karşı müdafaa etmeye bakar.

Bu müdafaa hususu enteresanmış...
Eeee, münevver, cemiyet karşısında nefsini müdafaa etmek durumunda. Belirsizlik ve karanlık içinde yaşamaya alışkın kimselere karşı yani.

BARIŞÇIL DELİLİK

Romanın başka ne gibi fonksiyonları var?
Hayal ile hakikati buluşturur roman. İsabetli hayaller kurmaya yöneltir bizi. Birey ve toplum olarak gerçeği neresinden tutup nasıl değiştireceğimizi fark etmemizi sağlar.

İyi bir eser verebilmenin başlıca koşulu nedir?
Sanat eserini güçlü ve zengin kılan şey barışçıl bir deliliktir.

Yazarların neye dikkat etmesi gerek sizce?
Yazarın eserini kalabalıkların beğeneceği bir şekle sokmaya çalışması abestir. Doğrusu, toplumun yazarı anlayacak seviyeye taşınmasıdır. Aksi takdirde yazar da toplum da zarara uğrar.

Bu durumda yazarlara tavsiyeniz?..
Anlaşılmamaktan ve kötülenmekten ötürü üzülmesinler. İleride onları anlamadan övenler çoğalacaktır!

Yazar ile iktidar ilişkisine nasıl bakıyorsunuz?
Hükümdarlar karşısında sanatçı gururunu en iyi ifade eden kişi Voltaire veya Hugo değil Fuzuli'dir. Der ki:
"Her cihetten fariğim, âlemde hâşâ kim ola
Rızk için ehl-i beka ehli fenanın çâkeri"

Yani?
Her bakımdan rahat ve yüceyim ben, dünyada
Ölümsüzler kul olmaz fanilere rızk uğruna.

Fakat muktedirlere yakın duran yazarların sayısı hiç de az değil?
Peh... Entelektüeller, otoriter idareye müsamaha etseler bile, o idare tarafından makbul görülmezler.

Ya müsamaha göstermekten öte, otoriter idareye râm olanlar?
Eh, onlar zaten makbul olmadıklarını bu tutumlarıyla ispat etmişlerdir.

Sanırım, güçlünün yanında durunca emniyette hissediyor, ödüllendirileceklerini umuyorlar… Demek ki yüreksiz oldukları kadar beyinsizler de. Yahu bize iyi bir gelecek vaat edenler, çoğunlukla kendi geleceklerinden habersizdirler. Açık söyleyeyim...

'YARIN' CADDESİ, 'DAHA SONRA' SOKAĞI, 'HİÇBİR ŞEY' ŞATOSU

Edebiyat teorisine yaklaşımınız nasıl?
Her şeyden ziyade esere bakmayı önemserim. Zira sanatta kuramların doğruluğunu eserler kanıtlar.

Marcel Proust'u sevdiğiniz malum. Yerli yazarlardan kimi çok seversiniz?
Yakup Kadri Bey'i.

Ne yapsak, hayattan beyhudeliği tümden silemiyoruz...
Orası öyle. Kendimizi oyalamak ve avutmak için yapabileceğimiz en iyi şey çalışmaktır.

Çalışmayı salık vermek... Klişe olmadı mı üstat?
O takdirde biraz açayım: Müjdeler ve iyi sürprizleri cezbeder çalışmak. Piyangoyla, avantayla yaşanan hayatta canlılık bulunmaz. Senin emeğinin, eserinin etkilerinden doğan beklenmedik sonuçlardadır hayatın tadı. Senin asıl hayatın odur. Sevdiğim bir İspanyol atasözü vardır...

Nedir?
"Yarın Caddesi ve Daha Sonra Sokağı, insanı Hiçbir Şey Şatosu'na götürür!"

KÜÇÜK SEBEPLER, BÜYÜK NETİCELER

İyiymiş. Yani diyorsunuz ki...

Eşe dosta, daha doğrusu şeytana uyup da çalışmayı ihmal etmeyiniz!

Piyangodan kötü bir şeymiş gibi bahsettiniz az önce. Neden?

Talih ve talihsizliği ayırt edemeyiz bazen.

Ve?

Kaybedenler bazen kazananlara benzer.

Bir insan çalışmadan, hak etmediği, emeğinin karşılığı olmayan bir servete konuverse fena mı?

Hak edilmemiş kazanç, tüm insanlıkla dostluğumuzu, bitirir. Yalnız ve yabancı bir mahluka dönüştürür bizi.

Ooovvvv, fenaymış hakikaten.

Hayatın kârı nerede biter, iflası nerede başlar?.. Bunu kim bilebilir?..

Tabiatı tahrip ede ede güzel manzaralardan, seslerden ve kokulardan mahrum kaldık... Etikten, erdemden uzak, bilgisiz ve bilinçsiz olmak yaşam kalitemizi düşürüyor, ha?
Daha da acayibi, kimileri yaşamıyor da hâlâ bir 'yaşama hazırlanma' devresinde bulunuyor.

Problemler de, çözümler de basit görünüyor… Yani sizin sözleriniz bana böyle düşündürdü.
Öyle… Çok da karmaşık değil. Sebeplerin küçüklüğüne karşılık neticelerin büyüklüğü… Bu fark karıştırıyor kafamızı.

Hayatlarımız arasında farktan ziyade benzerlik mi var dersiniz?
Kesinlikle evet. İnsanlar başlarına gelenlerle değil, bunlara verdikleri reaksiyonlarla birbirlerinden ayrılır.

OHHH... BURANIN MANZARASI HÂLÂ GÖZÜ GÖNLÜ OKŞUYOR...
İNSANIN CENNETİ ÇOCUKLUĞUNUN GEÇTİĞİ YERLERDİR.
ORADA, DÜNYANIN BAŞKA BİR YERİNDE RASTGELMEYECEĞİMİZ BİR MUCİZE BULURUZ.
SAHİDEN ÖYLE GALİBA...
İSTANBUL'DA YAŞAYANLAR İKİ ŞEYİ HİSSEDERLER: TARİH VE TABİAT.
BU İKİSİNİ YAŞATABİLİRSEK İSTANBUL SAĞLIĞINI KORUR ANCAK.

İstanbul'u bunca sevmenizin nedeni...
İstanbul, insanı gafletten uyandırır, ona bilinç aşılar. İstanbul'u evliyaya benzeyen bir akrabayı seven çocuk gibi severiz.

Sizin çocukluğunuzdaki İstanbul'u biz eski romanlardan biliyoruz. Fakat bizim fark edemediğimiz bir özelliği var sanki o İstanbul'un...
Fark edemediğinizi fark etmeniz takdire şayan. Eski İstanbul'da tabii güzellikler daha çoktu, hava daha temizdi, nüfus daha azdı, köyden göç etmiş kişiler şehre hakim olmamıştı... fakat hakikaten sizlerin kolay saptayamayacağınız bir özelliği daha vardı şehrin.

Neydi o?
İstanbul dağınıktı. Yani semtlerin birbiriyle irtibatı yoktu. Fatih ile Harbiye birbirine sahiden uzaktı. Hem bunca bina yoktu hem de otomobil yoktu!

Biz trafik sıkışıklığından kahroluyoruz. Tüm arabalar bir anda yok oluverse, hiç fena olmazmış...
Semtlerin birbirine uzak olması, onlara ayrı bir değer katardı. İstanbul'un her mahallesi diğerlerine merak besler, sanki hasret çekerdi. Biz İstanbul'un herhangi bir yerinde, başka bir semtin daüssılasını duyardık.

Sürat, bazı şeylerin tadını kaçırdı, ha?
Hislerimizin hiçbirini doya doya duymaya, işlemeye vaktimiz kalmıyor. Şehir hayatı, günlerimizi birer göç arabası gibi her çeşit yüklerle tıklım tıklım dolduruyor.

Böylece?
Günlerimiz duygudan yana fakirleşiyor, acınacak şey.

Mimari de sorunlu maalesef.

Şehrin, insanı tabiattan büsbütün koparması bir felakettir. Şehir ağaçsızlık, çiçeksizlik demek midir? İstanbul'da artık insanlar mevsimlerin değişmesini bile idrak edemiyorlar. Halbuki mevsimler bizim tattığımız zevkleri değiştirir. Mesela hayvanları sevecek, onları düşünecek halimiz kalmadı. Çok yazık…

Sizin durduğunuz yerden bakınca, her şey daha hüzünlü, daha moral bozucu görünüyor anlaşılan.
Belki de… Öyle gafil yaşarız ki, çok kere saadetimizi kaybettikten ve felaketimizi geçtikten sonra fark ederiz.

Bilgi çağında bile duygu ve düşüncelerimizi netleştiremiyoruz. Aydınlanmak şaşılacak derecede zor. Neden böyle?
İnsanız çünkü. Bir insan kafası bütün ömrü boyunca ancak beş on defa böyle tamamen uyanır, aydınlanır ve her şeyi anlar. Fakat zarar yok, çünkü talihimiz hakkında vuzuhlu bir fikir edinmemiz için işte bu kadarı bize yarar ve yeter.

SADAKATİN ŞARTI AYRILIK

Toplum ile birey arasında ne fark var? Yani birey iyi de toplum mu kötü?
Size bir şey söyleyeyim mi… Cemiyetimiz her ferdiyle ıstırap çekiyor bana sorarsanız. Ve bu hal karşısında enikonu aciziz.

Aciz miyiz?
E öyle… Kaderimizin sınırlarını hissettiğimizi düşünüyorum. Hayata söz dinletemiyoruz, kafa tutamıyoruz.

Günümüzde motivasyon çok önemseniyor. Herkese, hepimize "Yapabilirsin, başarabilirsin, değerlisin…" deniliyor…
Züğürt tesellisi, zavallı beşeriyetin başlıca gıdasıdır.

Hay Allah... Umutlu, iç açıcı bir söz lütfedin üstat.
Şunu söyleyebilirim: Yoksulluk muhtaç olmayı gerektirmez. Hüzün de mutsuzluk değildir.

Sizin de ümitleriniz, hayalleriniz var, değil mi?
Elbette, hepimiz geleceğe dair hayaller kurarız. Hatta ömrümüzün bir kısmı o hayal âleminde geçer.

Neymiş bu hayaller?
Bilhassa aşka dair hayaller... Asla kavuşamayacak kadınlar ve erkekler, birbirlerine uzaktan öpücükler gönderirler.

Uzaktan öpücük mü? Yakınlaşınca hayaller dağılıp gidiyor mu, nedir?
Ne yazık ki. Sevgililerimiz arasında en çok, elimizi eline hiç değmediğimiz ve sonra izini tümden kaybettiklerimize sadık kalır gönlümüz.

Fazlasıyla tuhaf... Sadakat, ayrılıkla mı mukayyet?!
Üstüne bastınız.

Sizin zamanınızda erkekler ile kadınlar pek biraraya gelemiyordu, ha?
Cumhuriyetten sonra İstanbul bir nebze nefes aldı. Öncesinde bir kadın vücudunun bir zerresini görebilmek, teleskopla göklerde Merih veya Zühre'nin bir parçasını görmek kadar nadir ve tesirliydi.

SEVGİLİM SAĞ OLSUN DA...

Gene de eserlerinizde nostalji hakim. Mazide pek de heyecan yokmuş aslında?
Yaşadığımız zamanın bize mutluluk veremediği hissiyle, mutluluğu ya geçmişte yahut gelecekte hayal ederiz. Burada mühim olan tasavvurdur. İnsanın zihninde mutluluk sahneleri olması iyidir yani.

Sizin gönlünüzdeki sevgili nasıl biri?
Boyumuzu aşan şeyleri, elle tutamadığımız ruhları, hülasa kendimizden yüksek mefhumları sevmeye alışkınız ve erişemeyeceğimiz sevgililere âşığızdır.

Bir sevgiliden ne beklemeliyiz?
Sevgilimizin bize yapabileceği en büyük iyilik, sıhhatini muhafaza etmesidir.

Hep böyle görülemeyen, ulaşılamayan, erişilemeyen, yapılamayan şeylerle mi dolu hayat?
Değil mi? Asıl sözlerimiz de söylenmemiş kalanlardır. Başkalarının duymadıkları ve eğer söyleyebilmiş olsak hem onları, hem de kendimizi şaşırtacak olanlardır. Bunları hiçbir zaman söyleyemeyiz.

O halde ömrün yarıdan fazlası hayalle, ümitle, aldanışla geçiyor?

Dünyayı ve hayatı herkes kendine göre tefsir eder. Birçok ahmaklar dünyanın kendi kafalarına göre kurulup düzeleceğini beklerler. Birçok beceriksizler de iş başına kendileri geldi mi, hemen her işin yoluna gireceğini zannederler. Birçok yabaniler kendi dehâlarına inanırlar.

Ah yazık ya...

Hayalci birçok müflisler zengin olmak ve birçok ölüm döşeğindeki birçok hastalar şifa bulmak arifesinde yaşadıklarını sanırlar. Birçok mütekaitler takdir olunmamış faziletlerinin manevi iradıyla geçinerek şereflerinin servetini bol bol tadarlar.

HAYAT KURTARAN YARI-DELİLİK

Hayal iki çeşit mi acaba? Yani gerçeği dönüştürme hazırlığı niteliğindeki hayal ile gerçeği çarpıtıp bizi yanılgıya sürükleyen hayal?
İsabet buyurdunuz. Lakin bilgi de hayal kadar yanıltır bazen.

Nasıl?
Bilgimiz ve görgümüz arttıkça, olayların arkasında zekice planlar olduğunu düşünürüz. Olup bitenin ahmaklık ve bayağılıktan neşet ettiğini göremeyiz.

Hah hah haaa... Akıllılar, aptalları zeki zannediyor yani?
Dengeli görülenler de yarı deli, yarı iradelidir. Belki bizi kurtaran da bu yarı deliliğimizdir.

Çok acayipmiş...
Sıhhatimizin ve zihnimizin dengesi bir ince tel üstünde perendeler atan bir cambazın dengesine benzer. Bozulmaya hazırdır.

Herkes dengesini zaman zaman veya en nihayetinde kaybeder mi dersiniz?
Hayata, vücut gibi, zihin de dayanamıyor. Zihin bozulunca bütün oyun değişiyor. Hayat bir felaket oluyor.

Tecrübelerimiz bizi maddi ve manevi bakımlardan sağlamlaştırmaz mı peki?
Tecrübe acı derslerden edindiğimiz bilgidir daha ziyade. Bu bilgiye de tam güvenemeyiz. Yani ders alma kabiliyetimiz eksiktir. Böylece belalar tekerrür eder. Tecrübeler hep ziyan olur.

Devir değiştikçe, zaman ilerledikçe tecrübeyle gelen bilgi kökleşmez mi?
Nasıl kökleşsin? Tecrübeler babalara kâr etse bile oğullara

miras kalmaz ki. Bir nesil öteki neslin aldığı derslerden haberdar bile olamaz. Onun da her acı tecrübeyi bizzat tekrar etmesi lâzım gelir.

AHMAKLAR DAHA AHMAK, ZEKİLER DAHA ZEKİ

Hemen herkesin düştüğü bir duruma örnek verebilir misiniz?
Mesela... Maziye bakınca çoğu kere aklımızın yetmediğini idrak ederiz.

Bu da değiştiğimiz anlamına geliyor sanırım?
Elbette. Hayat duygu ve düşüncelerimizi yoğurup değiştirir.

Değişmeyi, evrilmeyi, dönüşmeyi olumsuz sayanlara ne demeli?
Değişimi inkar etmek, hayata karşı ölümle ittifak kurmaya varır.

Hayata tat katan sürprizleri, çalışkanlıktan başka hangi erden davet eder?
Cömertlik. Açgözlü, cimri ve eline para geçirmiş kimselerin tek kazancı, ölümün kucağına tok gitmektir.

Sevgili Abdülhak Şinasi Bey, bana insanlar hakkında hep aklımda tutmam gereken, yararlı bir bilgi verebilir misiniz?
İnsanların çoğu zannettiğimiz kadar ahmak ve ahlaksız değildirler. Zannettiğimizden daha ahmak ve ahlaksızdırlar. Buna karşılık bir kısmı da zannettiğimiz kadar iyi ve zeki değildirler. Zannettiğimizden daha iyi ve zekidirler.

A-ha? Bu sözünüz cidden zihnimde kıvılcımlar çaktırdı. Peki hayata dair ilginç bir gözleminiz...
Gördüğüm kadarıyla cesaret için acemilik, başarı içinse cesaret gerekiyor!

Ah hah hah haaa! Az önce gençken okuduğumuz kitapların yazarlarını üstat kabul ettiğimizi söylediniz ya. Ona takıldım. Hakikaten öyle oluyor. Bu hususta bir ikazınız var mı?
İnsanları bir inancın veya ideolojinin aşılmaz öncüleri, anıtsal kahramanları değil 'kişi' olarak görünüz.

Bilerek veya bilmeyerek birbirimizi aldatıyor muyuz?
Bu, meselenin bir yönü. Bir de… insan en uzun süre kendini aldatabiliyor.

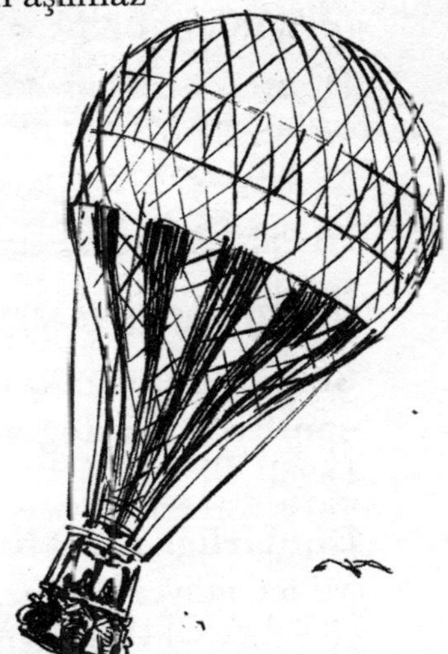

BİR TUTAM RÜYA MAYASI

Sizin muhafazakar, dindar biri olduğunuz sanılıyor. Bu doğru mu?
Değil.

Dindarlığa nasıl bakıyorsunuz?
Mütemadiyen namaz, oruç gibi dinin emirlerini yerine getirmeye dikkat eden, bu hususta pek ihtiyatlı görünen kimselerin çok azında sıhhatli bir ruhun zarafetine rastladım. Dinibütün olmakla insan tamam olmuyor. İnanca sıkı yapışmakla kemale ereceğini düşünen kimselerde daimî bir noksanlık kalıyor.

Bir yazar olarak yanlış anlaşıldığınızı düşünüyor musunuz?
Hiç şüphesiz! Sanırız ki düşüncemizi takdir edecekler, sözümüzü anlayacaklar; doğru hareket edersek, lehimize şahadet edeceklerdir. Aldanırız! Hemen daima bunun aksi sabit olur. Hayatımızın her anında yapayalnız kalırız. Çağırırız ve hiç kimse imdadımıza gelmez. Muhitimiz bize karşı her an kör, sağır ve şuursuzdur.

Peki sonuç?
N§ice yorgun ıstıraplar veya hummalı ihtiraslarla geçen bir hayattan, hafızalarda pek az bir şey kalıyor! Ateşten

arta kalan küller gibi… Vücut toprağa ancak birkaç avuç toprak daha katıyor! Ve her ruh hafızalarda ancak bir tutam rüya mayası bırakıyor!

Ve de?..

Biz, tüm insanlar, yeryüzünün en büyük suçluları gibi ölüm cezasına mahkumuz.

GALAKSİ BEYEFENDİSİ
ISAAC ASIMOV
1971, Galaksi kırsalı.
3 ROBOT YASASI
ROBOT İNSANA ZARAR VERMEZ. ZARAR VERİLMESİNE GÖZ YUMMAZ
1. KURALLA ÇELİŞMEDİKÇE İNSANIN EMİRLERİNİ YERİNE GETİRİR
İLK İKİ KURALLA ÇELİŞMEDİKÇE KENDİ VARLIĞINI KORUR.
ODR 10
1970'LERE BAYILIYORUM.
ASIMOV
FOUNDATION TRILOGY
HIH... BUGÜNÜN DÜNYASI 30 YIL SONRASININ ÇOCUKLARINA HİÇBİR ŞEY İFADE ETMEYECEK.

Isaac Asimow [1920-1992]
Dünyanın en ilginç yazarlarından. 500'den fazla kitap yazdı. Bilim-kurgu edebiyatının en önemli ustası kabul edilir. Nebula Ödülü ve Hugo Ödülü'nü defalarca aldı. Biyo-kimya uzmanıydı. Romanları, bilimsel gelişmelere yön vermiş, katkı sunmuştur. Robotlar hakkında yazdıkları, bu konudaki en etkili ve etkileyici eserlerdir. *Vakıf* serisiyle, dünya dışında sürdürülen insan hayatını romanlaştırdı. Asimov'un hayalleri ve öngörüleri, gerçekleşmeye devam ediyor.

ESRARENGİZ BİR SANAT: OKURYAZARLIK

Pekala... yazarlık nedir?
Birçok şeydir. Fakat hepsinden ziyade yazarlık, bir yalnızlık mesleğidir.

Yazarın başlıca özelliği nedir?
Bir yazar, yazmaya daima hazır olmalıdır.

Yazmaya meraklı biri kendini nasıl geliştirebilir?
Başka yazarları okuyarak. Okumak, yazmaktan daha

önemlidir. Herkes birşeyler okur, birşeyler yazar. Fakat gerçek okuryazarlık esrarengiz bir sanattır.

Roman yazarken not tutar mısınız?
Daktilo başında değilken de zihnimden yazılar akar. Hiçbir şeyi unutmadığım için not tutmam gerekmez.

Fütürist romanlar, hikayeler yazdınız. Fakat üslubunuz biraz... eski mi ne?
Aynen öyle. Dumas'nın, Dickens'ın eserlerini 5'er, 6'şar kez okudum. 19. yy. İngiliz romanlarının birçoğunu hatmettim. Agatha Christie ve P.G. Wodehouse'ı severim. Modern romanları pek okumadım. Bu nedenle, eski tarz bir anlatımla bilim-kurgu romanları yazıyorum.

Yazmayı çok seviyorsunuz...
Çünkü ne yazacağımı bilmiyorum. Sonunu merak ediyorum. Yazmakta olduğum kitaba okur gözüyle bakıyorum yani. Daktilom mıknatıs gibi çekiyor beni. Doktorum 6 ay ömrüm kaldığını söylese, daha hızlı yazardım.

1966'de *Vakıf* serisiyle, J.R.R. Tolkien'in *Yüzüklerin*

***Efendisi*'ni geride bırakarak Hugo Ödülü aldınız. Nebula Ödülü, Büyük Usta Ödülü... ve daha 10'larca ödül...**
Evet... Uçak korkum olmasa, daha çok seyahat edebilsem, daha fazla ödülüm olacaktı, heh heh...

SAÇ STİLİM SAYESİNDE MEŞHURUM

Kitaplarınız 50'den fazla dile çevrildi. Türkçe'de de 100'e yakın kitabınız var...
Evet... Gösterişli favorilerim sayesinde de her yerde tanınıyorum.

***Asimov'un Mizah Hazinesi* adlı bir fıkra kitabı yazmanız beni şaşırtmıştı.**
Komik, değil mi?

Çocuklara yönelik kitaplar da yazdınız...
Evet. Onları küçük görmediğiniz takdirde, çocuklar için kitap yazmak kolaydır.

Bir yazar sizin hakkınızda "Kendi kitaplarının tümünü okumaya kalksa, yazmaya zamanı kalmaz" demişti...
Ha ha ha... Aslında, başkalarının kitaplarını okumaya da zaman bulamıyorum. Hah haaa...

Aynı anda iki roman yazdığınız doğru mu Mr. Asimov? İki masada birer daktilo varmış ve siz tekerlekli sandalyede oturuyormuşsunuz. Roman yazarken takılacak olursanız, diğer masaya geçip öbür romanı yazıyormuşsunuz?
Enteresan, değil mi?! Bu yöntemi uyguladığım oldu, evet. Fakat her zaman değil.

Müzikle aranız nasıl? En sevdiğiniz besteci kim?
Çaykovski. Beni mutlu den bir müzik duyduğumda bilirim ki bu Çaykovski'dir.

OKULLARI HEP SINIF ATLAYARAK OKUDUNUZ. ÜSTÜN ZEKALI BİR ÇOCUK MUYDUNUZ?
HÂLÂ ÖYLEYİM.
FOTOGRAFİK HAFIZA?
VAR, OLMAZ MI? HEH HEH...

BİRÇOKLARINA GÖRE GELMİŞ GEÇMİŞ EN BÜYÜK BİLİMKURGU YAZARISINIZ. FAKAT AYNI ZAMANDA BİR BİLİM İNSANISINIZ. SİZE GÖRE BİLİMKURGUYU ÖNEMLİ KILAN NE?
BİLİMKURGU, TOPLUMLARIN DEĞİŞECEĞİ FİKRİNİ BARINDIRIYOR.
DÜŞÜNCE, DUYGU, İFADE VE DAVRANIŞ BİÇİMLERİ DEĞİŞMİŞ BİR TOPLUMA, BİLİMKURGU SAYESİNDE BAKIYORUZ.
FANTEZİ DEĞİL, GERÇEĞİ ARAYAN BİR AKIL YÜRÜTME SÖZ KONUSU.
STRAND BOOKSTORE
OLD RARE NEW
STRAND BOOKSTOR
HEPSİ BU MU?
BİLİMKURGU, SİHRİN EĞLENCESİ İLE BİLİMİN DİSİPLİNİNİ BİRARADA SUNAR.
BİLİM SİZİN İÇİN NE İFADE EDİYOR?
KESİN OLAN ŞU Kİ, İNSANLIĞA EN BÜYÜK FAYDAYI BİLİM SUNMUŞTUR. BİLGİ YALNIZCA GÜÇ DEĞİL, AYNI ZAMANDA MUTLULUKTUR. BİLGİNİN SİZE SUNULMASI İSE SEVİLMEKLE EŞDEĞERDİR.
VE?
BİLİMSEL GERÇEKLİK HER TÜRLÜ İHANETİN VE SADAKATİN ÖTESİNDEDİR.

BİLİM İNSANLARI "BULDUM! BULDUM!" DEMEZ

Bilimin temel özelliği ne?
Carl Sagan'ın da dediği gibi "Bilim bir bilgi yığını değil, bir düşünme biçimidir."

Bilimsel düşünmek derken...
Olgular, teoriler ve yasalar eşliğinde düşünmekten söz ediyorum.

Bilimsel çalışmalar, hayatın bir parçası. Dolayısıyla bilimin de bir hikayesi var, yanılıyor muyum?
Haklısınız, Murat. Bilimsel faaliyetler beşerî olanaklar içinde yürütülüyor. Öte yandan, bilime dışarıdan bakarken öykü klişelerini bir kenara bırakmak iyi olur.

Ne gibi?
Bilim insanları yeni bir şey keşfedip heyecanlandıklarında "Buldum, buldum!" demezler mesela.

Ne derler?
"Hoppalaaa! Bu amma acayip bir şey!" derler. Hah hah haaa!

Bilimin, fen bilimleriyle iştigal etmeyen bizlere katkısını net göremiyoruz sanırım...
Buna itiraz etmeyeceğim. Düşünün ki bilim dünya nüfusunun büyük çoğunluğuna eğitim ve sanatın ulaşmasını sağlamıştır.

Bilim-kurgu yazarı ve biyokimya uzmanısınız. Bu ikisi arasındaki bağdan bahsetseniz...
En etkili güç, bilgi ile hayalgücünün ittifakından doğar. Bilimsel çalışma, ümitlerin, endişelerin, ideallerin... etkisiyle biçimlenir.

Bilim insanlarının bir derdin devasını aramak veya bir sevinci yaygınlaştırmak gibi motivasyonları var, ha?

Kesinlikle. Mucize beklemek hem kolaycılık hem tembelliktir. Etik bakımdan sorunlu bir tutum yani. Fakat bir ideal uğruna sistemli bir çalışma, bizi iyiye yaklaştırır.

Güzel söylediniz Üstat Asimov...
Kaldı ki mucizeler gerçekleşmez, idealler gerçekleşir.

CEHALET, DEMOKRATİK BİR HAK DEĞİLDİR

Şüphenin değerine sık sık vurgu yapıyorsunuz...
Evet. Çok şükür, şüpheci biriyim. Fakat belirtmem gerekir ki bilgiden kaynaklanan şüphe ile cehaletten doğan şüphe birbirinden tümüyle farklıdır.

Cehalet, hayatımızda çok fazla yer kaplıyor, ha?
Maalesef... Shakespeare gibi ben de dünyanın bir sahne olduğunu düşünüyorum. Bu oyunda kahraman bilim, kötü adam ise cehalet.

Cehalet sizi çok rahatsız ediyor...
Üzüyor da. Cehaletle ebedi nikah kıymış insanlar... kabuğundan çıkmadığı için tüm evreni yeşil sanan bezelye taneleri gibiler.

Peki cahil kimseler bu hayatta nasıl tutunabiliyor, hatta servete, makama, üne kavuşuyor?
Çünkü çoğunluktalar. Cahil ve önyargılı toplumumuz, neye alışmışsa onu "en iyi" kabul ediyor.

Birçok olgu da yanlış anlaşılıyor, değil mi?
Hem de nasıl! Bilime ve düşünceye karşı çıkmayı; savaşı yüceltmeyi, ırkçılığı, baskıcılığı... insani ve meşru görenler var, baksanıza.

Savaş demişken, savaşlar nasıl son bulur?
Dünyadaki tüm savaşlarda yenilen ordunun komutanlarını derhal idam etme kuralı konsa, savaşların sayısı epey azalır.

Emin misiniz?
Hiç kuşkusuz. Savaş, birtakım açgözlülerin, ölümü gençlere reva görmesidir.

Cehaleti demokratik hak gibi görenlere dönersek...
"Benim cehaletim, sizin bilginiz kadar iyidir" iddiasında bulunan kimseyi şımartmakta bir yarar göremiyorum.

YALNIZLIĞA SÜRÜKLEYEN BİLGİSİZLİK

Fakat bilim cahillerin de hizmetinde?..
Kuşkusuz öyle. Bilim sayesinde şifa bulan, dünyanın bir ucundan diğerine giden, iletişim kuran... kimseler pekala bilime 'şüpheyle' yaklaşabiliyor. Karanlıkta yaşayanların ışığı reddetmesi, ışığa ihtiyaç duymadıkları manasına gelmez. Bilgisizliğe dayalı inat hiçbir şey kanıtlamaz.

Sonuçta sadece gevezelik etmiş mi oluyorlar?
Zaman kaybettiriyorlar. Gelgelelim aptallık enerjisiyle ulaşılamayacak bölgeler vardır. Bunu bilmek beni ferahlatıyor.

Gene de biraz gıcık kapıyorsunuz galiba?
E herhalde! Ne zaman birisi belli bir alanda pek bilgi sahibi olmadığını söyleyerek konuya girse, hemen ardından o konudaki kesin fikrini belirtiyor!

Yazık aslında...
Yazık elbet. Aynı zamanda moral bozucu. Bakınız, insana güvenmek 'medeni cesaret' gerektirir. Medeni cesaretin ardında özgüven vardır. Onun da destekçisi bilgidir. Bizleri yalnızlığa sürükleyen, bilgisizlikten doğan güvensizlik ve ödlekliktir. Böylece insan insandan korkar. Bu mesnetsiz korkuyla boşa geçirilen zaman içinde, çoğu kimse açgözlü, kıskanç ve saldırgan yaratıklara dönüşür.

Dahası?
Ateşe körükle giden kişi, bir alev göremezse yangını kendisi çıkarır.

Ve?
Her şeyi bildiğini sananlar baş belasıdır.

Zamanla değişiyor insanlar fakat?
O da doğru. Fakat kimileri değişse de iyi bir insana dönüşmüyor.

Cahillerin çoğunlukta olduğunu söylediniz. Bu tespitiniz, toplumsal sorunların çokluğunu açıklıyor sanki?
Sorumluluktan ve özgürlükten köşe bucak kaçıyorlar. Bir toplum hata yaptığında bu sadece o topluma zarar vermez. Sonraki nesilleri de etkiler. Vaziyetin vahametini görüyorsunuz değil mi?

YÜKSEK SESLE TEKRARLANAN YALANLAR

Toplum bireylerden oluştuğuna göre... Birey olarak bağlı kalacağımız ve topluma fayda sağlayacak ilke...
Kararlarımızın ve eylemlerimizin sorumluluğunu başkalarının sırtına yüklememek. Bununla birlikte, bizim adımıza başkalarının karar alıp bize emir vermesine hevesli olmamak.

Başka?
Korkularımızın kararlarımızı etkilemesine izin vermemeliyiz.

Üç etti. Dördüncüsü?
Kendinizi eğlenceye ve kedere kaptırmayacak kadar metanetli olmaya bakınız.

Beşincisi?

Geleneksel kabulleriniz, doğru davranmanızı ve doğruyu söylemenizi engellemesin.

Bir de cömert olsak mı?
"Vermek, almaktan daha iyi" derdim, şayet bunlar iki ayrı eylem olsaydı. Halbuki birine sevgi, neşe, bilgi verdiğinizde siz de müspet hislere kavuşursunuz.

"Toplum" diyoruz fakat daha ziyade "kitle" hatta "sürü" konumundayız sanki. Neden böyle?
Yüksek sesle ve sık söylenen bariz yalanlara inanıveriyoruz da ondan.

İnsanlık tehlikede mi dersiniz?
İnsanlığın kendi kendini yok etme kapasitesine sahip olduğu muhakkak.

Yaşatma yetimizi de pek kullanmıyoruz... mu?
Homo Sapiens'in doğada hakim tür oluşu ona hayati bir mesuliyet yüklüyor: Biz insanlar tüm yaşam formlarına karşı mesulüz. Ve buna uygun davranmıyoruz. Dünyayı ve hayatı korumak için pek az şey yapıyoruz.

DÜNYAYI KURTARMAK İÇİN UZAYA AÇILMALIYIZ

İyi insan kimdir?
Bir başkasını mutlu edebilen kişidir. Bir başka insanı, bir ağacı, köpeği, güvercini...

Aklı başında insan kimdir?
Kendi sınırlarını bilen kişidir.

İnsanlar hakkında karamsar mısınız?
Bazen veya bazı konularda evet. Fakat esasen... kötü davranışlarda bulunanların bile özünde iyi olduğunu düşünürüm. Bu inanç, hayatımdaki neşe ve mutluluğu arttırıyor.

Kötümser değil misiniz? Az önce insanlığın kendini yok edebileceğini söylediniz?
Size, insanlığın yok olmasının kötü olduğunu düşündüren ne? Öyle bir durumda, diğer yaşam formları için daha hayırlı işler yapan bir tür öne çıkacaktır. Kötümser değilim. Kötümserlik hayattan zevk almayı engeller.

Bir keresinde "Dünya er geç yok olacak" demiştiniz?
N'olmuş?

Hiiiç?..

Sizin romanlarınızdaki gibi, katrilyonlarca insanın yaşadığı galaktik imparatorluklar mı kurulacak?
Ona daha var sanırım.... Dünyayı tümden kaybetmek istemiyorsak yapabileceğimiz en iyi iş hammadde ve yerleşim için uzaya açılmaktır. Böylece dünyada tarım alanları mahvedilmeyecek, işgaller ve sömürü ortadan kalkacaktır. Gezegenimizin kurtuluşuna ancak hümanistler öncülük edebilir. Arkasına yaslanıp mucize bekleyenler veya milliyetçi bir tutumla içe kapananlarda umut yok.

Nasıl olacak bu işler Sayın Asimov? Evrende bir zerreciğiz...
Fakat bu sonsuzluğun içinde oyun oynamıyoruz. Çalışıyoruz!

HİÇLİKTEN RANDIMAN ALAMAZSIN

Açıkçası, en çok siz bilim insanları çalışıyorsunuz. Biz daha ziyade kendimizi dinliyoruz. Bir sineğin vızıltısı da, gökyüzünde yalnız gezen yıldızlar da kederlendiriyor bizi...
Size ilginç bir şey söyleyeyim mi?

Lütfen.
İnsani duyguların en mühimi merhamet, en mühim davranış ise affetmektir.

Bunun evrenle ilgisi?..
Evrene olumlu mesajlar gönderirseniz, yıldızlar sizin hatırınız için şekilden şekle girer ve talihinizi açarlar.

Ne?! Şaka mı ediyorsunuz!?
Şaka tabii! Astroloji su katılmamış bir sahtekarlıktır. Fakat merhamet ve affetme konusunda ciddiyim. Merhamet, ilişkilerinize yumuşaklık getirir. Affetmek ise manevi yüklerden kurtarır sizi. Böylece doğru düzgün çalışabilirsiniz.

Astroloji, alternatif tıp, numeroloji gibi sözde-bilimlere neden itibar ediliyor?
Sanırım, aşamayacağı zorluklarla karşılaşan insanlar gerçeklikten uzaklaşıyorlar. Halbuki...

Halbuki ne?
Hiçlikten randıman alamazsınız.

Kurumsal dinleri de reddediyorsunuz...
Reddetmekten ziyade, kabul edemiyorum... "Bunlar Tanrı'nın sözleridir" diyen kimseye sorulacak ahlaki soru şudur: "Nereden biliyorsun?"

Dinî inanç ile bilim arasındaki ilişki hakkında ne söylersiniz?
Avrupa'daki katedrallerin tepesine paratoner takıldığında, rahiplerin bile kendi kutsiyetlerine değil de bilime güvendiklerini herkes gördü.

Hepsi bu mu?
Bilimsel kazanımları, dinle uyumlu kılmaya çabası, rahiplerin o asık suratlı hiyerarşisine taviz vermeye varır. Bu da etik değil, sorumsuzcadır. Müesses dinin üstünlük iddiası, bilimin ahlaki niteliğiyle çelişir.

MEZARA YEMEK SERVİSİ

Bilim, başından beri inanç sistemlerinden bir kopuş ve uzaklaşma faaliyeti mi?
Şu kadarını söyleyeyim, Hipokrat'a "Tıbbın babası" denir çünkü M.Ö. 5. asırda hastalığın "ilahi bir ceza" olduğu fikrini reddetmiştir.

Fakat dinî kabuller de insanlığın gelişiminin bir parçası, değil mi?
Meteorolojik ölçümler yapamıyor ve örneğin bulut tohumlama yoluyla yağış sağlayamıyorsanız, yağmur duasına çıkarsınız.

Bu kadar basit mi?
Bir düşün dostum, M.Ö. 200 bin civarında, ölüyle birlikte yiyecek ve içecekler de gömülüyordu. Görünüşe bakılırsa, Neandertaller hayatın ölümden sonra devam ettiği duygusu taşıyorlardı. Bunu dinin ortaya çıkışı

olarak düşünebiliriz. İşin aslı, evrende duyularımızla algıladığımızdan fazlasının olduğu fikri yabana atılacak bir şey değil. Fakat gerçeği keşfetme yolunda temennilerle ilerlemek ne yazık ki imkansızdır. Bir tek insanın his, tahmin veya hayalle vardığı sonucun, başkalarını alakadar etmesi beklenemez.

Peki ya peygamberler, kutsal kitaplar?
Kutsal kitaplar, dikkatle okuyan herkesi müthiş bir güçle ateizme iter.

Dolayısıyla siz de ateistsiniz...
Ben rasyonalist ve hümanistim. 'Ateist' kelimesini sevmiyorum. 'Tanrı karşıtı' değilim. Tanrı'yı aramıyorum da. Tanrı benden çok daha bilgili ve zeki olduğuna göre, o beni bulmalı.

Bir Tanrı kavramınız var anlaşılan?
Neden olmasın? Bence bir Tanrı, cehenneme ruhsat vermez.

Gene de varlığına inanmıyorsunuz?
Tanrı'nın, samimi bir inançsıza gücenmeyeceğini düşünüyorum.

CENNETTEKİ DAKTİLO

Musevi asıllısınız...
Evet. Bu da en çok Yahudilikteki akıl-dışı ögelere karşı olduğum anlamına gelir.

Kurumsal dinleri reddetmenizin asıl sebebi Yahudilik mi?
Benim için insan olmak ve insanlık mirasını üstlenmek önemli, Yahudi olmak değil. Bence hiçbir dinsel miras sayesinde kendimizi özel hissedip, bize insanlık mirasının sunduğu katkıyı görmezden gelmemeliyiz.

1984'te Amerikan Hümanistler Derneği'nin Başkanı seçildiniz...
Evet. İnsanların çoğu aslında hümanisttir bence. Fakat çocukluk şartlandırmaları veya toplum baskısı yüzünden dine bağlıymış gibi görünürler.

Öbür dünya?.. Cehennem, cennet ilginizi çekmiyor mu?
Cehennemde azap, cennette can sıkıntısı var. Dünyayı tercih ederim.

Cennet size sıkıcı mı görünüyor cidden?
Hem de nasıl! Kutsal metinlerdeki tariflere bakılırsa, enikonu bir mahrumiyet bölgesi. Entelektüel biri, cennetin her bölgesinde sıkıntıdan patlar.

Cenneti sıkıcılıktan kurtaracak şey ne olurdu?
Geçenlerde rüyamda, ölüp cennete gittiğimi gördüm...

A-ha?
Yaaa... Karşımdaki melek "Cennete hoşgeldiniz" dedi. "Fakat bir yanlışlık olmalı. Ben ateisttim?" dedim. Melek "Yanlışlık yok, kimin buraya kabul edileceğine biz karar veririz, sen değil" diye kestirip attı. Etrafa bakındım ve sordum: "Buralarda kullanabileceğim bir daktilo var mı?"

BİR İNSANIN YAPABİLECEKLERİ YAPTIKLARINDAN ÖNEMLİDİR

Hepimiz yaşlanıyoruz Mr. Asimov. Ve hayatın doğal akışı içinde çaresizleşiyoruz...
Ne yapalım?.. Yaşlılıkta ilginç bir yön var...

Nedir?
Gençliğinizden beri tanıyanlar sizi yaşlı biri olarak görmez. Onların gözünde gençsinizdir. Fakat arkadaşlarınızdan biri ölünce, sizin de gençliğinizin bir parçası yok olur...

Sizinle aynı dünya görüşünü paylaşmayan dostlarınız var mı?

Var, evet. Kimi dostlarım zamanla aşırı muhafazakar, hatta faşist bir tutumu benimsedi. Beni çileden çıkarıyorlar. Gene de aramızdaki sevgi bağı nedeniyle onlardan tümüyle kopamadım.

Tüm insanları değerli sayıyorsunuz, öyle mi?

Tüm insanlık, hiçbirini horgörmeye hakkımız olmayan komşularımızdır. Hiç kimse sorunlarının tümünü kendi başına çözemez. Mutsuzluktan tek başına kurtulmaya çabalamak, içinde bulunduğu bataklığı sopayla dövmeye benzer. Yani evet, kimseyi hiçe saymamak ve terk etmemek gerektiği fikrindeyim.

Bir insanı doğru tanımak için ne yapmalıyız?
Onun gelecekte, imkan bulduğunda neler yapabileceğini düşünün. Kapasitesi, potansiyeli, eğilimleri neye elveriyor? Sorun çıkaran, bozguncu, işlerin kötüye gitmesine sebep olacak biri mi? Yoksa harika işler başaracak, elindekini paylaşacak, yapıcı biri mi?

Yani yaptıklarına değil, yapabileceklerine mi bakmak gerek?
Bir insanın yaptıklarına bakarak hakkında hüküm vermek, tam anlamıyla yargıçlık taslamaktır. Onu yaşayan, değişme ve gelişme imkanına sahip bir varlık olarak görmemektir.

KENDİ KENDİNE ÖĞREN

Büyük işler başarmak için ne yapmalı?
Tarih yazmak istiyorsanız tarih okuyun.

Tarih mi?
Evet. Tarihten bir ipucu bulup çektiğinizde gerisi çorap söküğü gibi gelir.

Böylece mutluluğa erer miyiz?
Tarihte mutlu sonlar yoktur. Fakat bunu fark etmek iyidir.

Başkalarının desteği olmadan tüm sorunlarımızı çözemeyeceğimizi söylediniz. Öğrenmek için de geçerli mi bu?
Hayır. Öğrenmede kişinin kendi talebi ve çabası esastır. Kesinlikle inanıyorum ki asıl öğrenim insanın kendi kendine öğrenmesidir.

Herkes herşeyi öğrenemez yani?
Öyle demedim. Aksine, normal bir beyni olan herkesin çok şey öğrenebileceğine ve üst düzey entelektüel olabileceğine inanıyorum. Ne yazık ki çoğu kimse öğrenmek için sosyal teşvik veya onay bekliyor. Toplum da öğrenmeyi pek az destekliyor.

Ebeveynlerin, çocukları teşvik etmesi...
Lüzumlu tabii. Akıldan çıkarmamak gerekir ki çocuklarımız sahip olduğumuz birer mal değildir. Kimi anne-babaların bunu anlaması uzun zaman alıyor.

Biz ebeveynler, neyi gözden kaçırıyoruz?
Üstün başarı gibi, isabetli başarısızlık da vardır... Yani başarısızlık, başarıya giden yolda bir basamak olabilir. Bir yetersizlik, başka bir yeterliliğin işareti de olabilir.

HÜMANİST ROBOTLAR

Ebeveyn demişken, annenizle ilgili bir anekdot vardı... Neydi o, anlatır mısınız?
Memnuniyetle... Annem İngilizce yazma kursuna gitmişti. Yazmayı kısa zamanda öğrendi. Birgün öğretmeni sormuş: "Bayan Asimov, Isaac Asimov'la bir akrabalığınız var mı?" Annem de "Isaac benim sevgili oğlumdur" diye cevap vermiş. Öğretmen "Nasıl bu kadar iyi yazdığınız şimdi anlaşıldı" demiş. Bunun üzerine annem "Asıl, Isaac'in nasıl

iyi yazdığının anlaşılmış olması lazım" demiş. Hah haaa!

1950'de yayımlanan *Ben Robot*'ta öne sürdüğünüz Robotun Üç Yasası... Robotlar bu yasalara göre üretiliyor ve diğer bilimkurgu yazarları da sizin koyduğunuz üç yasaya uygun yazıyor hikayelerini...

Evet... Bir mimarlık dergisinde, bu yasaların insanın kullandığı tüm aletler için geçerli olduğunu yazdı biri. Robot yasaları, Frankenstein faktöründen kaçınabilmek için var... 1970'lerde, robotların kendilerini insan olarak gördüğü hikaye yazdım. Böylece robotların üç yasası, insanların üç yasasına dönüştü. Hümanizmi robotlara aşılamış olduk!

Robot Yasaları nasıl ortaya çıktı?

Editörüm John Campbell'ın fikriydi.

John Campbell da bu yasaların sizin öykülerinizde zaten uygulandığını söylüyor?

Evet ama övgülerin tümünün benim payıma düşmesinden huzursuzum.

Sizce robotlar en çok hangi alanda faydalı olabilirler?

Kamu idareciliği! Robot Kanunları'na göre insanlara zarar vermez, tiranlık etmez, rüşvet almaz, önyargılı davranmaz, saçma sapan yasalar çıkartamazlar. Ve dönemi başarıyla tamamladıktan sonra [ölümsüz olmalarına rağmen] görevi başkasına devrederler. Robotlar bu iş için biçilmiş kaftandır.

İnsanlar kamu yönetiminde neden robotlar kadar yetkin olamıyor sizce?

İnsan bir kez emir verecek konuma ulaştı mı, sanki doğuştan gelen bir hakmış gibi habire emir yağdırıyor. Muhatapları da emir almaya şartlanmış oldukları için, hep itaat ediyorlar. Böylece suçun ve savaşın kısırdöngüleri başlıyor.

Bunun da sebebi gücün temerküz etmesi yani tek elde veya dar bir çevrenin elinde toplanması, ha?
Politikada yenilikçiler değil, muhafazakarlar avantajlıdır. Zira toplum, geleneklere uygun yaşayanları seçme eğilimindedir. Oysa tevazu konservatistlere özgü bir erdem değil. Hatta onlarda tevazu gibi görünen şey, çoğunlukla, güce kavuşana dek elden bırakmadıkları itaatkârlıktan ibaret.

Sıradanlığın kötülüğe yol açtığını mı söylüyorsunuz?
Ne yazık ki bilimin gelişme hızı ile insanların bu gelişimi anlama ve ona adapte olma hızı aynı değil. "Sıradan" derken gerçeklerle bağı gevşek birini kastediyoruz. Bu koşullarda kötülük yürürlükte kalıyor. Ondan da beteri, kötülük 'iyilik' diye sunuluyor.

Sıradanlıktan kurtulmak için yapılması gereken ilk şey ne?
Hiçbir şeyi sırf muktedir öyle dedi diye kabul etmemek.

Ya güçlüler bizimle aynı ideolojiden yana iseler?
İdeolojik kabuller dünyaya baktığımız pencerelerdir. Arada bir silmezseniz içeri ışık girmez.

Politik bağnazlığa karşısınız...
Evet, kesinlikle. Bu tür bir teslimiyetten zararlı çıkarsınız. Bağnazlığın aptallığından doğan propaganda, onu seslendirenleri de er geç korkutur.

İlginç?..
Her türlü bağnazlığın berisinde korkular vardır. Ve korkakların ömrü, cesurların dedikodusunu yapmakla geçer.

İktidarı özünde zayıf mı buluyorsunuz?
Şöyle söyleyeyim: İktidarın büyüsü asla tutmaz.

Ne demek bu?
Kitleleri etkilemek lidere iyi hissettirir, fakat kitleler vefasızdır.

1970'TE İKİ CİLTLİK ASIMOV'UN SHAKESPEARE REHBERİ ADLI KİTABI YAZDINIZ...
EVET, YAZMAKTAN EN ÇOK KEYİF ALDIĞIM KİTABIM...
ÇOCUKLUĞUMDAN BERİ SHAKESPEARE HAYRANIYIM. TÜM ESERLERİNİ SATIR SATIR, NOTLAR ALARAK OKUDUM.
SHAKESPEARE BENCE ZAMANDA VE UZAYDA EHEMMİYETİNİ SONSUZA DEK KORUYACAK.

GALAKSİDEN GALAKSİYE GİDEN İNSANLARIN HİKAYELERİNİ YAZIYORSUNUZ. FAKAT UÇAĞA BİNMİYORSUNUZ...
EVET... GÜLÜNÇ DEĞİL Mİ?
ESTAĞFURULLAH...
UÇAK KAZASI FİKRİ BENİ ENGELLİYOR..
SEYAHAT ETMEYİ PEK SEVMİYORUM ZATEN.
BENİ DAKTİLOMDAN UZAK TUTUYOR.

BİLİMKURGU YAZARLARI UZAY ARAÇLARINA BİNDİRİLİP BAŞKA GALAKSİLERE YOLLANSA GİTMEZSİNİZ YANİ?
YO, SANMIYORUM. GİDEMEM. BU İŞ İÇİN YAŞLIYIM. AYRICA ÇOK KORKARIM.
ŞU ANDA BİR HİKAYENİN İÇİNDEYİZ MR. ASIMOV.
HAKAN BİZİ IŞINLAYIVERİR.
VE SİZ İSTEDİĞİNİZİ YAPABİLİRSİNİZ.
HİKAYELER GİBİSİ YOK.

Mazlumlardan yana mısınız Mr. Asimov?
Zalimliğe karşıyım. Fakat bu mazlumlara bayıldığımı düşündürtmesin size.

Nasıl yani?
Zulme uğrayanlar, sırf mazlum oldukları için harika insanlardır diyemeyiz. Zayıftırlar, orası kesin. Fakat güçlü olsalardı, belki onlar da zulmedecekti.

1950'lerde sanatçıların büyük baskı gördüğü McCarthy'cilik döneminde hiç sorun yaşamadınız?
Doğru. Fakat baskıya boyun eğdiğim anlamına gelmiyor bu. Nitekim bilim-kurgu insan hak ve özgürlüklerinin savunulduğu son kaleydi. Sansürcüler, bilim-kurgu okumuyordu. Okusalar da anlamıyor, neyi yasaklayacaklarını bilemiyorlardı.

Tabiata nasıl bakıyorsunuz?
Modern çağın bütün dertlerinin kaynağı, doğadan uzaklaşılmış olmasıdır.

Cenneti sıkıcı bulan biri için ilginç sözler?
Konuyu saptırmayın lütfen. Ormanlar, tıbbi ilaçların büyük hammadde kaynağıdır. Sağlığımızı da tedavi imkanlarımızı da ormanlarla birlikte yok ediyoruz.

Gezegeni düşünecek kadar geniş bir bakış açısı tutturamıyoruz...
Öyle... Kendi sınırlarımızın ötesini görebilsek... Radyasyona maruz kalmak; sigara tüttürmek, içki içmek, fazla yemek gibi haz verse ona da pek itiraz eden çıkmazdı.

Ne olacak peki?
Eğer işler şimdiki gibi devam ederse, son gülen Şeytan olacak.

Doğa ile insan arasındaki satranç maçını kaybedeceğiz demek?
İnsanın kaybı, hayatın sona ereceği anlamına gelmez. Hayat denen oyun, satrançtan farklı olarak şah-mat'tan sonra da devam eder.

SUSAN SONTAG

TOPLUM, YAZARI ALNINDAN ÖPMEZ

1983, New York...

Susan Sontag [1933-2004]
Amerikalı romancı, filozof… Başkalarının acılarını sadece seyrederek, onlarla bağ kurduğumuz yanılsamasına kapıldığımızı vurguladı. İşgal sırasında, 1993'te dokuz sefer Bosna'ya gitti. Saraybosna'da bir meydana onun adı verildi.

Zelig
PEPSI
SONY
WOODY ALLEN
MIA FARROW
ZELIG
SANAT ESERİNİ YORUMLAMAYI BİLMEK GEREK, HA?
BENCE SANATI ANLAMAK İÇİN BİZE GEREKEN ŞEY YORUM-BİLİM DEĞİL, SEVGİ-BİLİMDİR.
YAZAR KİMDİR?

W45 ST
Enjoy
HOWARD
YAZAR, ÇEKTİĞİ ACIYI, SANATSAL BİR KAZANIMA DÖNÜŞTÜRMENİN YOLUNU KEŞFETMİŞ KİŞİDİR.

Aydınlanma çabası nedir?
Aydınlanmak sersemleticidir. Bilgeliğe doğru ilk adım, kendinden hoşnutsuz olmakla atılır.

Yazmak nedir?
Yazmayı kendini ifade yolu olarak görmeyi çok kaba buluyorum. Yazarken yaptığım işin kendimi ifade etmek olduğunu düşünseydim, daktilomu çöpe atardım. Yazmak bundan çok daha karmaşık bir eylemdir.

Karmaşık derken?..
Yazmak, gizemli bir iş. Yazarken hem bilinçli hem saf olabilmelisiniz.

Siz neden yazıyorsunuz?
Kendimi tanımlamak için yazıyorum, bir kendini yaratma eylemi olarak. Varolma sürecinin bir parçası bu. Kendimle diyalog içindeyim, sevdiğim yaşayan ve ölü yazarlarla, ideal okurlarla...

"Kendini yaratma" eylemi mi?
Yazarın genelde kendini ifade etmeye çalıştığı ya da başkalarını değişmeye yönlendirdiği düşünülür. Ancak bu iki model bana uymuyor. Ben aslında kendimi değiştirmek için yazıyorum.

Yazarın temel işi ne sizce?
Yazar ayrımcılığın klişeleriyle mücadele eder.

Nasıl yapar bunu? Veya nasıl yapmalı?
İnsanların ne yapması gerektiğin söylemeye pek istekli değilim. Zira insanların beni şaşırtacak farklı şeyler yapmasını umuyorum.

YAZMAK, DİKKATLE OKUMAKTIR

Kime "yazar" dersiniz?
Yazar dört kişi olmalı: Çılgın, saf, üslupçu ve eleştirmen.

Çılgın, fikirleri temin eder. Saf, bunun kayda geçmesine izin verir. Üslupçu özel tadı sağlar. Eleştirmen ise zeka katar.

Yazmak ile okumak arasında ne gibi bir etkileşim var?
Yazmak yoğunlaşarak ve dikkatle okuma sanatıdır aslında. Kendi yazdıklarınızı okur ve iyi olup olmadıklarını görürsünüz.

Yazmak, fazlasıyla zaman alıyor, haksız mıyım? Yaşamı emiyor adeta...
Eh... Hayatını yazmaya adamak, kendi kendini köleleştirmek gibi. Hem köle hem de efendi oluyorsunuz. Yazarlık fazla ihtiras içeriyor.

Hangi özellik yazarın kişiliğine zarar verir?
Kükreyen ego, iyi bir yazarı budalalığa sürükler.

Saygın bir yazar olarak siz neyi kaygı verici buluyorsunuz?
Mesela, bir yazarın okurlarında minnet duygusu uyandırması tehlikelidir.

Neden?
Çünkü minnet, çok güçlü, ama aynı zamanda çok kısa ömürlü bir duygudur.

Kurmaca anlatıların gerçeklerle ne tür bir ilgisi var?
Bir eser dünyayı nasıl gördüğünüze ve kendinizi nereye koyduğunuza dair birşeyler söyler. Kurmaca kitaplar fotoğraf gibidir. Fakat fotoğrafın gösterdiği şey, onu çekenin gördüğüdür. Arkasında insan vardır yani. Kurmaca anlatı, gerçeği değil, hakikati sunar.

KİBİR HAPİSHANESİNDEN KAÇIŞ

Yazıyı fotoğrafa benzetmeniz ilginç. İkisi arasında büyük fark olduğunu sanırdım...
Kesinlikle var. Hatta fotoğrafın, yazarın görme biçimi ile

rekabet halinde olduğunu düşünüyorum. Birçok insan gördüğü şeyi sözle ifade edemez. İlginç bir olaya şahit olunca "Keşke fotoğraf makinem yanımda olsaydı" der. Anlatım becerilerinde genel bir kırılma var ve çok az insan güzel bir şekilde hikaye anlatıyor artık.

Okumanın sizin için anlamı ne?
Dünyaya katlanamadığım zamanlar bir kitap alıp battaniyenin altına kıvrılırım. Beni her şeyden uzaklaştıran küçük bir uzay gemisi gibidir.

Okumayı dünyadan, insanlardan bir 'kaçış' olarak mı görüyorsunuz?
Aslında tam tersi. Her uzaklaşma, kaçış değildir.

O halde, kitap okumamayı 'kişinin kendinden kaçması' sayıyorsunuz?
Evet. Kitap okumayan kimse kendinden kaçıyordur. Okumak, insan olmamızın, kendimiz olmamızın bir yoludur.

Yazar adayına bir öneriniz?
İlham beklemeyin. Toplumun sizi alnınızdan öpmesini de.

Başka?
Asla alaycı ve yapmacık olmayın. Ama bu espritüel olmanızı önlemesin.

Ve de?..
Dikkatli olun. Dikkat, zindeliktir.

Edebiyat nedir?
Edebiyat, insanların canlı olana ve can çekişene verdiği cevapların tarihidir.

Siz tam olarak neye karşılık verdiniz? Edebiyatın sizin için anlamı ne?
Edebiyat benim için ulusal kibir, dar görüşlülük, mecburi taşralılık, anlamsız müfredat eğitimi ve tıkanmış kaderden oluşan hapishaneden kaçmaktı. Edebiyat bir özgürlük alanına giriş pasaportuydu.

Üslup?
Üslup sanatçının bireyselliğini ve özgünlüğünü yansıtır. İçerikten ayrı düşünülemez. Ayrıca esere bütünlük temin eder. Üslup epistemolojik bir karardır.

AŞKI GENELEVDE ARAMAK

Esaslı bir roman nasıl olmalı?

"Esaslı" bir roman bilgece ve oyunbaz olmalıdır. Duygudaşlık yetisini geliştirmeli, hayatın gerçeklerinin kaydını tutmalı ve aykırı düşünceler içermelidir.

Sizi cezbetmeyen kitaplar var mı?

Bilgelik projeme katkı sağlamayacağını düşündüğüm kitaplarla ilgilenemem.

Bilgelik projesi mi?.. Bu sizi muhtemelen "sosyal" biri olmaktan alıkoyar, ha?

Orası öyle... Dünyaya karışmak ahlaki bir düşüş gibi geliyor bana. Bir genelevde aşkı aramak gibi.

Aramak demişken, aradığınız başka ne var?

Doğrusu, hayatım boyunca konuşacak zeki birini aradım.

İnsanın değerini zeka seviyesi mi belirler?

Düşünmenin önemli olduğunu söylemekle

yetineyim. Emerson şöyle demişti: "İnsan, gün boyu düşündüklerinden ibarettir."

Düşüncenin başlıca fonksiyonu...
Düşünceler, hayatın hizasını bozar.

Bir kültürün en önemli özelliği nedir?
Cömertlik. Cömertliğin olmadığı yerde gerçek bir kültürün varlığından söz edilemez.

Sözleriniz biraz muğlak Sayın Sontag. Kastınızı tam anlayamıyorum...
İnsanlar varlar ve gerçekler. Ama hepsi bu kadar. Neredeyse etkisiz, neredeyse cansız, hissetmeyen, düşünmeyen varlıklar. Nasıl düşünmek, yaşamak gerektiği hakkında onlara destek olmak zorundayım. Konuşacak birine, sevecek birine ancak bu şekilde kavuşabilirim. İronik, değil mi?

YABANCIYA SEMPATİ

Kendinizden de pek hoşnut değilsiniz sanki?
Temelde kendimi gerçekten seviyorum. Yalnızca, başka insanların beni sevemeyeceğini düşünüyorum. Ve onların bakış açısını anlıyorum.

Biraz... acayipmiş... Hüzünlü yani.
Fakat kendi kendime yüksek sesle konuşmam. Çünkü o zaman gerçekten yalnız olduğumu anlıyorum.

A-ha?.. Ünlü bir şarkı sözü vardır: *"Sevmek korkulu rüya / Yalnızlık büyük acı..."* Neden böyle?
İnsanoğlu hâlâ Platon'un mağarasında kös kös oturuyor ve gerçekliğe sırtını dönüp gerçekliğin görüntüleriyle oyalanıyor da ondan.

İyi de artık Platon'un mağarasında değiliz ki? Metropollerde yaşıyoruz?
Ah... Modern toplum hem doğaya hem de her türlü varlığa karşı sürekli saldırı halinde. Saldırganlık modern yaşamın çekirdeği. Yani, hayatın ritminin bir parçası olan olağan bir saldırganlık var.

Yani... Biz insan değil miyiz? İnsan olamamakta mıyız?
Bizden olmayanlara karşı sempati besleyemezsek nasıl insanlar oluruz? Bazen kendimizi unutmayı başaramazsak nasıl kendimiz oluruz? Yaşadıklarımızdan ders çıkarmayı bilemezsek nasıl iyi insan oluruz? Ya affetmeyi bilmezsek? O zaman insandan başka bir şey haline gelmez miyiz?

Gerçekliği sevgiyle irtibatlı mı sayıyorsunuz?
Murat... Terkedilmişsen, sevilmiyorsan, yalnızsan, sevecek kimsen yoksa, dünyadaki en korkunç şey başına gelmiş demektir. Dibi gördün. Üstelik hâlâ hayattasın...

Sevgisizlik bizim varoluşumuzu tehdit ediyor... doğru anlamış mıyım?

Aşkta daima yetersiz, değişmekte tereddütlü, ölüm karşısında acizsek var olmak nasıl mümkün olsun?

Bu koşullarda siz kendinizi nasıl koruyorsunuz?
Kimse tarafından derinden üzülmeyeceğim ya da incitilmeyeceğim bir hayat kurdum kendime.

Aşktan söz ederken biraz geriliyorsunuz sanki?
Orası öyle… Aşka dair yazmak da konuşmak da cesaret gerektiriyor. Çünkü kendinden bahseder gibi oluyorsun.

Konuşmayınca da olmaz ki?
Öyle mi acaba?.. Bazı şeyler ancak insanların arasındaki sessizlikte ortaya çıkar.

İlişkiler, iki taraf birbirine pek ilişmediği takdirde yürüyor galiba?
Birçokları gibi siz de "ilişkilerin yürümesinden" bahsediyorsunuz. Sanki ilişki denen şey yürütülecek bir işlem. Kafalarımız bu türden imgeler ve beklentilerle dolu.

Israr etmiyorum, fakat ilişkilerinizde faydasını gördüğünüz bir tutumunuzu söylerseniz memnun olurum.
Hımmm… İlişkilerimde kendimi kurban olarak görmekten nefret ederim. Ve başkalarını suçlamayı sevmem.

Aşk insanın akli dengesini de sarsıyor…
Akıl sağlığı, bir pembe yalandır.

Cinsel yakınlığın ilişkileri karmaşıklaştırmasının sebebi ne?
Cinsellik içgüdüsel olmanın ötesinde elbette güzel olabilir. Gelgelelim tehlikeye de kolayca kapı açabilir. Çünkü bir sırrı açığa vurmayı ve çözmeyi içerir. Kişinin kendine biçtiği değere bağlı bir duygu pazarlığı başlayabilir. Bu da evet, karmaşa demektir. Cinselliğin de aşkın da karşılıklı, dengeli ve sürekli olması zor…

YANİ AŞK BİR ALGI VE ANLAYIŞ PROBLEMİ? DOLAYISIYLA DA KARŞILIKSIZ?
ÖYLE GÖRÜNÜYOR... ZATEN KARŞILIKSIZ AŞKIN CAZİBESİNE BİLİNÇLİ BİR ŞEKİLDE BOYUN EĞİYORUZ.
HAY ALLAH. FENAYMIŞ...

MODERN AŞK, DUYGULARIN YİTİRİLMESİNDEN DOĞAN ENDİŞE İÇİNDE DİDİNİP DURMAKTAN İBARET.

ROMAN KAHRAMANLARINI POLİSE İHBAR ETME

Düşünce ile duyguyu yan yana, iç içe ele alıyor gibisiniz...
Bu doğru... Düşünce ile duygu arasındaki ayrıma şüpheyle bakıyorum. Kalp ile beyin, düşünce ile his, hayal gücü ile muhakeme ayrımı... Bunları doğru bulmuyorum. Düşünmek, hissetmenin bir hali bence, nitekim hissetmek de düşünmenin bir hali.

Ve?
Düşünmek endişe verici ihtimalleri çağırmaktır.

Endişeden kaçış yok mu? Her şey o kadar korkunç mu sahi?
Hıh... Ahlaksızca davranışlarla her karşılaşışında serseme dönen, insanın insana zulmü karşısında hayal kırıklığına uğrayan [hatta, gördüklerinden kuşku duyan] kişi, bu çağın yetişkini değildir.

Ahlaksızlık demişken, ahlakçılık hakkında ne düşünüyorsunuz?
Ahlakçılık geçmişten gelir, geleceği yönetmeye kalkışır ve "bugün köprüsünü" geçmeyi zorlaştırır.

Sanat eserlerinin ahlak merceğiyle incelenmesine ne dersiniz?
Sanat eserine ahlakçı bir tutumla yaklaşmak sorunludur. Sanatın eleştirisi estetik alanında kalarak yapılmalı.

Örnek verebilir misiniz?
Komşum eşini öldürse ve ceza almasa buna tepki gösteririm. Buna karşılık Norman Mailer'ın *Amerikan Rüyası* romanındaki, karısını öldüren fakat cezalandırılmayan adama kızmam.

Sanat ile ahlakın bir ilgisi yok mu?
Sanat hassasiyet itibariyle ahlakla örtüşür. Estetik deneyim;

çıkar gözetmeme, yoğunlaşarak düşünme, özenlilik ve duygu uyandırma bakımından ahlakidir.

Eser?
Sanat eseri ise zarafeti, zekası, ifade gücü, enerjisi bakımından temelde ahlakidir.

Aşırılık, müstehcenlik, şiddet içeren yapıtlara ne demeli?
Ciddi misiniz Murat?.. "Yapıt" diyorsunuz işte. Sanat ile gerçek arasındaki mesafeyi gözardı etmemeniz gerekir. Hem sonra... Rilke der ki "Şeytanlarımı benden alırsanız, meleklerim de onlarla gider."

MÜNZEVİ BİR AYLAK

Anladım... Ah Leydi Sontag, yalnızlığı da gidermiyoruz, ha? Eser hâlâ bir çığlık mı dersiniz? Bana sadece bir sinyal gibi görünüyor. Hüzünden umutsuzluğa geçiveriyoruz da ne oluyor?
Hiç... Romantik bir imge karşısında gene hipnotize oluyoruz.

Büyülenmek işe yarıyor mu ki?
Ne gezer... Kişilik kazanmaya çabalayıp nihayet kendim olmaktan yorgun düştüğümü anladım.

İnsan olmak, olabilmek tat vermedi mi?
Bir dağ, ağaç, bir taş olmak isterdim.

Afedersiniz ama sözün burasında söyleyebileceğim tek şey şu: "Haydaaa!"
İnsanları seyretmekten hoşlanıyorum ama onlarla konuşmak, ilişki kurmak, eğlenmek veya çatışmak istemiyorum.

Hiç mi umut yok?
Münzevi bir aylak olmak... tek çözüm gibi görünüyor.

Hatıralarla avunabiliriz belki?

Zor... Hatırlamak derinlere kök salmaktır, acı verir.

Gene mi acı?
Modern insanın geçmişle ilgili tutumu, onu büyük ölçüde geride bırakmak, unutmaktır. Geçmiş, eylemi sekteye uğratır, enerjiyi tüketir. Bir yüktür... Acıdan kaçmanın mümkün ve gerekli olduğundan emin değilim.

Yaşayıp gitmek yerine hayatın ille bir anlamı olsun istiyoruz. O da yok gibi. Akli çaba deliliğe mi yaklaştırıyor nedir? Fazla akıllı biri, delirince mi ferahlar anca?
Kimse deliliğin daha iyi olduğunu söylemiyor. Fakat düşünürün ve sanatçının yalnızlığı, başlıbaşına bir delilik motifi. Büyük bir sanatçının değeri; aykırılığı göze almasına, kimsesizliğe katlanmasına ve delilikle alışverişine bağlı bence.

O zaman da marjinalleşir, anlaşılmazsınız veya dışlanırsınız?
Bence dünya marjinal insanlar için güvenli bir yere dönüşmeli. İyi bir toplumun vazgeçilemez özelliklerinden biri de insanlara marjinal olma hakkı tanımasıdır.

Günümüz toplumumunun temelinde ne var?
Toplumumuzun temelinde... nihilizm var; televizyon nihilizmdir.

TERKEDİLMENİN ACISINDAN DOĞAN HAKİMİYET

Galiba sokaktaki vatandaş ile entelektüel sanatçı arasında ortak bir yön var: Sıradan insanın gözü doymazken, entelektüelin gönlü doymuyor. Sonuçta ikisi de tatmin olamıyor, ha?
Trajedimizin büyüklüğü, küçük bir işlem hatasından mı kaynaklanıyor dersiniz? Sahip olamadığını istemek,

eline geçirdiğinden çabucak sıkılmak... Bir şey elimizden alınınca onu yeniden arzuluyoruz. Kaybetmek, ayrılmak ve kopmak bizi canlandırıyor...

Galiba mutluluk ve huzur, zenginlik ve güvenlik filan aslında herkesi ölgünleştiriyor. Kaybetmenin hissettirdiği yalnızlık ile sanatçının biricikliğinden doğan yalnızlık türdeş. "Düşünmek endişe verici ihtimalleri çağırmaktır" dediniz ya... Endişe sayesinde zindelik kazanıyor, umutsuzluktaki umuttan besleniyoruz.
Bu çelişkiler arasındaki ilişkiyi kendi içimize bakarak test edebiliriz. Şahsen terkedilmişliğin acısının yanında bir tür hakimiyet de hissediyorum.

Pekala... Yaşamın önemli olayları nelerdir?
Yeni duygular hissetmeyi sağlayan bir olay, önemli deneyimdir.

Yeni duygular hissetmek de belki düşüncelerimizi yenilemeyi gerektiriyor, ha?
Onu çok az kişi başarabilir. En büyük meselemiz de bu zaten.

Neden değişemiyoruz? Kim değişmek istemez ki?
Unutmayın ki katlanmak, değişmekten daha kolaydır.

Nasıl olur?.. Değişmeyi erteliyoruz belki?
Fazla uzatılan erteleme de kendiliğinden bir tercihe, kabule dönüşüyor.

Fakat?..
Fakat insan bir kere değişince, onca derde neden katlandığına şaşar.

Kimse kimseye şefkat de göstermiyor...
Maalesef. Nefretin, kinin karşıtı olan şefkat aynı zamanda istikrarsız, gelgeç bir duygu. Eğer eyleme dökülemezse, yok olup gider.

Hayat zor Sayın Sontag...
Eee... Sakince sevebilmek, tereddütsüzce güvenebilmek, kendini hiçe saymadan umut edebilmek ve perişan olmadan esaslı işler başarabilmek kolay değildir.

14 YAŞINDA HİSSEDEN İHTİYARLAR

Trajedimizi zekice analiz etmekten fazlasına gücümüz yetmez mi?
Normal şartlarda ancak 70-80 yıl canlı kalabilecek bir bedende, tuzağa düşmüş haldeyiz. Vücut, bir aşamadan sonra çürüyor ve hayatının yarısını, belki daha bile fazlasını kendi çürüyüşünü izleyerek geçiriyorsun. Yapabileceğin hiçbir şey yok.

Pek moral vermiyorsunuz açıkçası.
Öyle bir vaatte bulunmadım zaten.

Devam ediniz lütfen.
60-70 yaşındaki yakınlarına kendilerini kaç yaşında hissettiklerini sorsan, 14 yaşındaymış gibi hissettiklerini söylerler. Sonra aynaya bakar, yaşlanmış yüzlerini görürler. Müflis bir vücuda hapsolmuş 14 yaşındaki biri gibi hissediyorlardır kendilerini! Bu, yeterince yaşayan herkesin başına gelir. Al sana vahim bir deneyim.

Ne yapmalıyız?
Teselli arayabiliriz anca. Kendi alanını yaratmalı insan, uzun sessizlikler ve bolca kitapla.

İnzivayı ve sessizliği önemsiyorsunuz...
Elbette. Gelgelelim insanlar "sözün bittiği yer"den uzun uzun bahsediyorlar.

Öyle hakikaten.
Modern sanat da susma çağrılarının oluşturduğu gürültüyle dolu.

"Bolca kitap" dediniz. Kitaplarla en derin bağı kimler kurar?
Gençler. Gençken okuduğun kitaplar senin bir parçan olur.

Günümüzde gençler kitap okudukça, kitlesel aydınlanma yaşanıyor sanki, yanılıyor muyum?
Sanmam… Bence insanlar hâlâ son derece entelektüellik karşıtı.

Bir görgüsüzlük sorunu da mı var dersiniz?
Maalesef evet. Görgü, her şeyden önce, farklı bakış açıları olduğunu bilmektir.

FOTOĞRAF ÇEKMEK BİR SALDIRIDIR

Fotoğraf çeker misiniz?
Fotoğraf makinem yok. Bir fotoğraf müptelasıyım ama fotoğraf çekmek istemem.

Neden?
Muhtemelen kendimi kaptıracağım için.

Niçin fotoğraf hakkında yazdınız?
Duyarlılığın evrimi açısından, fotoğraf makinesinin icadı belki matbaanın icadından bile daha önemliydi bence.

Resim ile fotoğraf arasındaki ilişki de ilginç…
Çok. Resimleri, fotoğrafları sayesinde tanıyoruz artık.

Fotoğraf dünyayı nasıl değiştirir?
Uzaklardaki başkalarına ait sonsuz sayıda deneyimi bize vererek. Bu deneyimlerin yanlı ve ideolojik bir seçkisini yaparak. Fotoğrafın kapsayamayacağı hiçbir şey yok gibi görünüyor. Ve fotoğraflanamayan her şey önemsiz sayılıyor.

Fotoğrafın da önemsendiğinden emin değilim.
Ben de. Gene de günümüzde her şey bir fotoğrafta sona ermek için var.

Fotoğraf çekmek 'sonlandırmak' demek o halde?
Kameranın kullanımı, saldırganlığın modern biçimlerinden. Bir tür el koyma eylemi. Ve insanlara gayet normal ve arzulanası geliyor. Çünkü fotoğraf makineleri var ve bir şeyi beğendiklerinde, eve götürmek istediklerinde, bu eylemi onu fotoğrafa dönüştürerek gerçekleştiriyorlar. Dünyanın koleksiyonunu yapıyorlar.

ŞEHİDE BİR GAZİNİN GÖZÜYLE BAK

John Berger gibi siz de fotoğrafı ölümle irtibatlandırıyorsunuz.
Öyle. 1839'da kameranın icat edilişinden beri, fotoğraf sanatı ölümle hep haşır neşir olmuştur.

Nasıl mesela?
Bir insanın şehit olduğunu söylemek kolay ve ferahlatıcıdır. Onun vurulduktan sonra çekilmiş fotoğrafına bakmak ise zordur ve huzur bozar.

Savaş hakkında ne söylersiniz?
İnsanlar savaşı durdurabileceklerine inanmıyorlar. Bu yanlış. Bir ülkede savaş çıktı mı, diğer ülkelerdeki insanlar oraya barış götürmek için harekete geçmeli. Aksi tavır, yangını söndürmeyip seyretmeye benzer.

Haklısınız. Neden 'yangını' seyrediyoruz? Aptal mıyız?
Savaşın gerçekte ne olduğunu idrak edemiyoruz. Ateş altında kalmış ve yanıbaşında insanlar vurulup düşerken ölümün pençesinden kurtulmuş bir asker gibi hissedip düşünmeyi öğrenmeliyiz.

TEHLİKELİ TUTUNAMAYAN

Oğuz Atay [1934-1977]
1972'de yayımlanan ilk romanı *Tutunamayanlar*'ın algılanması ve anlaşılması 10 yıldan fazla sürdü.
Bu özgün, yerli ve yenilikçi eser, yazarın vefatından sonra, çığır açıcı bir başyapıt olarak kabul gördü.
Tehlikeli Oyunlar, Korkuyu Beklerken, Oyunlarla Yaşayanlar…
Oğuz Atay'ın tüm eserlerinde entelektüel bir yüzleşme ve vicdani bir hesaplaşma söz konusudur.
Yaşadığı dönemde hiçbir kitabı ikinci kez basılmayan Atay, 43 yaşında vefat ettiğinde, *Türkiye'nin Ruhu* adlı bir roman üzerinde çalışıyordu.

HAKAN BURAYA NEDEN GELDİK?
ŞİMDİ ANLARSIN.

A-HA?! OĞUZ ATAY!
OĞUZ BEY!
ROMANDAN BAHSETSENİZ ...
ROMAN TEHLİKELİ BİR TÜR. ÇÜNKÜ OYUNU FARKETMEMİZİ, ONA KARŞI ÇIKMAMIZI SAĞLAR. ROMANDA GERÇEĞİ TÜM ACILIĞIYLA YAZMALI. ONU HAFİFLETME İŞİ, KAHRAMANLARA BIRAKILMALI.
TUTUNAMAYANLAR OĞUZ ATAY
TEHLİKELİ OYUNLAR OĞUZ ATAY
ROMAN ACI VE ACITICI MI OLMALI YANİ?
İNSANI ANLATIYORUZ. ONU SEVİYORSAK, ÇİZDİĞİMİZ RESİM BİR AYDINLIK TAŞIR.
YEŞİLKÖY

TUTUNAMAYANLARA SAYGIM BÜYÜKTÜR

Romanlarınız nasıl bir tutumun ürünü?
Sanırım... yalnız bırakıldığımı hissettiğim zaman kendi çapımda mesele çıkarıyorum.

Siz, romanınızda insanları 'tutunamayan' olmaya çağırıyordunuz. Yanılıyor muyum?
Bir arkadaşım da aynı şeyi söyledi. Fakat... Çağrıma henüz bir karşılık alamadım.

Neden herkes başarı vaat ederken siz tutunamayanlığı önerdiniz?
Çünkü başarı insanı sevimsizleştirir.

Tutunamayanlık bir dünya görüşü veya yaşam biçimi mi?
Aslında roman kahramanlarını peşinden koşturacağım büyük ülkülerim yok. Bununla birlikte, insanlara, özellikle tutunamayanlara saygım büyüktür.

Varoluşçular gibi siz de meselenizi ancak romanla anlatabileceğinizi düşünüyordunuz sanki?
Haklısınız... Tutunamayanlığın makale, inceleme, deneme gibi yazı türlerinin konusu olduğunu sanıyorum.

YAZDIKLARIM BU COĞRAFYANIN ÜRÜNÜ

Dostoyevski ve Kafka'yla akraba sayılıyorsunuz...
Dostoyevski'yi seviyorum. O, büyük ustalarımızdan biri... İnsan, Kafka'yı okumazsa, bitiktir işi. Kafka'nın duyduğu dehşet, metafizik bir dehşet değildi. Onun romanlarındaki insanlar, evrendeki baş aşağı gidişin farkındadırlar.

Ayrıca Stendhal, Laclos, George Eliot, Henry James, Melville ve Nabokov'u seviyorsunuz.
Evet. Doğru. Roman yazma arzusu ile başka romanlar karşısında duyulan heyecan... Bu ikisi birbirini besliyor.

Tahminimce... Ivan Gonçarov'un *Oblomov*'unu çok beğenmiştiniz...
Tam isabet! *Oblomov*'u okuyunca derinden sarsılmıştım.

Eserlerinizde düşünceye ağırlık verdiniz. Sürekli bir sorgulama ve eleştiri hattı var...
Evet ama belki de edebiyatı değerlendiremiyorum? Elias Canetti, Jean Rhys, Jacov Lind, Paul Bailey, John Fowles gibi sevdiğim yazarlar kimseyi ilgilendirmiyor.

Türkiye sizin romanlarınızın değişmez kahramanı bence. Buna ne dersiniz?
Böyle bir yorumdan memnuniyet duyarım. Zira yazdıklarımın insanımızı ve sorunlarımızı aksettirme bakımından ve duyarlık itibariyle bu coğrafyanın ürünü olduğunu sanıyorum...

SIRADAN FAKAT ACIKLI BECERİKSİZLİK

Türkiye'yi "yoksul düşmüş bir soylu"ya benzetmeniz ilginç...

Ülkemiz birbirine benzemeyen birçok medeniyetin beşiği olmuştur. Bu beşikte birçok medeniyet sallanmıştır. Son kurulan medeniyet ekmek medeniyetidir.

Yani epey düşmüş durumdayız?

Eh... Sıradan fakat acıklı bir beceriksizliğin örnekleriyle dolu hayatımız.

Buna karşılık eserlerinizde mizaha yer veriyorsunuz.

Mizah, benim durumumdaki biri için tehlikeli bir çare.

Günlüğünüzde bahsettiğiniz "fakirliğin kültürü" nedir?

İçinde bulunduğu şartları değiştirmede ümitsizliğe kapılmış insanın ifade biçimidir. Fakirlik ortadan kalkınca bile fakirlik kültürü silinmez. Ve fakirler, ruh bozukluklarına hoşgörüyle bakar.

Bir insanı diğerinden ayıran hususiyet nedir?

Kazanç ve kayıp hakkındaki telakkisidir.

Haksızlık etmekten kaçındığımız için kaybediyorsak ne yapmalıyız?

Gülümseyeceksin... Bekleyeceksin... Ve hiçbir zaman beklentiye kapılmayacaksın.

Böyle bir durum ıstıraplı olmaz mıydı?

Aramızda asıl ıstırap çekenler, düşünmeyi henüz unutmayanlardır. Düşünce artık onlara hayatlarını düzenlemede yararı olmayan bir yüktür.

Öyle diyorsunuz ama aydını da epey eleştiriyorsunuz. Aydına yazık değil mi?

Bir bakıma evet... Aslında aydınımız, toplum ahlaken

yenilenmeden, eski bozuk düzeni kişisel hayatında yıkmaya çalışıyor. Bu da onun dramı.

TESADÜFİ, İRRASYONEL VE KEYFÎ

Aydınlar da toplum da pek iyi durumda değil, ha?
Bizim trajedimiz irrasyonel bir biçimde gelişiyor. Durumumuzun farkında bile değiliz. Çok güzel yaşayıp gittiğimizi zannediyoruz. Aydınlar da toplumsal bağlamda konuşuyor. Meselenin psikolojik yönü boşlukta kalıyor.

Türkiye'nin sorunu psikolojik mi yani?
Öyle görünüyor. Neyin suç, neyin makbul olduğu belli değil. Suçluluk duygularıyla yaşıyor insanımız. Başı önünde geziyor. Cezalandırılmadığında; hoş görüldüğünü, bağışlandığını düşünüyor.

Yurdumuzda güvensizlik ve hep sözünü etiğiniz korku hakim demek?
Toplumumuzda da devletimizde de tesadüfi, irrasyonel ve keyfî yönler çoktur. Ne kurumlara güvenebilirsiniz ne de insanlara.

Dolayısıyla?
Yazılar, sözler, sizinle şu konuşmamız bile korkunun onayından geçiyor.

Cezalandırılma korkusuyla ne yapıyoruz?
Sorumluluktan köşe bucak kaçıyoruz. Kimi yarı-aydınlar da bu atmosfere pek yakışan ucuz romantizmi paraya çeviriyor.

Gene aydınlara çattınız. Kemal Tahir'den başka sevdiğiniz yerli aydın yok mu?
Mehmet Âkif'in gücüne, sevgisine hayran oldum. Fakat ona da sağcılar sahip çıkıyor.

Başka?
Orhan Veli... Şiirlerine uygun olarak gerçek bir

tutunamayandı. Sevdiği küçük insanların dünyasında bile yabancıydı. Sözünün eriydi, huzursuzluğunun eri.

BATI KARŞITLIĞI BİZİM EVRENSELLİĞİMİZE UYMUYOR

Bildiğim kadarıyla, Halit Ziya'yı da önemsiyorsunuz?
Halit Ziya, Türkiye'nin Batıya açıldığı dönemin insanını anlatır. Böylece bugünkü Türkiye'nin de önemli bölümünü aydınlatır. Halit Ziya'nın kahramanları ne kadar piyanoda Chopin çalsalar; Alexandre Dumas okusalar, redingot giyseler ve XIV. Louis mobilyalarıyla evlerini döşeseler de bizim insanımızdır.

Batı demişken, Batı hakkında siz ne düşünüyorsunuz?
Batı, diğer kültürleri "inceler" ancak. Biz ise samimiyetimizle benimseriz. Batı bilgiyi istismar eder, kaliteyi sömürür. Edebiyatı bile Batı 'değerlendirir' biz ise 'severiz'.

Bir dakika, Batı karşıtı mısınız?
Batı karşıtlığı bizim evrenselliğimize uymuyor. Türkler olarak kişiliğimizi savunmak için Batıya karşı çıkıyoruz. Batılılara iftiralar ederek, kendimizi temize çıkarmak için didiniyoruz. Doğuya da Batıya da sahip çıkabiliriz oysa.

Gene de 'Batıcı' değilsiniz besbelli?
Batının bizi hiçbir zaman anlayamayacağını hissediyorum. Biz de onların mantığını kullandıkça kendimizi derinlemesine anlayamayacağız. Batıcılık bir tembelliğe sürüklüyor bizi. Orijinal düşünce üretmeyip kolaya kaçıyoruz.

"Roman tehlikeli bir tür" dediniz... O halde romancılar da tehlikeli insanlar?

Bir işi iyi yapınca tehlikeli oluyorsun. Esaslı bir eser verdiğin için seni tehlikeli bulurlar. Ve olmadık bir şekilde suçlarlar. Bana "Batı hayranı" dediler mesela.

Sonra?
Sonra da Amerika'ya onlar gittiler!

DEVLET DİYOR Kİ "BİREY DE KİM OLUYOR?"

Aydınlara dönelim...
Aydınlarımız da yargılayıcı. İlerici sözler edip kendi muhitlerinde tutucu davranıyorlar.

"İnsana karşı katıyız" yazmıştınız. Nasıl bir şey bu katılık?
İnsanı insafsızca yalnız bırakıyoruz.

Aydın ile halkın ortak bir yönü var mı peki?
Her şeyi yarım yamalak yaptıkları halde,
her şeyden usanmışlar.

Ve?
İki taraf da şunu söyleyebilir: "Bizi kimse anlamadı, biz de kimseyi anlamıyoruz."

Devlet bu işe ne diyor?
Devlet diyor ki "Birey de kim oluyor?"

Devletin bireyle ve toplumla ilişkisi neden sıhhatli olamıyor?
Çünkü devlet her türlü eleştiriye kapalıdır.

Onun da sebebi?..
Felsefe geleneğimiz yok. Tek felsefe, bireyin yok oluşu.

Birey hiçe sayılmaya, yok edilmeye dirense ya?
Keşke… ama çoğu kimse sorumluluk üstlenmektense, suçu, cezayı kabul etmeye hazır.

Gerçekten mi?
Evet… İnsanımız başkasına isyan etmektense kendini cezalandırmayı seçer.

İNANCI BAYRAK YAPARLAR, ASLINDA İNANÇSIZDIRLAR

Felsefe noksanlığından yalnızca birey mi zararlı çıkıyor?
Medeniyetle ilgili tartışmalarımız da şiddete dönüşüyor. Barbarlığa meylediyoruz.

Devlet katlarındakiler, topluma fayda sunabiliyor mu?
Pek öyle görünmüyor... Açıkçası, kendi evini düzene koyamayanlar, toplumu yönetmeye kalkıyorlar.

Muhalefete ne dersiniz?
Hayatımızdaki olumsuzlukları sadece dile getirmek 'muhalefet etmek' sanılıyor. İnsanlar bir yanlış anlamalar düzeni içinde anlaşıp gidiyorlar.

Tarih epey popüler. Tarihimizde olup bitenlere dair tartışmalar dinmiyor. Bu konuda ne söylersiniz?
Evet, herkes tarih okuyor. Bugüne değer veren kalmadı. Hafıza önemli elbet, ama o da esasen zekanın bir

unsurudur. Güçlüler ise dağılmalarını örtbas etmek ve kendi varlığını meşrulaştırmak amacıyla tarihi tahrip ediyorlar.

Osmanlı?
Osmanlı kuralları ciddiye aldı. İnsanı ciddiye almadı.

"Üçkağıtçılıkla ne devrim olur ne de ümmet-i İslam kurulur" yazmıştınız. Muhafazakar aydınlardan ümitli misiniz?
Onlar da, Mehmet Âkif gibi ender şahsiyetler hariç, 'kurumsal aydın' konumundalar.

Yani?
Kendini yenileme gereği duymuyorlar. Mevkisinden memnun kimseler.

Onlar da mı korkuyor?
Hem de çok... Yaşamaktan, eğlenmekten korkarlar. İnsanı, özellikle de kadını tanımaktan korkarlar. İnancı bayrak yapmalarına rağmen aslında inançsızdırlar.

ŞAHİT OLDUĞUMUZ ŞEY, YAŞAMA KORKUSUDUR

Edebiyatta ve hayatta temel problemlerimiz neler sizce?
Kişiliktir. İnsanımız, kişilik kazanmanın önemini henüz kavramamış görünüyor. Halka büyük doğrular adına yalan söylemekten kurtulamamaktır. Sevgisizliktir. Duyarsızlıktır. Kötü romanları büyük sözlerle yutturacağını sanma yanılgısıdır. Bir edebiyat çetesine yaslanmanın verdiği rahatlıkla yıllar boyunca bir arpa boyu ilerleyememenin zavallılığıdır. Düzenden yana olanın da, düzene karşı olanın da aynı sularda çırpınmasıdır. Haksız olana karşı çıkanın da haksız olduğu bir ortam bu.

Sevgili Oğuz Atay, kişilik sahibi olmamız imkansız mı?
Burada kişi önemsizdir. Dolayısıyla kişilik de önemsiz. İnsanımız asker veya memura dönüştürülüyor.

Siz de üzülüp duruyorsunuz, ha?
Doğru… İnsanların gündelik sözleri beni incitmeye başladı.

Çaresizliğin en kötü tarafı ne sizce?
Çaresizlik yüzünden birçok şeyin anlamı kayboluyor.

Kurumları, aydınları, düşünceleri eleştiriyorsunuz. Fakat sevgiye özel bir

anlam yüklüyorsunuz sanki. Neden?
Çünkü akıl, tutucu; sevgi ilericidir.

Sevgimizi kime sunmalıyız?
Onurlu kişilere. Onlarla birlikte çaba harcamalı, başkaldırmalıyız.

İşte şimdi konuşmaya başladınız Sayın Atay.
Beni gayriciddiye alıyorsunuz.

Aman efendim, estağfurullah...

İKİNCİ DERECEDEN BİLİNMEYEN GÜZELLİKLER

Peki bu gidişle ileride ne olacak dersiniz?
Birgün bu çiçekler o kadar büyüyecek ki tüm reklam panolarını örtecek. Sarmaşıklar tüm medeniyeti yutacak.

Bir mühendis romancı için ziyadesiyle şairane sözler...
Hayatın asıl tadı tuzu olan 'ikinci dereceden bilinmeyen güzellikler'i fark etmeli insan.

Esasen merhametli birisiniz...
Galiba evet... Bizi de bu acımak mahvediyor. Başkalarına acımak, kendimize acımaya varıyor. Kendimize acımaktan, işlere zaman kalmıyor.

Eric Berne'in Hayat Denen Oyun dediği bu macerada...
Soğukkanlı ve acımasızların kaybettiği pek görülmemiştir, maalesef.

Bu konunun içinden çıkamayacağız herhalde...
Alice'in dünyasında kahramanlar bir konunun içinden çıkamayınca, hemen başka bir konuya geçerler. Biz de öyle yapalım.

Bu neyi halleder?
Aslında... İlk yalanı söyledikten sonra bir daha konuşmamalı insan.

Fakat zamanla hatalarımızı görür, düzeltir ve gelişiriz... Yanılıyor muyum?
İnsanın geliştiği filan yok. Yalnız kusurlarına alışıyor o kadar.

Gelişmeyi ne durdurur?
Kendini beğenmişlik.

Nasıl?
Halinden memnun kimse kusurlarını göremez ve düzeltemez. Ama daha acayip olan şu ki...

Nedir?
Meziyetlerinin de farkına varamaz. Geri kalmamızın esas sebebi bu: İmkanlarımızı fark edememek.

İYİ YARINLARI HAYAL ETMEKTEN BİLE ACİZİZ

Galiba başkalarının meziyetlerini, iyi yanlarını da göremiyoruz?
Maalesef. Didişip duruyoruz. Bir ömür kavga etmeyi marifet sanıyoruz. Ölülerimizi bile anlaşmazlıkları üzerinden anıyoruz.

O kadar kötü mü?
Değil mi? Yarını düşünmeden yalan söylüyoruz. Her şeyi yıkıyoruz. Ve bilinci küçümsüyoruz. İyi yarınları hayal etmekten bile aciziz.

Sizi karamsarlığa sürükleyen tüm bu görüşlerinizin doğruluğundan emin misiniz?
Açıkçası… her şeyi hem görüyor hem de ümitsizce öyle olmadığının söylenmesini bekliyorum.

Az da olsa ümitlisiniz fakat?
Eh… bana dayanılmaz gelen acı ümitler içindeyim.

Tatlı ümidin zerresi de mi yok?
Çelişkilerimizden ümitliyim. İnsanımız tiyatroyu soytarılık, resmi günah sayar. Öte yandan, meyhanede rastladığım balıkhane memuru Nikolay Gogol'den bahsedip beni şaşırttı.

Ülkemizde ellerini temiz tutan, açık zihinli insanlar yaşıyor, ha?
Yaşı kaç olursa olsun, kafası yüreği genç kalmış insanlar, sorunlar üstüne düşünür… Gerçekleri okuyarak, düşünerek, kendi bilinciyle anlayacak insanlar vardır bu ülkede…

Gerçekleri "kendi bilinciyle" anlamanın yolu nedir?

Kitabı karşısına alıp araya hiçbir bezirgan sokmadan, kitapla tek başına hesaplaşmak...

GALİBA BİRBİRİMZİ HEP BÖYLE ANLAMADAN SEVDİK

Siz sonuçta yeterince, layıkıyla anlaşılmadığınızı düşünüyorsunuz...
İçimden geçenleri bilselerdi... İnsanları dinlerken sıkıntılı bir görünüşüm vardı. Bana kalırsa bu görünüş çok aldatıcıydı. "Bana kalırsa bana kalırsa..." Ne yazık hiç kalmadı bana. Belki de anlaşılacak, önemsenecek bir şey yazmadım?.. Sadece yazı hayatı denen çamura bulaştım, yeni öfkeler edindim o kadar.

Yoo, yoo, kitaplarınız memlekette elden ele geziyor, çokça okunuyor. Herkes size hayran...
Bunun ne yararı var?.. Neler kurdum, ne kadarını gerçekleştirebildim ayrı mesele. Belki, bir iki kişinin dediği gibi ancak kendini ve aklına nasıl geliyorsa öyle yazan biriydim. Düşüncem geç gelişti, biraz geç başladım; biraz da erken bırakmak durumunda kaldım. Geleceğini kaybetmek, yaşanan zamanı da boşlaştırıyor.

"Ben buradayım sevgili okuyucum, sen neredesin acaba?" diye soruyordunuz *Demiryolu Hikayecileri*'nin sonunda. Artık, "Sevgili okuyucum da burada" diyebilir misiniz?
Ne evet ne hayır… Ben yalnız kalmalıyım, başka çarem yok. Para kazanamayacağımı, insanları sevemeyeceğimi anlayınca uzaklara gittim, kimse beni bulamasın diye.

Ama insanlar sizi sevdiler? Kabul edin ki –aksini söyleseniz bile- siz de insanları sevdiniz?
Tamam, haklı olabilirsiniz…

Eee?
Eee'si… Galiba biz birbirimizi hep böyle anlamadan sevdik.

Ve?
Maruzatım bundan ibarettir. Ekmek; suyla undan ibarettir.

SON BİR ŞEY... GÖRÜŞLERİNİ DEĞİŞTİRMEKLE ELEŞTİRİLEN KEMAL TAHİR'İ NEDEN SAVUNDUNUZ?
ÇÜNKÜ HEPİMİZ FİKİR DEĞİŞTİRİYORUZ.
NE VAR Kİ BUNU KENDİMİZDE BAĞIŞLIYOR, BAŞKALARINDA AFFETMİYORUZ.

TOMRİS UYAR

AŞK SONSUZ DEĞİL İSE SONSUZLUK NEYE YARAR

Tomris Uyar [1941-2003], 11 öykü kitabı yazdı.
Uyar'ın öyküleri felsefi tespitler, sosyolojik gözlemler ve psikolojik analizlerle örülüdür.
Gündökümü adıyla yayımlanan günlüklerinde, [Prof. Dr. Handan İnci'nin derlediği yazılardan oluşan] *Kitapla Direniş* ve *Aşkın Yıpranma Payı* adlı eserlerinde zarif, özenli ve yetkin bir anlatım göze çarpar. Bununla birlikte Uyar'ın mizaç itibariyle muzip ve coşkulu biri olduğu hissedilir.
"Bir yazarın anlaşılmasını sağlamak kendine değil, yaşadığı ortama düşer" diyen Tomris Uyar'ın özel hayatına, eserlerinden daha çok ilgi gösterilmesi bana hazin görünüyor...
Uyar, 60'tan fazla eseri dilimize kazandırdı.
Birçok yazarın yetişmesinde doğrudan ve dolaylı katkılarda bulunmuştur.

1979, istanbul...
NEDEN BURADAYIZ TOMRİS HANIM?
YÜREĞİMİN AĞZIMA GELMESİNİ SEVİYORUM GALİBA!

Yazar ile okur birbirine denk mi?
Elbette. Okumak da yazmak kadar ciddi bir uğraş. Okurun en az sizin kadar akıllı ve birikimli olduğunu düşünmelisiniz. Aksi takdirde edebiyatın geliştirici, ilerletici işlevi ortadan kalkar. Metnin değeri yiter yani.

Peki okur hikayeye, romana nasıl yaklaşmalı?
Her yapıtta kendi yaşamını, her edebiyat kahramanında kendi kişiliğini bulmaya çalışmamalı.

Yazarın en büyük sorumluluğu...
Dili iyi bilmesi ve kullanması.

Türkçe'nin felsefeye ve edebiyata elverişli olmadığını söyleyenler var...
Bir yazar Türkçe'nin yeterli bir dil olmadığını düşünüyorsa lütfen yazmasın!

Yazar ve çevirmen olarak Türkçe'nin gelişkin bir dil olduğunu düşünüyorsunuz, öyle mi?
Tabii ki. Benim için Türkiye Türkçe'dir. Türkiye'yi, her şeyden evvel, Türkçe'yi sevdiğim için seviyorum.

"Dili iyi bilmek ve kullanmak" derken, üslup yaratmayı mı kastettiniz?
Üslup yazarın kendisidir. Epik de yazsa lirik de yazsa "Bu, şu yazardır" dedirtebilmesi gerekir bir yazarın.

Yazarlığa varan yolda nasıl ilerlenir?
Yazarak. Denize girmeden yüzmeyi öğrenemezsiniz.

EDEBİYAT YOKSA YALNIZLIK SALDIRGANLIĞA DÖNÜŞÜR

Edebiyatın belirgin faydası nedir?
Edebiyat bize bir tek insanın yaşamının sınırlarına sığmayacak binlerce dünya ve kişilikte yaşama olanağı tanır.

Ve?
Bizi maddi manevi bütün sıkıntılara karşı dayanıklı kılar. Bize yaşama sevinci aşılar.

Edebiyatın düşünceye katkısı nedir?
Yaşamı, yerinde kullanılan sözcükler sayesinde doğru ve sıkı kavrarız.

Edebiyatla hiç ilgilenmeyip işine gücüne bakan biri...

Yazıyla, sözle bağ kurmadan hiçbir meslekte tam manasıyla başarılı olunamayacağı fikrindeyim.

Aha? Toplumsal sorunların da temelinde bu "yazıdan uzak durma" mı var dersiniz?
Bir toplum ifade gücünden yoksun ise herhangi bir alanda güç kazanabilir mi? Gerek toplum gerekse birey kendi tarihiyle bağını da esasen edebiyat sayesinde kurar.

"İfade gücümüz" yoksa, iletişim, bilgilenme, ilerleme… her şey zorlaşıyor, tıkanıyor demek?
Dahası, edebiyatsızlık, insanların yalnızlığının saldırganlığa dönüşmesine sebep oluyor.

Tomris Hanım, yazılacak her şey yazıldı belki de?
"Güneşin altında söylenmemiş söz yoktur" derler…
Güneşin her gün yeniden doğduğu da bir gerçek, Murat.

Yazarlıkta sizi teskin eden, teselli eden yön ne?
Ölümün silgisi, yazıları çok daha güç siliyor. Daha ne olsun?

Ekim 1977, George Washington Üniversitesi
Amiri Baraka'nın odası
BENCE BİR YAZARIN ASLA YAPMAMASI GEREKEN İKİ ŞEY VAR:
SORGULAMADAN KABUL ETMEK, BİLMEDEN REDDETMEK. DİYALEKTİĞE TERS.
HAKLISINIZ MR. BARAKA.
HEM SONRA... YAŞAMA EHLİYETİNİ KENDİMİZE ANCAK BİZ VEREBİLİRİZ.

Konuya biraz duygusal yaklaştınız sanki?
Düşünmeyle duygulanmanın birbirinden kesin çizgilerle ayrılamayacağına inanıyorum.

Hislerin ehemmiyeti büyük mü sizce?
Yanlış anlaşılmasın. Toplumsal sorunlar üzerinden daimi bir duygu sömürüsünü sürdürenlere karşıyım.

Sizi inciten veya kızdıran ne?
Yozlaşmış bir düzende yaşamak. Bu adlı adınca bir hastalık bence.

İnsanların kişiliğini tahrip eden bir hastalık, doğru anlamış mıyım?
Evet. Her insanın teşhis edilmiş kişiliğinin yanısıra, sahip olmak istediği kişiliği de bir o kadar önem taşır. Toplum, bireyin bu değişimine, gelişimine olanak sağlamalı.

KONFORU ÖZGÜRLÜKTEN ÜSTÜN TUTUYORUZ

Dışsal baskılara rağmen kişilik kazanmak mümkün mü dersiniz?

Mümkün. Direnmelisiniz. Siz "siz" oldukça başkaları da sizi o "siz" olarak görmeye başlayacaklardır. Yeter ki kişiliğinizin, kendiliğinizin sınırlarını bilinçle ve kendiniz saptayın.

Kendimiz olabilmek için enikonu mücadele etmemiz gerekmesi de amma acayip?

Eeee, öyle... Fakat insanoğlu yürüdükçe, kendisine kurulan tuzakları bir bir atlattıkça daha bir akıllı, dayanıklı olur

Özgürlük nedir?

"Hayır" diyebilme imkanıdır. Reddettiğiniz şey size dayatılıyorsa, özgürlüğünüz elinizden alınıyor demektir.

Hangi sanatçılar "Hayır" der?

Kendine yani ürünlerine güvenen soylu sanatçılar, içinde 'yaratıcı ahlakı' taşıyan kişiler "hayır" der.

"Çoğumuz nasıl bir özgürlük peşinde olduğumuzu bilmiyoruz" yazmıştınız...

Evet... Rahatı özgürlükten üstün tuttuğumuzun farkında değiliz.

"Hayır!" demeyi, tavır koymayı, itiraz etmeyi önemsiyorsunuz...

Tepkisiz kimseler özgür olsalar ne çıkar? Yani öyle ot gibiyken?

Özgürlüğü 'bahşedilen" değil, sahip çıkılan ve hassasiyetle korunması gereken bir değer sayıyorsunuz besbelli.... Peki, bilge kişilere özgü sakinlik de tepkisizlik midir?

Bilgelik gevşekliğe dönüşmemeli bence.

Özgürlüğün temeli olan itiraz ve direniş nasıl başlar?

Sorgulamayla. Değerleri sorgulamalı. Namus nedir, ahlak, aşk, sevgi nedir? Bunlara verilen cevapları değişmez sanıyoruz. Acaba bize öğretilen her şey doğru mu?

ÖZELEŞTİRİ, KENDİMİZİ TANIMAMIZI SAĞLAR

Ahlakın ne olduğunu bilmiyor muyuz?
Ahlakı savunmak kolay da, kendi ahlakını sorgulamak zor. Bilinçsizlikle gelen ahlaksızlık gizli kalıyor. Kendini ahlaklı sanan kimseler, hallerinden memnun yaşayıp gidiyorlar.

Bu tür sorgulamalara neden girişilmiyor?
Başkalarını sigaya çekmekten kendilerine soru soracak zamanları kalmıyor. Eh, yeni bir ahlak da kolay bulunmuyor!

Yenilik şart mı? Bazı şeyler de eski olsa?
Yenilik, değer üretmekle ilgili. İlericilik her geçen gün yeni yorumlar ister. Bir de gelenek var tabii.

Nedir gelenek?
Gelenek "eskimez eski"dir. Ve bize "kalıcı yeni"nin ipuçlarını verir. Gelenek aşırılığı frenlerken, değişime yakıt sağlar.

Galiba biz eski değerleri yaşatmada da pek iddialı değiliz, ha?
Maalesef. Onca tutucumuz, gericimiz, bağnazımız var da sağlam muhafazakarlarımız yok. Gelenekten süzülüp gelen, yenilenmeye, yorumlanmaya elverişli değerleri, sanatı ve yaşama kültürünü korumayı düşünen yok.

"Sağlam muhafazakarlarımızın olmaması" sizin gibi devrimci bir entelektüeli neden rahatsız eder ki?
Ne demek? Dünya görüşünü benimsemediğimiz

kişilerde de sağlamlık ararız. Aksi takdirde bizim nerede durduğumuz da belirginleşemiyor. Eski köklere bağlı kalınmadığı için yeniliğin filizlenmesi mümkün olamıyor.

Muhafazakarı devrimcisiyle entelektüellerin en büyük eksiği ne sizce?
Özeleştiri erdemi.

Özeleştiri bir erdem midir cidden?
Kesinlikle evet. Ayrıca özeleştiri, insanın kendini anlaması bakımından vazgeçilmezdir.

Aydınlara neyi borçluyuz mesela?
Çağımızın olanaklarını ve gereklerini kavramamızı sağlar aydınlar. Yaşadığımız dönemin ruhunu belirleyen de büyük ölçüde sanatçılardır.

Çağdaş toplum nedir, nasıldır?
Çağdaş toplum, haksızlıklar getiren yanlışlar, belirsizlikler ve kaypaklıklardan paçasını kurtarmış toplumdur.

Çağdaş olmanın gerekleri?
Çağdaşlık; yanılgıları, çelişkileri ve riskleri tanımayı gerektirir.

Çağdaşlıktan kaytarıyor muyuz?
Çoğunlukla.

Nasıl?
Seçmelerimizin sorumluluğunu başkasına yükleyerek.

"YASAL AŞK" VAR, "YASAK AŞK" VAR, "AŞK" YOK

Tek sorunumuz sorumsuzluk mu?
Önyargı da var tabii. Önyargılı olmayı hiçbirimiz kabul etmeyiz. Fakat şöyle bir yoklayalım kendimizi. En açık görüşlü olanımız bile birtakım önyargıların etkisinde. Sudan ipuçlarından genellemelere varmaya düşkünüz çoğumuz.

Sorumsuzluk ve önyargıya eklemek istediğiniz bir şey?
Var: İstediğimiz kadar gelişmiş, çağdaş olalım, yüreğimizde yine de bir hoşgörüsüzlük tohumu kalıyor çoğu zaman.

Niye böyle?
Hoşgörüyü "savunulacak hiçbir değeri olmamak" sanmaktan.

Hoşgörüsüzlüğün özünde ne var?
Bahanelerle desteklenen bir bencillik.

Dilden bahsedelim. Sizce dil nedir?
Dil bir konuyu aktarmanın aracı değil, iç dünyaların yansıtılmasında ön koşul sayılabilecek bir varoluş sorunudur.

Bir dil ne zaman kirlenir?
Yalnızca bir iletişim aracı sayıldığında. Solunan bir dünya olduğu gözden kaçırıldığında; özellikle de tınısı ecnebileştiğinde.

Fakat dildeki bozulmaya rağmen insanlar gayet tutarlı bir hayat sürüyorlar?
Bana öyle geliyor ki çoğu kimse beş yüz kelime içinde dolaştığından böyle tutarlı kalabiliyor!

DİLİN BOZULMASINA GÖZ YUMULUNCA, DİL, İNSANLARDAN İNTİKAM ALIR.
NASIL?
İNSANLAR GÖNÜL İLİŞKİLERİ KURAMAZLAR ÖRNEĞİN, AŞKSIZLIK SANCISI ÇEKER DURURLAR.
A-HA?
EEEE... HER ŞEYİN SARKTIĞI BİR TOPLUMDA AŞK'IN DA SARKMASI DOGAL.
AŞK'IN DA KALİTESİ DÜŞTÜ, ÖYLE Mİ?
BENCE ÖYLE. AŞK'TA SERÜVEN PAYINI YOK SAYIYORUZ. AŞKI "YASAL" VE "YASAK" OLARAK İKİYE AYIRIYORUZ. SIFATSIZ BİR AŞKI BENİMSEYEMİYORUZ.

DÜŞÜNCELERİNİ ANLATIP DUYGULARINI ANLATAMAYANLAR

Aşkla ilgili, insanların kafasını karıştıracak, kolay katılmayacakları fakat "Acaba mı?" diye tereddüt edecekleri bir söz söyler misiniz?
Sürekli ve sağlam beraberliklerde kafa ve duygu birliği, bir insanı benimsemek söz konusudur. Öbür adı "alışkanlık."

Ne?! Alışkanlığı, kalıcı aşk olarak mı görüyorsunuz?
Evet. Alışkanlık asıl çetrefil ve büyük tutkudur.

Vay canına? Bu kadarını beklemiyordum... Ömür boyu süren aşk var mıdır?
Yoktur. Her ilişkinin bitmesi gereken bir yer vardır.

Ne yapabiliriz. Yani... bu koşullar altında?
Aşk'ın sevgisizliğe dönüşmemesi için özen göstermeli.

Sevgi ne de olsa daha dayanıklı aşktan.

Zarif, kibar, nazik olmaktan söz ediyorsunuz sanırım?
Tabii ki. Kurt Vonnegut "Aşk bitebilir ama incelik yürürlüktedir" diyor. Gençlerimizin bu duyarlığa yabancı olmalarının sebebi sanırım aldıkları yanlış edebiyat eğitimi.

Sevgiyle ilgili gözden kaçan kritik bir husus var mı sizce?
Sevgi yalnızca bir duygu değildir, bilgi de gerektirir. Kendimden biliyorum. Sevgi savurganlığım yüzünden habire su vererek çürüttüğüm kaktüsler hâlâ aklımda.

Bilmeden, tanımadan, anlamadan sevilemez ha? Başka?
Sevgiyi soyut bir kavram olarak alıyoruz. Ve insan sevgisi, hayvan sevgisi, yurt sevgisi, bayrak sevgisi... gibi bin parçaya bölüyoruz. Bir tek varlığa veya nesneye vakfedilen ve geri kalan her şeyi hiçe sayan sevgiyi "gerçek sevgi" olarak niteleyemeyiz. Naziler bir yandan insanları yakıyor bir yandan hayvan besleyip çiçek yetiştiriyor ve klasik müzik dinliyorlardı.

Vay canına...
Başkalarının sorumluluklarını paylaşmaya götüren, insanı geliştiren, yaratıcı sevgi... Sevginin en önemli koşulu eşitliktir. Eşitliğin herhangi bir şekilde gözetilmediği ve giderek haksızlığın normalleştiği yerde sevginin zerresini bulamazsınız.

Aşk bittikten sonra sevgiyi koruyalım, tamam. Fakat âşıklara özgü yakınlık da sona eriyor, araya mesafeler giriyor...
Sevmeyi bilmek kadar, bir insanı anmayı bilmek de önemli. Yıllar sonra o kişiden nasıl bahsediyorsunuz? Anısını,

anılarınızı temiz tutabiliyor musunuz? Bu aslında insanın kendine duyduğu saygının tam bir yankısıdır.

Aşka, sevgiye dair bu kadar berrak ifadelere varabilmenize şaşırdım. Çoğumuz aşkı serinkanlı bir şekilde anlayamıyor, anlatamıyoruz halbuki?
Maalesef insanlarımız düşüncelerini anlatabilse de duygularını anlatamıyor. Kadınla erkek arasındaki ilişkiyi insan ile insan arasındaki ilişkilerin en doğalı, normali olarak görememekten sanırım. Romantizm ile gerçekçilik arasında ayrım yapmak hep ters gelmiştir bana. Ben romantik bir gerçekçiyim.

KIRILMAYA DEVAM EDEN KIRIKLAR

Sizce aşkı ne yoğunlaştırır, kıvamlı kılar?
Galiba güçlüklere birlikte karşı koymaya başladıktan sonra severiz asıl birbirimizi.

Aşkta yapılan en büyük hata?
İki kişinin birbirini düzeltmeye, yola getirmeye çalışması.

Neden?
Karşılıklı bir kısırlaştırma işlemine dönüşüyor da ondan.

Ayrılık acısı?
Üç günlük sıkı ve sürekli bir uykunun onaramayacağı yaralar üçü-beşi aşmaz.

Yapmayın lütfen. O kadar basit mi? Böyle düşünüyor olamazsınız?
Pekala, kabul, Murat... Bir insanı özlemek, mantıklı açıklamalara sığmıyor.

Hüsrandan, hasretten nasıl kurtulabiliriz?
Bilmiyorum. Bildiğim şu: Kırıklar, zamanında onarılmadı mı büsbütün kırılıyor, durmadan kırılıyor...

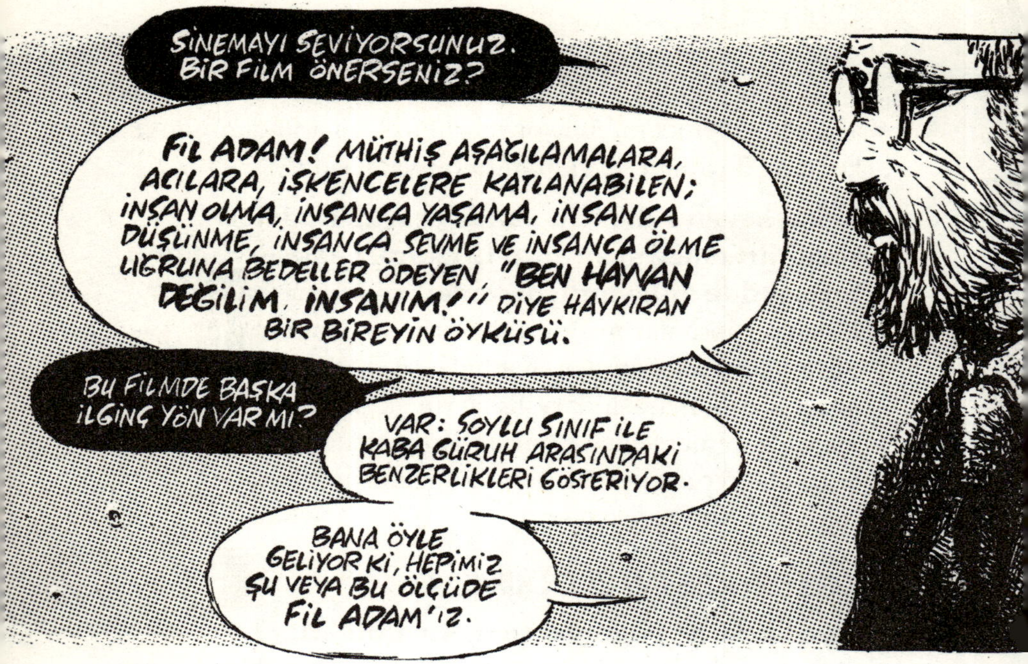

GENÇLERDEN KORKUYORLAR

Sinemanın en önemli özelliği ne sizce?
Sinema, yaşamı birkaç adım önden izleyen bir sanat.

Edebiyatla ilişkisi?
Nasıl edebiyat estetiğinde bir tür görsellikten söz edilebilirse, sinema estetiğinde de bir tür sözellikten söz edilebilir.

Popüler filmleri izliyor musunuz?
Truman Show'u sevmiştim, fikir çok iyiydi. Çok izlenen filmlerin öyküleri genellikle pek iyi değil. Efektler, hareket ve hıza ağırlık veriliyor. Böylece 'gösteri' öne çıkıyor, öykü geride kalıyor. Bu benim kişisel görüşüm değil. Jack Nicholson da aynı şeyi söylüyor.

Televizyon dizilerini izliyor musunuz?
İzlemiyorum. Senaryolarını edebiyattan habersiz

kimselerin yazdığı diziler çoğunlukta. Sinema da televizyon da insanları düşünmekten alıkoyan, uyuşturan yapımlarla dolup taşıyor.

İnsanları kimler neden uyuşturmak ister ki?
İktidar unsurları. Kendi çıkarlarını sağlama almak için, toplumu geri bırakan, topluma zaman kaybettiren bir strateji izliyorlar.

O niye?
Gençlerden korkuyorlar. Gençler, onların pörsümüş dünyasının bayat kurallarını yıkacak, rahatlarını bozacak diye korkuyorlar. Birçoğunun, bugün 14 yaşındaki çocuklar kadar bilgili olmadığı anlaşılır diye korkuyorlar.

İktidar ihtiyarların elinde, yani gerontokrasi var... Mesele bu mu?
Aslında ihtiyarlamak çağının gerisine düşmektir. Yaşla ilgisi yoktur.

Gençlere katkı sunmak yerine onlardan korkmak, onları baskılamak için çağın epey gerisine düşmek gerek, ha?
Öyle... Hayatımıza ilkel bile olamayan bir kitle söz geçiriyor.

Dolayısıyla?..
Şiddete, tedhişe başvuruyorlar. Amerika, Vietnam'ı işgal etmek için harcadığı parayı insanlara dağıtsa, her bir Vietnamlıya 200 dolar düşerdi.

HAYATI İNANDIRICI KILMAK

Edebiyat ile politika, yazar ile politikacı arasında bir karşılaştırma yapmak gerekse....
Politika sorumluluktan kaçma maratonuna dönüştü. Bu, onun etik boyutunu, saygınlığını ortadan kaldırıyor. Esaslı biri yazar okurdan / eleştirmenden övgü ya da onay değil tartışma bekler. Politikacı ise eleştirileri tehdit sayıyor. Özgüvensizliği yüzünden sahtelikle yol alıyor.

Şimdi görevde bulunan siyasetçiler bir röportajda en çok sevdikleri yazarlar arasında adınızı ansalar...
İyi ki böyle bir olasılık yok! Kara kara düşünürdüm.

Siyasi gücün meşruiyetinin işareti?..
John Kennedy'nin de dediği gibi "Bir ulusun büyüklüğü, en zayıf yurttaşına takındığı tavırdan belli olur."

Politik yozlaşma ve otoriterliğin sonuçlarından bahseder misiniz?
Düşünün ki toplumumuzda suya sabuna dokunmayanlar bile daha aşağılara çekiliyor. Bu durumda hayatımızı nasıl inandırıcı kılabiliriz?

"Hayatı inandırıcı kılmak..." böyle düşünmemiştim hiç, iyiymiş doğrusu.

Sonuçta toplumun esenliğine katkıda bulunma yetkinliğine erişememiş kimselerle dolup taşıyor ülke.

GİZLİ BİR İNAT

Otoriter politikalar toplumu, bireyleri, gençleri... yani herkesi hırpalıyor mu? Bu menfi tesirlerden kaçış, kurtuluş yok mu?
İçinde özgürlük tohumu taşıyan kişi, ona dayatılan kalıbı zorlayacaktır. O kalıbın içinde kalmakla yetinmeyecektir.

Ne zaman?
Nereden bileyim? Ben zaten karamsarım Murat. Bununla birlikte, insana inancı bir yana iterek insanı mutluluğa kavuşturmak olanaksızdır. İyi gözle bakmadığınız bir topluma esenlik yayamazsınız. Yırtına bozula düzelecek bu dünya.

Ne yapmalı? Sivil bir örgüt de yok ki gidip katılalım?
Katılmak isteyeceğiniz örgütün kurulmasını başkasından beklemeniz doğru mu?

Aykırı, uyumsuz insanlar mı olmalıyız?
Aykırı biri olmak da övünülecek bir şey değil... Fakat düşünsel bakımdan bir sağlamlığa ulaştıysanız, en ufak bir aykırılığınız mevcut düzendeki çok büyük yanlışları ortadan kaldırabilir.

Neyi kastediyorsunuz?
İlk bakışta Don Kişotça görülebilecek çabaların arkasından hakiki bir Don Kişot çıkma olasılığı yüksektir.

Yani toplumumuzda birileri kişiliğini ve kendiliğini inşa etme, koruma yeterliği gösteriyor?
Evet. Yıllarca yıkılmadan, acıları, yoksunluğu, yoksulluğu anlayışla karşılamayı, haksızlıklar karşısında

başkaldırmayıp bir süre susmayı yeğlememiz bence pısırıklıktan değil.

Neden peki?
Gizli bir inat bu. Bizim yaşama direncimiz.

Günlükleriniz *Gündökümü* adıyla yayımlandı. Alt başlık, *Bir uyumsuzun notları*. Uyumsuzluğun en zor tarafı ne peki?
Dostlarının kalbinde nasıl bir yer tuttuğunu kavrayamadığı zaman, kimsesizliğe benzer bir duygu sarıyor insanı.

Tomris Uyar, sizi anlamakta zorlanıyorum. Mücadeleci misiniz, kendi halinde bir yazar mısınız çözemedim.
İkisi de. Fakat... Dünya toplumlarına geniş bir açıdan bakmayı öğrendiniz mi, gençlikteki inançlarınız tavsıyor, eski kavgacılığınız kalmıyor.

FAYDASIZ AŞK

Aşka dönelim mi?
Neden? En ulvi konu aşk da ondan mı?

Bilmem? Belki. Aşk üzerine düşünürken fazla mı hataya düşüyoruz?
E tabii... Aşk'ın mekanını, zamanını, onu yaşayanların sınıfsal özelliklerini hesaba katmadan aşkı yüceltiyoruz. Böylece işler sarpa sarıyor.

Bir de mutluluğa kestirme yollardan ulaşılabileceğini sanıyoruz galiba?
Hem de nasıl! Hazır reçeteler, beylik "yaşama sevinci" formülleriyle ulaşılamaz mutluluğa. Yaşamı soylu ve çok daha ince bir imbikten geçirmeyi sağlayacak bilinçli bir yetiye varmak gerekir.

İyi ama biz işte bu kolaycı, duygularıyla hareket eden ve bilgisi kıt insanlarla birarada yaşıyoruz ve ister istemez onlardan birine âşık oluyoruz?
Böylece her sivriliği yumuşatma, her suçu bağışlama, her ayıbı örtme gibi üzücü beceriler ediniyoruz. Hem acıklı hem komik bir durum... Birey olamamış, yalnızca sınıfsal özellikleriyle sivrilen bir kukla olan kimselerin aşk'ından fayda yok.

Öyle diyorsunuz da, faydalı veya faydasız, uygun veya uygunsuz, dengeli veya dengesiz tüm aşkların ortak bir özelliği yok mudur?
Var. Her halükarda âşık olmak ile bir yakınını yitirmek arasında garip bir benzerlik var.

A-ha? Nedir?
İki durum da yaşam karşısında bocalamaya sebep oluyor.

AŞK İLE PORNOGRAFİ ARASINDA

Cinsellik de içinden çıkamadığımız bir konu...
İnsanların bu doğal olguyu bu kadar abartmasına şaşmamak elde değil.

Cinsellik algısındaki sorunlar nasıl çözülebilir?
Her şeyden önce özeleştiriyle. Bu konuda kendimizi ciddiyetle sorgulamalıyız. Bir de haklı çıkma hevesinden vazgeçmemiz lazım.

Aksi takdirde?
Erkekleri düşman olarak gören, içe kapanık, ürkek, çağ dışı genç kızlar ile aşağılık duyguları içinde bocalayan, saldırgan, saygısız ve somurtkan delikanlılar yetiştireceğiz.

Konunun aşkla ilgisi hakkında ne söylersiniz?
Cinsellik aşkın öz kaynağıdır. Bundan yoksun bırakıldığı nispette çıkmaza girer aşk.

Masum, çocuksu, meleksi bir aşk olamaz mı?
Olamaz. Aşkı cinsellikten ve erotizmden soyutlamak, pornografi salgınına yol açar!

Doğru söylüyorsunuz. Ama gene de...
Bir Amerikan şarkısı vardır: "Aşk sonsuza dek sürmüyorsa, sonsuzluk neye yarar?"

E şimdi bu cinsellikten uzak, pür romantik bir söz değil mi?
Romantizm ile cinselliği birbirinden ayrı ve uzak sanmayın. Flört de ilkgençlik çağına özgü bir ilişki türü, hatta geçici bir hastalık sayılıyor. Oysa...

Evet? Nedir flört?
Kişinin hayatını zenginleştiren kalıcı bir sanattır.

Flört, romantizm, erotizm, cinsellik, pornografi gibi kavramları yerli yerine oturtabilmek için ne gerekir?
Kadın ile erkek arasında yaşama saygınlık katacak bir dostluk kurulabilmesi. Kadını köşeye kıstırmayan, onun olanaklarını ezip bitirmeyen, kişiliğini geliştiren bir dostluk... Erkek de o zaman yerini bulur. İki cins arasında sahici, sağlam, insani bir denge kurulur.

Arızaların tümü kadını anlayamamaktan kaynaklanıyor demek?
Öyle değil mi? İlerlemenin yükü de kadına yükleniyor. Hep çağdaş kadının nasıl olması gerektiğini düşünüyoruz. Bir de çağdaş erkeğin bu kadın karşısında nasıl davranacağını düşünsek iyi olur.

Böylece?
Erkeğin açmazını da anlayabiliriz.

MUTSUZLUKTAN KURTULMAK İÇİN BAŞKA BİR MUTSUZLUĞU SEÇMEK

Kadın anne, erkek baba oluyor bir de. Ebeveynliğe nasıl bakıyorsunuz?
"Anne" sözcüğü çoğumuza erdemli, özverili, hakkı ödenmez bir 'dişi kuş'u çağrıştırır. Oysa "baba" denildiğinde yalnızca kendi babamızı düşünürüz. Anne kavramını soyutlayabilmişizdir, kendi annemizin bedeninden sıyırıp genelleyebilmişizdir de babayı kendi babamızdan ayrı görmeyiz.

"Baba" soyut bir kavram değil cidden. Çok ilginç...
Yaaa... Baba bir "patron" mudur? Yoksa yaşama uğraşında bilgilerini ve becerilerini çocuklarına aktaran bir "usta" mı? Dokunulabilen, öpülebilen, sıcaklığı yürekte duyulabilen, dertleşilebilen gerçek bir baba mı? Gönlümüzün ikinci tür babada karar kılması yetmiyor. O babanın bizzat ortaya çıkması da gerekiyor.

Konumlar belirsiz, ilişkiler çarpık, iletişim yetersiz...
İletişimi ne tıkıyor biliyor musun? Kalıp yargılar: "Kadın sevecen, erkek yiğittir" gibi bize normal görünen kabuller.

O zaman kişiliğin, kendiliğin ortaya çıkması da imkansızlaşıyor galiba? Birey olma çabası, kaosun içinde bir mücadeleye dönüşüyor besbelli?
Ve tam da bu sebeple, biraz gülümsemeyi, teşekkür etmeyi ödün vermek sanıyor insanlar. Dahası... sevilmemeyi rahatça kaldırabiliyoruz da sevilmek zor geliyor bize. Bir mutsuzluktan sıyrılmak için er geç bir başka mutsuzluğu seçiyoruz.

İkili ilişkilerde sizi en çok ne rahatsız eder?
Özverimin görev diye görülmesi. Bu beni çileden çıkarır.

Toplumda gıcık kaptığınız bir şey?
"Hanımefendi" hitabıyla başlayıp on dakika içinde "canım"a giden konuşmalar.

ANNEYE VERİLEBİLECEK EN GÜZEL HEDİYE

Saygın bir çevirmensiniz. Biraz da çeviriden, çevirmenlikten konuşalım.
Sevdiği yazarları çevirmekte direnen bir yazar-çevirmenseniz işiniz bitik demektir. Onca emek verip anadilinize aktardığınız yapıt, günün modasına, edebiyat yönsemelerine pek uymuyorsa arada kaynayıp gidecek, sizin elinizden de bir şey gelmeyecektir.

Çeviri yaparken başvurduğunuz özel bir yöntem var mı?
Yazarın fotoğraflarına, giyimine kuşamına bakarım.

Ne? Neden?
"Benim yerimde o olsaydı hangi kelimeyi seçerdi?" sorusunun cevabını kestirebilmek için.

Siz aynı zamanda annesiniz. Anneler Günü'nde alınan hediyeler, Babalar Günü'nde alınanlardan çok daha pahalı oluyor, malum...
Bir anneye verilebilecek en büyük armağan, kanı canı pahasına büyütüp okuttuğu çocuğunun çağdaş dünyada çağdaş birey onuruyla yaşayacağına dair güvencedir.

Çocuklarımızı gereği gibi sevebilmek için...
Çocuğu sevmek yetmez, çocuğu saymalıyız da.

BAYAĞILIKLARIN TUTARLILIĞI

"Çocukların yaşamını olabildiğince uzun süren bir şenliğe dönüştürmeliyiz" yazmıştınız. Halbuki yavrucaklar mutsuz. Özellikle de okulda.
Bizde eğitim, öğrenim mutluluğun tam karşıtı sanki.

İnsanın içini kıpır kıpır eden bir gönül eğitimini nasıl inşa edebiliriz? Okullarda mutluluğu hakim kılmayı başaramadıktan, bilgilenme ile sevinci örtüştüremedikten sonra çocuklarımız adına sahici bir umut besleyemeyiz.

İkide bir "çocuklar bizim geleceğimiz" diyoruz fakat bu sözün arkası yok. Neden böyle?
Dedim ya, çocuklarından korkan bir devlet ve toplum var. Benzer şekilde gelecekten de korkuyorlar. Bu nedenle hep geçmişle ilgileniyorlar. Geçmişi karalamak da göklere çıkarmak da gelecek korkusundan kaynaklanıyor. Burnumuzun dibindeki güncel sorunları görmekten kaçmanın bir yolu bu. Çocuklarımızı bu çağın insanlık değerleriyle donatmak için el ele verip çabalamayacak mıyız? Soru bu.

Sorulardan ve sorunlardan kaçmaya alıştık mı dersiniz?
İyi de, berbatlığını kanıksadığımız bir dünyayı, çocuklarımıza öylece devretmenin acısına da alışacak mıyız?

Kadınları üretime çağırmanın, bilinçlendirmenin önündeki engeller neler?
Toplumun katılıkları ve sindirilmiş, kişiliği hiçe sayılmış kadınların korkuları. Bunların hepsini yıkmak gerek. Kadınlara çağdaş bir dünyada insanca yaşama hakkı tanımamak da nesi? Toplum olarak çok yüksek hedeflere göz dikip, yanıbaşımızdaki vahameti görmememiz büyük bir ayıp.

Neden kadın hakları konusunda serinkanlı olunamıyor? Sosyopsikolojik bir sorun mu bu?
Yaşadığımız bayağılıklar her alana yayılıp garip bir tutarlılık kazanmış…

KOLAYLIK SAĞLAMAK UĞRUNA KOLAYA KAÇMAK

Kadının iç dünyasını kadın yazarın, erkeğin iç dünyasını erkek yazarın daha iyi anlatabileceği fikrine katılır mısınız?

Hayır. Aynı mantıkla ölüm olgusunu da en iyi ölülerin kaleminden okuyabiliriz!

Bir yazar olarak özellikle dikkat ettiğiniz bir husus...

Dedikoduyu sanata bulaştırmaktan kaçındım.

Aaa? Yazarlıkla ilgili bir tüyo vermenizi ummuştum.

Peki: Kolay anlaşılır olma özrüyle kolaya kaçmamalı yazar.

Dünya görüşünü anlaşılır kılmak için yazanlara ne dersiniz?

Edebiyatın dışına düşme tehlikesi büyük... İyi bir yazar dünya görüşünü sloganlarla anlatmaz.

Aşmayı istediğiniz yazarlar var mıydı? "Filancadan daha iyi yazmalıyım" diye düşünür müydünüz?

Yo, bence yazarların birbirlerini aşmaları söz konusu olamaz.

Mizah bizim edebiyatımızda o kadar yaygın değil fakat?
Çünkü güleç insanların ciddi olabileceğine inanmak zor geliyor çoğumuza.

Onun da sebebi?
Sınıflar arası uçurum, yoksulluk... Hiçbir umudu olmayan, yoksul kimse onurunu nasıl koruyabilir, nasıl taşıyabilir yüreğini yerli yerinde?

EMEL SAYIN'LA AYNI PARAYI KAZANMAK

Tomris Hanım, sormamda sakınca yoksa, kitaplarınızla, çevirilerinizle geçinebiliyor musunuz?
Kesinlikle hayır. Babaannemden kalan iki dairenin kira geliriyle geçiniyorum.

Hay Allah...
Böyle işte... Emekçilerin haklarını ateşli bir şekilde savunuruz da, yazar sıfatıyla telif hakkımızı istemeye utanırız. Halk da yazarın emeğini bir türlü görmez. Yazarın emeğinin maddi bir karşılığı olması gerektiğini anlamaz. Onlara göre, yazarlar, yazma hazzıyla yetinmeli, maddi bir karşılık beklememelidir.

Yazarların enikonu zengin olması...
Zenginlikten değil, geçimden bahsediyorum. Emel Sayın benim kazandığım parayı kazanacak değil tabii ki. Fakat aradaki farkın büyüklüğü incitici oluyor.

Arabeskten hoşlanmıyorsunuz. Neden?
Arabesk köylerin kentleşmesi yerine kentlerin köyleşmesine yol açan bir ideoloji görünümünde de ondan.

Arabeski hüzün değil de ajitasyon olarak görüyorsunuz...

Gerçek bu. "Hafif müzik" ve yabancı bestelere rastgele sözler uydurarak kotarılan aranjmanlar da sanatsal bir katkı getirmiyor. Ayrıca yakınmaktan, pişmanlıktan ve bunların getirdiği mızmızlıktan hoşlanmıyorum.

Düşünürken yanıldığımız gibi duygulanırken de yanılıyoruz, ha?
Öyle. Duygular dış etkilere çok açık. Daha çabuk zedeleniyorlar. Sözgelimi bir eşyayı ancak seller, depremler etkilerken duygular en ufak bir ayrıntıdan nem kapabiliyor. Bir de...

Nedir?
Biri geliyor hayatımıza makas atıyor; o yaşadığımız bölüm, bütünün dışına düşüyor.

E işte o zaman da arabesk dinliyoruz?
Avutulmayı reddedip iyileşmek istemeliyiz fakat.

Ne yapalım yani?
Sağlıksız hüzünleri kovun gitsin.

GÖNÜL BORÇLARINI GİZLEMEYİ SEVMEM

Ahlakı öncelediğiniz, önemsediğiniz halde dinî inanca mesafeliydiniz...
Küçükken 1 yıl kadar beş vakit namaz kıldım hiç sektirmeden. Dua etmeyi seviyordum.

Sonra? İnancın bireye ve topluma faydasız olduğu fikrine mi yaklaştınız?
Bu uzun ve çetrefil bir mevzu. Göz önünde bir gerçek var, inançlarda esnekliğe hak tanımazsak ikiyüzlülük kaçınılmazlaşıyor.

"İslamiyet bizim kültürel, millî köklerimizi oluşturuyor. Dinden uzaklaşınca kimlik kaybına uğruyoruz. Batı taklitçisi oluyoruz" şeklindeki yaklaşıma ne dersiniz?

Batı taklitçiliğini reddetme hassasiyeti bizi bir başka bağnazlığa sürükledi. Batı uygarlığının dünyaya ve bize önemli katkılarda bulunduğunu unutuyoruz. Ulusal değerler temelde öbür ulusların değerlerinden farklı değildir ki.

Biraz daha açar mısınız?
Hiç kimse dünyanın vardığı aşamaya varılmamış gibi davranılması yolunda bir öneriyle insanların karşısına çıkamaz.

Kimse tümüyle haklı değil mi sizce? Eleştirerek, tartışarak, uzlaşarak yol alabiliriz öyle mi?
Birbirimizden çok farklı gibi görünsek de, yaşamdaki biraradalığımızdan ötürü birbirimizi olumlu olumsuz etkiliyoruz. En uzak saydığımız kişiye de bir gönül borcumuz vardır. Gönül borçlarını gizlemeyi sevmem.

Çağdaş hayat değerlerini biz üretemediğimiz için galiba... Toplumsal ve politik konularda da arabesk bir tutuma mı yöneliyoruz? Düşünsel konularda duygusal veya içgüdüsel davranıyoruz belki? Bilimi, teknolojiyi üretmek şöyle dursun, alıp kullanmada bile zaafa uğruyoruz sanki?
Manzara ortada işte. Belli bir eğitim düzeyine gelmeyen kitleler, teknolojiyi kendilerini eğitmek için değil, kişisel doyuma ulaşmak ve gösteriş adına kullanıyorlar.

DÜELLOSUZLUKTAN ÖLEBİLİR İNSAN

Kedileri seviyorsunuz. Nedir, kimdir kedi?
Benim gibi kedi düşkünleri kediler hakkında genelleme yapamaz. Her bir kedi tek ve benzersizdir. Yeri başkalarıyla doldurulamaz.

"Nankör hayvan" derlerdi kediler için...
Kediyi nankör belleyenler, dostluklardaki dengeyi hep

kendi yararına değiştirmek isteyenlerdir. Düşünün, hangimiz kedi kadar bağımsız ve dünyayla barışığız?

Yalnızlıktan belki. Charles Dickens'ın dediği gibi "kalabalıklar içinde yalnızız."
Yalnızlığın da çeşitleri var. İki kişi yalnız kalmaktansa, kalabalıkta yalnız olmak çok daha kolay.

Bir de siz herkesin çift kişilikli olduğundan bahsediyordunuz...
Doğru... Galiba hepimizin ikinci kişiliği var. Kimi erkeklerin ikinci kişiliği kadın oluyor. Kimi kadınların ikinci kişiliği de erkek.

Belki sizin ikinci kişiliğiniz de erkek mi yani?
Olabilir... Hayatta en önemli şeyin düello olduğunu düşünürüm.

Düello mu?
Yüzleşmek anlamında söylüyorum. Türkiye'de kaçta kaçımız yaşadığımız şeyle yüzleşme gücüne sahibiz? Düelloda eşitlik var. Karşındaki, sana denk olmalı. Aksi takdirde düello değil aerobik olur o. Düelloda yalnız karşındakiyle değil kendinle de hesaplaşıyorsun.

Peki ya hayatımızda hiç kimseyle ve hiçbir şeyle yüzleşmiyorsak?
O zaman düellosuzluktan ölebilir insan.

BU ÇİÇEKLER SİZE.
TEŞEKKÜR EDERİM...
ÇİÇEKLERİ TANIMIYORUM PEK. ADLARINI BİLE DOĞRU DÜRÜST BİLMİYORUM. AMA AÇSINLAR İSTİYORUM.

SON BİR ŞEY...
GENÇ BİR YAZARA ÖĞÜDÜNÜZ NE OLURDU?
ÖLMÜŞ USTALARLA BAĞLANTIYI KOPARMASINLAR.

3.
CİLDİN
SONU...

BU KİTAP
KAĞIT VE KALEMDEN MÜREKKEP
BİR ZAMAN MAKİNESİ!

KONFÜÇYÜS
YUNUS EMRE
BALZAC
AHMET MİTHAT
ARTHUR CONAN DOYLE
HALİDE EDİB
THEODOR ADORNO
ORHAN KEMAL
ATTİLÂ İLHAN
URSULA K. LE GUIN
CEMAL SÜREYA
UMBERTO ECO
BRUCE LEE

ALFA | EDEBİYAT

MURAT MENTEŞ'ten

DERDE DEVA RANDEVU

№ 2

Çizen HAKAN KARATAŞ